*Traces of Violence*

# Traces of Violence



*Robert Desjarlais and Khalil Habrih*

UNIVERSITY OF CALIFORNIA PRESS

University of California Press
Oakland, California

© 2022 by Robert R. Desjarlais and Khalil Habrih

Cataloging-in-Publication Data is on file at the Library of Congress
ISBN 978-0-520-38245-9 (cloth : alk. paper)
ISBN 978-0-520-38246-6 (pbk. : alk. paper)
ISBN 978-0-520-38247-3 (ebook)

Grateful acknowledgment is made to the following publishers for permission
to reprint quotations from these works: University of Nebraska Press, *The
Writing of the Disaster*, by Maurice Blanchot, © 1986; Éditions Gallimard,
*L'Écriture du désastre*, by Maurice Blanchot, © 1980; State University of
New York Press, *The Step not Beyond*, by Maurice Blanchot, © 1992; Éditions
Gallimard, *Le pas au-delà*, by Maurice Blanchot, © 1973; University of
Chicago Press, *Writing and Difference*, by Jacques Derrida, © 1978; University
of Virginia Press, *Caribbean Discourse: Selected Essays, by* Édouard Glissant,
© 1989; Librairie François Maspero/Éditions la Découverte, Paris, *Les
Damnés de la terre*, by Frantz Fanon, © 1961, 2002. Grove/Atlantic,
*The Wretched of the Earth,* by Frantz Fanon, English translation © 1963
by *Présence Africaine*. Any third party use of this material, outside of this
publication, is prohibited.

31   30   29   28   27   26   25   24   23   22
10   9   8   7   6   5   4   3   2   1

. . . write in the thrall of the impossible real, that share of disaster wherein every reality, safe and sound, sinks.

MAURICE BLANCHOT,
*The Writing of the Disaster*

Would it be ridiculous to consider our lived history as a steadily advancing neurosis?

ÉDOUARD GLISSANT,
*Caribbean Discourse*

CONTENTS

# NOTE ON TRANSCRIPTION OF ARABIC TERMS

We use the Latin script commonly used by Darija-speaking communities (in Morocco, Algeria, Tunisia, and diasporic spaces in Western Europe and North America). With this script, certain sounds—notably the guttural letters—are replaced with Arabic numerals. For instance, the number 3 replaces the letter *'ayn* (ع), which does not have a phonetic equivalent in English.

## A guide to reading *Traces of Violence*

We must be several in order to write, and even to "perceive."
JACQUES DERRIDA,
*Writing and Difference*

Violence is expansive. It sneaks up on people, hits them hard, shears like shrapnel into bodies, mind, and matter. It sears through the world through vehicles of force, sight, and sound, and burrows into the memories of a life or a people. Remnant traces of violence can so easily get embedded in a landscape or urban terrain. Violent harm leaves marks, wounds, scars, absences, silences, potentialities. Violence is reiterative in time and space; it's often generative of further violence. Its very possibility is difficult at times to comprehend. At the same time, any history of violence is caught up in other histories of violence—genealogies of colonial conquest, imperial domination, genocide; chronicles of the tortured and disappeared, of saturation bombing and drone strikes, border surveillance, expulsions, internment camps; annals of military brutality, police harassment—a knotted tangle of violent histories that shadow a city mired in life, death, and wounding. In the midst of such harsh tracts of violence, where there are no easy answers or explanations, it's important to find ways to live generatively and co-constructively in relation to others.

On the night of 13 November 2015, a commando acting on behalf of the organization then known as the Islamic State perpetrated a string of attacks throughout the greater Paris area. Starting at 9:16pm, three explosions occurred outside the Stade de France, a national sports stadium just north of

Paris, resulting in four deaths, including three suicide bombers. In that same hour, armed gunmen approached several bars and restaurants in the 10th and 11th arrondissements and shot into the crowds gathered there, killing a number of people and wounding others. Three gunmen raided the Bataclan, a music venue on boulevard Voltaire, where they took hostages and shot at those attending a concert that night; hours later, police forces entered the Bataclan and fought with the hostage-takers. Ninety people were killed at the Bataclan and over two hundred were wounded. In all, the attacks that night resulted in 130 deaths. Some 413 people were injured, one hundred of whom were wounded seriously. Seven of the attackers also died when French police and security forces searched for the agents of the attacks and for accomplices. The Islamic State of Iraq and the Levant (ISIL), also known as the Islamic State of Iraq and Syria (ISIS), or Daesh, in line with its Arabic-language acronym, claimed responsibility for the attacks, stating they were in retaliation for the French airstrikes on ISIL targets in Syria and Iraq. The attacks, commonly known as *les attentats* in French, were reportedly planned in Syria and organized in Belgium.

The attacks caused concern and alarm throughout the world. Television and newspaper reports spoke in dramatic, mournful terms to shocked, distressed audiences. Much like with the *Charlie Hebdo* attacks in Paris in January 2015, the events took on a political and symbolic significance far beyond the specific lives and deaths involved.[1]

It was as if the space and values of the nation had been attacked, and the Republic responded with national acts of mourning and commemoration, combined with intensive security measures that sought to identify terroristic threats while shoring up the country's borders to protect its citizens. François Hollande, then president of France, called the attacks "an aggression against our . . . way of life" and an act of war by ISIL. On 14 November 2015 the French government declared a national state of emergency, a legal mandate that banned public demonstrations and allowed the police to carry out searches without a warrant and put anyone under house arrest without trial. With these sovereign powers in place, the government mobilized fifty thousand police officers, fifty thousand military police (*gendarmerie*), and seven thousand soldiers in order to find those responsible for the attacks. On 15 November France launched airstrikes against ISIL targets in Syria. Around dawn on 18 November a joint-police operation of the RAID and the BRI approached a building in Saint-Denis, north of Paris, where one of the alleged organizers of the attacks, Abdelhamid Abaaoud, was hiding. He was killed in the assault, along with two accomplices. By then, 296 home raids (*perquisitions*) had taken place and 114 people had been placed under house arrest (*assignation a résidence*). By July 2016 these figures had risen to over 3,500 home raids and four hundred house arrests.[2] These various operations are part of the broader ongoing Vigipirate program, in which security measures are undertaken to encourage vigilance at both the collective and individual level.

Many residents of Paris and its neighboring communities were deeply affected by the 13 November attacks, even if they did not experience them firsthand. More than a few would say that they were traumatized by the violence that occurred. The violent events affected different peoples in disparate ways, from those who directly mourned lives lost to the nervous residents of neighborhoods in north Paris and the *banlieue* suburbs, where French security forces were concentrated. In the weeks that followed, the focus of political violence moved from the site of the massacres to the stigmatization of particular urban spaces and the social groups that compose them, chiefly immigrant and French Muslim communities. France became a society supposedly at war in Syria and Iraq, at war within its own borders. Relying on existing legal, police, and military protocols, these operations have worked alongside broader discursive and affective constructions. They have allowed for a retracing of national borders, as lines of demarcation between the "civilized" and the "barbarian," between the French nation and the lurking "internal enemy," come to be signified anew. Out of the sequence of events of 13 November 2015—in the wake of previous attacks and foreboding future acts of violence—thus emerged a landscape of phantasms: a phantasmagoria of terrorist threats and enmity and governmental responses.

This book is concerned with the aftermath of the attacks. The writing tracks how certain trace elements of the violent events of 13 November 2015 have come to exist, recur, erode, or vanish altogether in the streets, bodies, inscriptions, archives, memorials, and collective memories within the cityscape of Paris. It gives thought to the ways in which certain marks of violence come to be effaced or denied, often for complicated political reasons. These considerations lead, in time, to a broader reflection on the ways in which certain histories of violence, from the French colonial era on into the contemporary moment, shape the contours of life and death in Paris.

Several key themes guide this inquiry, including: the disastrous effects and charged potentialities of violence in people's lives; forms of militarized vigilance and state security in contemporary life; the politics of traces, archives, and collective memorialization; demeaning and oppressive police strategies of harassment and forceful control of marginalized residents of north Paris; dynamics of haunting, phantasms, and spectrality; and the lingering wounds of (post)coloniality. These themes recur throughout the text, either implicitly within the narratives and images at hand, or in more overt conceptual statements. The book entails an integrative, interdisciplinary reflection on processes and effects of collective violence in Paris, France, and elsewhere, with the book's motifs conveyed through a historically complex terrain of traces, marks and inscriptions, spectral hauntings, wounds and scars.

It's worth noting several themes and methods integral to this work, so that readers have a clearer understanding of the book's organization.

*1. Collaborative anthropology.* The work is a collaborative effort in anthropological-sociological inquiry, in which we, the two authors, draw from our respective research engagements in Paris to reflect on forms and histories of violence in France and elsewhere. While such a collaborative anthropology has often been called for, there are surprisingly few examples of published works in which two or more authors write in an integrative way on a particular subject of ethnographic inquiry—especially when the authors come from different sociocultural backgrounds and political circumstances.[3] More specifically, few works attest to collaboration as a work of coauthorship, wherein reflexivity and dialogue work toward a constant questioning of the way the authors construe their object of study. In these pages, the co-construction of the object of study is articulated through an exchange in methods and in concepts. This book is the product of this process of contrasting and using each other's tools to sharpen one another's gaze.

Significantly, the approach undertaken here is a decidedly *dialogical* one, in which the two authors write in response to each other, making for a work of interlacing voices and displacements. Specifically, the main text of each chapter is followed by an "interruption" that works in relation to, or against the grain of, the main body of that chapter. Each text and interruption is written by one of the two authors, as indicated by the initials found at the end of each text (i.e., "K. H." or "R. D."). The authors bring to this dialogue distinct but nonetheless interlinked perspectives, academic traditions, sociopolitical and cultural worlds, and universes of meaning.

Khalil Habrih was born in Glasgow, Scotland, in 1995 and was raised between Villejuif (south of Paris), Toronto, and Ottawa. His father is the son of Algerian emigrants who progressively settled in France starting in the early 1950s; his mother, the eldest daughter of Romanian socialist lawyers, immigrated to France shortly after the December 1989 Revolution. Habrih was educated in the French national education system, in a French lycée in Canada, and later at the Paris Institute of Political Studies. A visiting student at Oberlin College in 2014, he arrived in Paris in 2015. Between 2015 and 2017 he engaged in ethnographic research on policing in Paris and began a master's program at the École des hautes études en sciences sociales (EHESS). His current research engages with the fields of surveillance, racialization, and gender, with a focus on ethnographic methods and sociohistory. As of this writing, Habrih is a doctoral candidate in anthropology at the University of Ottawa.

Robert Desjarlais, in turn, hails from a secular Catholic, culturally American, middle-class family of Quebecois-Polish heritage in western Massachusetts. A student of state universities in Massachusetts and California, and once a research fellow at Harvard University, he has taught for some twenty-five years at Sarah Lawrence College in New York. An anthropologist by training, Desjarlais has conducted ethnographic research in Nepal, the United States, and now in France. Over time he has become increasingly ambivalent about the ethics and politics of ethnographic research, and he has sought out alternative modes of anthropological thought, writing, and image-making.

The two authors first met after Desjarlais had already written draft versions of several of the chapters that now appear in this book (in greatly revised form).[4] This was in March 2017, at a time when Habrih was conducting ethnographic research on police practices and strategies in the Barbès–Goutte d'Or areas of Paris and Desjarlais was conducting research of his own on the aftermath of the violence of November 2015. We met at the EHESS, where Desjarlais was presenting on his research during one session of a year-long academic seminar.[5] We met again several weeks later. While taking a long, drifting walk together through parts of north Paris we began to exchange thoughts on life and violence in France and elsewhere. A few weeks later, in the summer of 2017, Habrih wrote a paper for the year-long seminar, which he was taking for academic credit. This reflective essay narrated aspects of that conversation-in-movement and its conceptual implications. He then forwarded a copy to Desjarlais in New York. (A trace record of this seminar paper, translated into English, can be found at the start of chapter 7). Finding that Habrih's ongoing research and thought opened up significant realms of generative perspectives of pressing relevance to his own efforts, Desjarlais invited him to join the writing of the book-in-progress. In the months that followed we began to work together on the manuscript, with Habrih adding texts of his own and Desjarlais writing further on the themes in question. From the preface and counter-preface on, the book's composition reflects the contrapuntal movement of this dialogic process.

The book thus entails an uncommon writing strategy, in which the two authors draw from their distinct but interrelated research inquiries in Paris—as well as their respective intellectual heritages and subject positions—in writing on life and violence in the metropole. The writing proceeds in interwoven ways, with distinct texts essayed by Habrih and Desjarlais working in dialogue with one another—and with some passages serving as "interruptions" to the main texts found in each chapter. What emerges from this joint effort is an intensive inquiry into processes and reverberations of violence, phenomena of importance to so many in today's world.

*2. A critical phenomenology of traces.* Central to the inquiry of this work is a critical phenomenology of traces, in which traces of violence are situated within complex vectors of time, space, history, and cultural and political formations. We also consider ways in which certain violent events are not preserved in lasting traces of such events. We write of inscriptions in Paris, a city engrained within a long, complicated history of inscriptions, be they the *graff* marks of graffiti, monuments and memorials, historical events and acts of violence sited in particular urban spaces, or, more viscerally, and metaphorically, wounds and scars of violence, from colonial times on to the contemporary moment. We do not take traces as being natural phenomena in the world, but rather the product of complex processes of materiality, inscription, semiosis, and perception. In consideration here are the ways in which fear and vigilance become inscribed in people's lives and fissures of the city; the archival, commemorative work of the French state; scriptive acts of police and military soldiers; acts of counterinscription; and the tracework of violence, cruelty, disaster, and creativity that runs through it all. Through this urban ichnology we write, in effect, of the politics of traces.

This focus on traces helps to explain the methods and motives of Desjarlais's research in Paris. From the start of his inquiry into the aftereffects of the violent attacks in November 2015, he was interested in tracking and retracing "traces" of violence perceived or grasped. In relation to this, and for complex reasons, he did not undertake any formal interviews with residents of Paris in regard to any violence perceived or experienced. Instead, he attended primarily to what he encountered through quiet, low-key engagements while residing in Paris—conversations overhead, incidental encounters, perspectives voiced in everyday conversations, newspaper entries, films and photographs, remnant marks of graffiti and street art, the eerie presence of armed soldiers in Parisian streets, and myriad other trace effects. In many respects, this ethnographic method is inspired by Walter Benjamin's writings on European cities (Paris and Berlin, most notably), in which Benjamin drew from numerous forms of historical artifacts and sensate perceptions to convey a sense of the cultural and political forms of life in these cities. Benjamin's archival impulse and historical materialist method was one of "ragpicking," as with the *chiffonnier* (ragpicker) that Charles Baudelaire wrote of in his portraits of figures of nineteenth-century Paris.

> Here we have a man whose job it is to gather the day's rubbage in the capital. He collects and catalogues everything that the great city has cast off, everything it has lost, and discarded, and broken. He goes through the archives of debauchery, and the jumbled array of refuse. He makes a selection, an intelligent choice; like a miser hoarding treasure, he collects the garbage that will become objects of utility or pleasure when refurbished by Industrial magic.[6]

The ragpicker is like an urban archaeologist, concerned with "excavation and memory" and the "phantasmagoria" of modern life, gathering up so many shards of urban detritus, the ruins of modernity, recycling that which holds the potential for further use.[7] Benjamin invoked such themes in his description of German writer Siegfried Kracauer: "A ragpicker at daybreak, lancing with his stick scraps of language and tatters of speech in order to throw them into his cart, grumblingly, stubbornly, somewhat the worse for drink, and not without now and again letting one or other of these fading calicoes—'humanity,' 'inner nature,' 'enrichment'—flutter ironically in the dawn breeze."[8] Such inclinations could readily apply when refashioned to Desjarlais's method of perusing the streets of Paris, looking for scraps of speech, remnant images and affective intensities, discarded fliers—"liberty," "security," "vigilance"—and specters of death and life.

We realize this is an unorthodox method of anthropological research, in which formal interviews play no part. But once Desjarlais got going with this practice he wanted to stay with it, to see how far it could go as a mode of ethnographic comprehension. He therefore relied on the same ragpicker's method during stays in Paris from 2017 through 2020. An objection might be raised that the style Desjarlais adopts as an ethnographer in the early chapters of this book—the shifting perceptions of a "spectral anthropologist," of sorts—leads to a focus on his processes of thinking through the afterlives of violence as opposed to the experiences of those who live in the city or experienced the violence firsthand. Yet our sense is that Desjarlais's observations, which work in relation to Habrih's research, are consistent with how many have experienced the aftermath of the violence of November 2015. In contrast, Habrih's ethnographic research in the Goutte d'Or (uninterrupted from 2015 to 2017, and again more sporadically in 2018 and 2019) draws from a number of formal and informal interviews, participant observation and less collective methods of observations such as "urban drifting" (*dérive urbaine*), as well as other forms of autoethnographic writing that describe his relationship to policed and surveilled urban space. This form of ethnography relies on living *in situ* and is largely drawn from the work of reflexive sociology and organic ethnology undertaken by French-Algerian sociologist Abdelmalek Sayad. Through dialogue, extensive interviews often cited at length without interpretive interruptions, Sayad centered the experiences and universes of meaning of Algerian (post)colonial immigrants to France. In so doing, he worked to *make sense* of the sociopolitical and affective reverberations of categories of (non)citizenship, from the *sensi*bility of the stigmatized, rather than the sense-making of state discourses.[9] Habrih's engagement with field research was in that sense committed to participants' testimonies and analyses and to formulating a critique of French Republican institutions. The authors' differing methods and their underlying normative commitments are part of the collaborative work and dialogue involved.

*3. Emergence of understanding.* The book reflects a process of research and writing in which there is an emergence of understanding of the conditions and histories of violence in contemporary Paris. This emergence, at once epistemic, affective, ethical, political, and intersubjective in scope, relates in part to changes in perspective that Desjarlais underwent through his research and writing efforts, in large part through his engagements with Habrih. In effect, there is a narrative structure implicit in Desjarlais's writings in this book, in which his initial encounters with traces of violence associated with November 2015 lead to a greater understanding of the complexities of violence, particularly the ways in which histories of state-supported violence in the contemporary world relate to violent events so often deemed acts of "terrorism." Habrih, meanwhile, progressively incorporated Desjarlais's phenomenological approach and vocabulary into his sociological method. Habrih began by systematically exploring concepts, such as immigrant centrality, spatialities, urban rhythms, collective memory, historicities of displacement, race-making, and the like. The constant "rubbing of shoulders" with phenomenology allowed Habrih to turn to the body in order to document, in a sociological and ethnographic way, what Frantz Fanon dubbed the "historico-racial schema" of phenomena and embodiment.[10] Desjarlais's critical phenomenology provided an analytic for Habrih to study his own corporeal and affective experiences with policing in Paris. Conversely, critical phenomenology and sociology allowed for an interesting experiment in historicization, as Habrih moved from the intersubjective into the historical and back again.

While this narrative structure is distinct from the structure of most scholarly works—in which a main thesis or argument is advanced from the start, and the rest of the text supports that thesis—the narrative stays true to the spirit of the thought involved. In some ways, the structure is more like that found in many novels, in which certain situations and understandings emerge through the narrative-temporal flow of the writing and reading involved. Imagine, if you will, an intertextual, polyphonic ethnography penned by the likes of Assia Djebar and Abdelkebir Khatibi, or Édouard Glissant and Patrick Chamoiseau, and one starts to get close to the patterns of language involved.

*4. Specters, phantasms, hauntings.* A key feature of the book's subject matter are the ways in which sundry events, memories, images, traces, and non-traces appear in spectral, phantasmal ways in the places, temporalities, histories, and trace-work in Paris. These themes relate to a growing interest in "hauntology" in the social sciences and the humanities—the study of ghostly hauntings, spectral resonances, phantasms, and phantoms. Resounding the work of Jacques Derrida, Avery Gordon, and others, we consider the hauntological dimensions of violence, ghostly hauntings, and specters in life and death, as much as any clear-cut ontologies of being, identity, and state formation.[11] We also consider the phantasms invested in certain discourses and sensibilities of everyday life, governmental practices, state or terroristic violence, and violent deaths.[12] Fredric Jameson once wrote that "Spectrality is not difficult to circumscribe, as what makes the present waver: like the vibrations of a heat wave through the massiveness of the object world—indeed of matter itself—now shimmers like a mirage."[13] A reader would not be mistaken to find that many of the images and materialities noted in these pages shimmer like mirages within the fissures of Paris, a place where present, past, and future waver.

*5. Palimpsest of violence.* In attending to various forms of violence that shape the lives of so many living in Paris and elsewhere, the book is in quiet conversation with important reflections on violence, from Frantz Fanon's and Hannah Arendt's writings "on violence" to more recent works by anthropologists on the causes and effects of violence in a number of sociocultural worlds.[14] Here, we pay particular attention to the ways in which forms of state, police, and terroristic violence affect the bodies, memories, spaces, temporalities, sensorial and affective sensibilities, and lives and deaths of residents of Paris and its *banlieues*. The City of Light holds a palimpsest of violence, in which myriad histories, marks, scars, wounds, and erasures of violence are caught up in complicated, cross-cutting trajectories within multiple temporalities and spatialities.[15] Each chapter of this book is palimpsestic in form, for the language, reflections, marks, images, and interruptions imply a plurality of intersecting inscriptions, erasures, reinscriptions and reerasures, graphed and ungraphed by the hands of many.

Such are some of the concerns, methods, and tracework of the pages that follow. This book is far from comprehensive, especially when it comes to considerations of violence and its aftereffects in France or elsewhere. Its pages are marked by gaps, lacunae, fleeting traces, partial knowings, and obscure neuralgic indications as much as they are by tangible perceptions and clear statements. Then again, much of life today proceeds in wavering, uncertain terms. With this palimpsest of a heterogeneous text we write in a spirit of relation and co-composition. We would like to think that the book is in accord with emergent possibilities of reciprocity and mutuality in life, as encouraged by Achille Mbembe and others—and Frantz Fanon, before us— in anticipating an open-ended potentiality that can mark a spirit of transfiguration, one that promises a return to life, against the powers of death.[16] This would entail an ethics and politics of amity, in contrast to the politics of enmity that plagues so much of the world today.

*R. D. and K. H.*
*New York, Ottawa, Paris*
*December 2020*

## Blue flight terminal

*Tuesday, 22 January 2019*

I didn't know that I would come to study violence. I didn't know I would walk the streets of Paris like an itinerant ghost, looking for traces of harm and loss. I didn't know I would write incessantly in the pages of notebooks, trying to comprehend it all while never really comprehending much at all. I didn't know of the archive of traces that I would cobble together out of words and images, a ragpicker's collection motivated not so much by any logical, well-defined inquiry but, rather, by a circuit of bafflement, sympathetic concern, and obsessive interest, stuck in the need to know something that could not be known. This unofficial archive, half-formed and nearly irrational, contained the strands of a historically complex set of encounters, perceptions, remnant traces. Photographs, drawings. Scraps of paper. Newspaper clippings. Letters left on a sidewalk, later scanned into an archive. Memorials chiseled into stone. And writings on the disaster: military soldiers on the lookout for acts of terror; walks through the security zones of north Paris; remnant images from 17 October 1961. At first, like others, I did not grasp the significance of that date within the aphasic history of Paris. I didn't know what I didn't know. I didn't know that encountering one scene of violence would lead me to go back in time to other scenes of violence. I did not know that I would retrace scars and wounds recurrent to postcolonial subjection and so come to taste fear, hatred, and the sad, miserable forces of violence and counterviolence. In tracking a trail of violence I would end up haunting places and be haunted in turn.

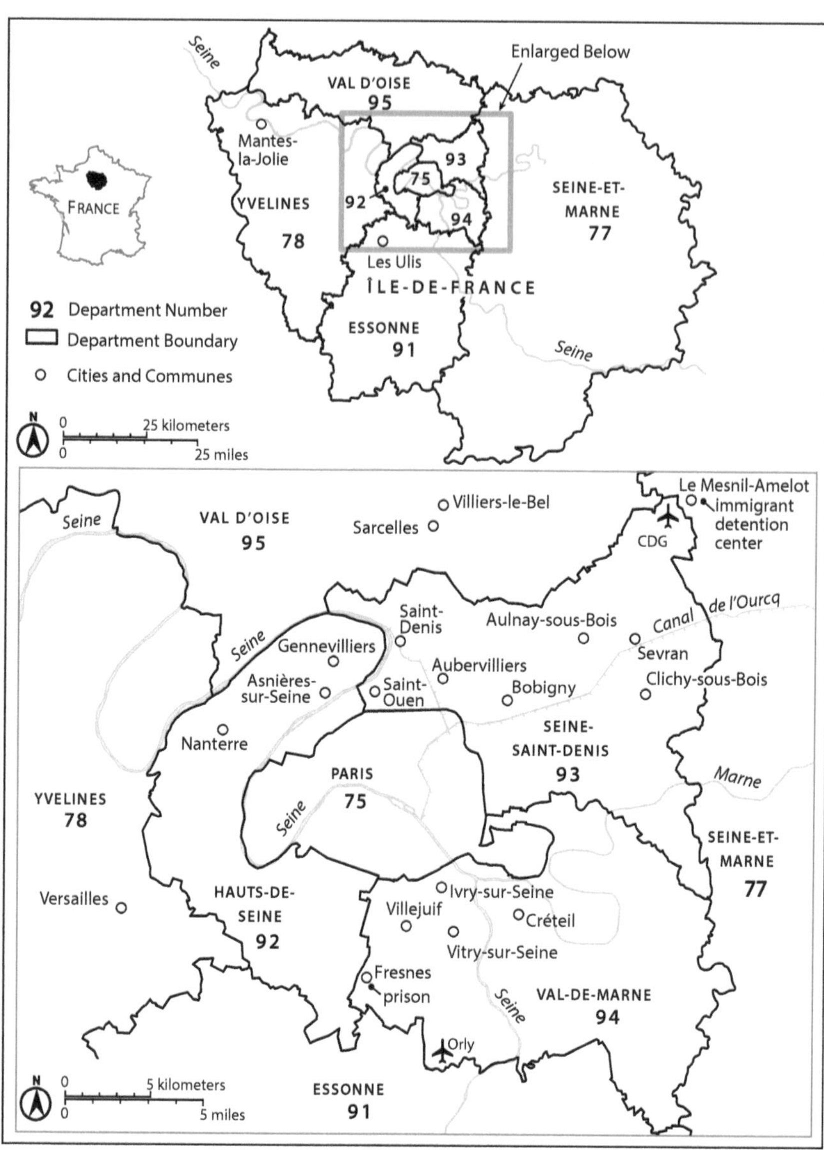


MAP 1. Île-de-France region (Map by Pease Press).

I knew none of this as one night in March 2016 I drove beneath an Albuquerque sky that was shifting from magenta to a deep, blackening blue. By the time I reached the airport, the desert sun had vanished into the west and the empty roadways were lit by the yellowish glow of streetlamps. I had been traveling through New Mexico, enjoying a meandering road trip

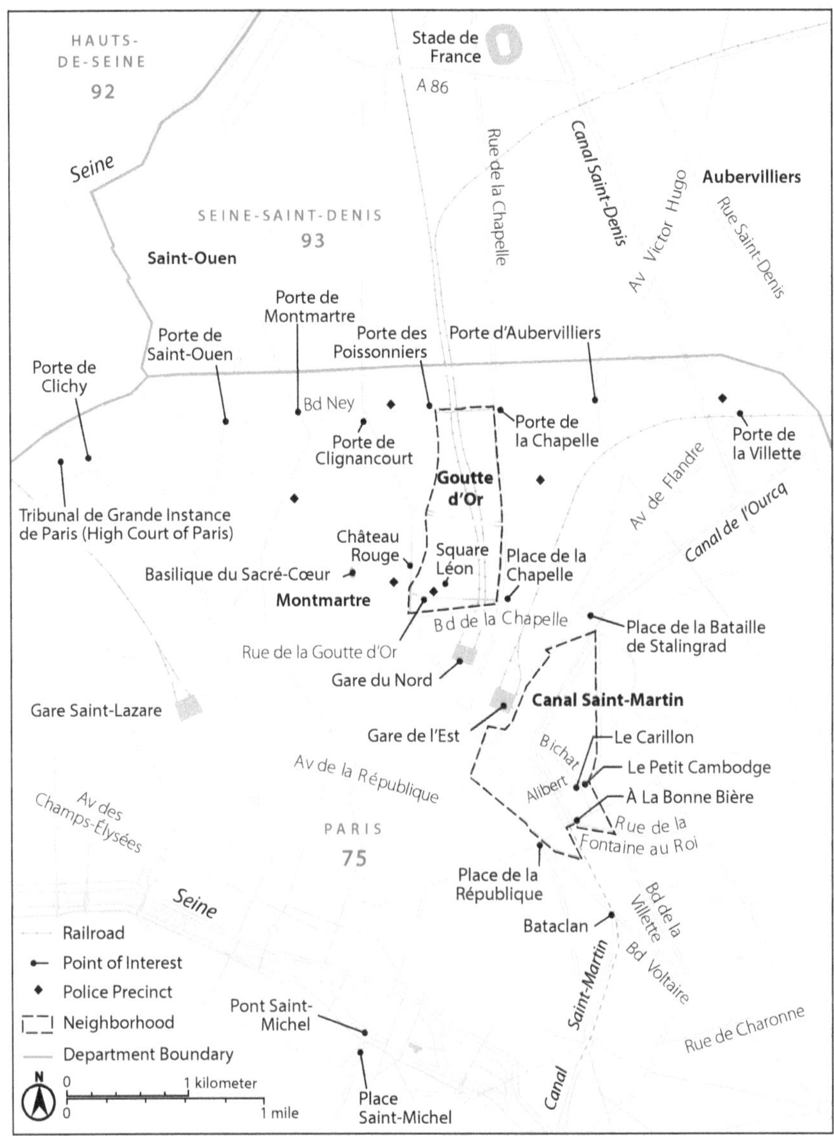


MAP 2. North Paris (Map by Pease Press).

through desert lands and mining towns. Now I was heading home. Soon I was in an airport terminal, waiting for my midnight flight. *Welcome to JetBlue airways. Flight number sixty-six to JFK is now boarding.* Painless take-off into dark clouds and then we were gliding through the continental night. The central cabin was illuminated with the subdued radiance of a deep blue tone seeping through narrow tubes of light. Each seat came equipped with a video console fixed to the back of the seat before it. The channels included live cable news programs. Around the turn of an hour one of the CNN newscasters said they had just received reports of explosions outside the airport in Brussels. It was unclear what had happened. No video feeds, yet. A gap in knowing in the dark shifting night. Within minutes reports came in of explosions at one of the departure halls at the airport in Zaventem. This is how it starts: the first words of something wrong and a mind braces for the brutality of a vision.

Streaming images appeared on the small screen set inches from my eyes, a few shaky videos taken with handheld phones inside the departure hall moments after the blasts. As the newscasters chatted nervously one video looped continuously on the television screen: white grey dust coating everything within the airport hall, baggage carts splayed on the ground, bodies walking past, the repeated cries of an unseen woman, one voice saying over and over, "It's okay. It's okay." The setting was familiar but marked by devastation; metal stands and check-in counters, travelers draped in winter coats trying to stand upright. As the JetBlue flight sped past Missouri and Indiana the disaster videos recurred, loop after loop of filmed white dust. I tried to catch patches of sleep with a blanket pulled over my face as violent images blurred into vague omens in dreams. I woke to televised dispatches of an explosion at a metro station in Brussels. By the time we reached the eastern seaboard a fiery red orb was rising from the ocean and a few things had become clearer in Belgium. At 07:58 two suicide bombers set off explosives packed into large suitcases in a departure hall at the airport in Zaventem. Another bomb was detonated at the Maalbeek metro station, around 09:10. A number of people had been killed, including the suicide bombers, and many others were injured.

The plane circled above the wetlands south of the city, waiting for a signal to land. I wondered if there would be more intensive security and armed police patrols stationed in the halls of JFK. The plane paced the sky in wide arcs and I thought of that November night in Paris when a series of coordinated attacks damaged the so-called city of light. That Friday evening I was in Manhattan, dining with a friend at a Korean restaurant in the Flatiron. We had just finished another round of rice beer when I noticed an email message from a friend in London. "Perhaps you've learned by now of the terrible events in Paris tonight," she wrote. "Some of the attacks were very close to where we met last summer." I brought up newspaper feeds on my phone and I saw headlines on death and maiming. I showed the small black script and images to my friend. We left the restaurant and began to walk along Fifth Avenue. The friend gave a nervous laugh and said, "I think this is going to be a very violent century."

On the train ride home that night I thought of those I knew in Paris and hoped they were okay. Past midnight I lay on a sofa in my apartment and with a sinking heart watched images rolling in from Paris, flickering loop after loop of emergency vehicles flashing alarm in the night and glimpses of people rushing past, until the shades of dreams replaced that churning phantasmagoria of violence. Not shown on the screen but spectrally present were acts of violence related at least indirectly to the horrific scenes in Paris—drone attacks in Afghanistan and the Middle East, bombs dropped from Air Force planes, the military surveillance and occupancy of lands in ways unwanted by many who lived in those places, as well as rites of exclusion and police harassment faced by those who live on the margins of cities in Western Europe. Through that night, and on to the next, media phantasms of sudden killings and violent explosions were entangled with mirages in a life, until it was impossible to know where the violence began or ended. The world was shot through with murderous intent, going back centuries, ghosting years to come.

And now again I was returning home, after leaving JFK that March morning, past a gauntlet of state security and red terror alerts. I watched unceasing videos of explosive concussion. As circuits of violence streamed past I tried to think on the sources of such violence, and those thoughts led me into the dark beast, the history of exploitation by colonial and imperialist powers. I thought of how nation-states like France and Belgium were haunted by their violent pasts, with reiterative returns of terror. But nothing was certain, and like so many others, my mind was vague on this.

Perhaps it was then, within the tired, despondent fugue of a post-terror morning, that I started to dwell on the disasters of violence, of the sort encountered in so many places. But I doubt it. The spectral wandering and obsessive writing came later. Most likely it was when I returned to Paris that summer, in June 2016. Soon after arriving I walked to sites of violence and met with the incomprehensibility of it all. Perhaps it was then, in those quiet, nervous moments when I sat on a terrace and jotted perceptions into a notebook, that I began to work on an archive of traces.

For some time I wrote on my own, spinning strands of writing that slowly formed into uneven bundles of thought. Only later did someone else join me in this endeavor; this took the writing into new domains of thought and perception. Months into the effort I met a scholar of north Paris, a sociologist from cultural and political histories and intellectual genealogies different from my own, who showed me parts of the city that I knew little about. As we walked in drifting ways through a series of neighborhoods in north Paris, we talked of the histories, wounds, and spectral hauntings embedded there. These excursions led to further conversations together and further researches into the formations of violence. Such interruptive engagements were most welcome. For one, I had come to realize that I could not grasp the force of violence on my own; my political subjectivity and interpretive frameworks were tied to certain perspectives and forms of attentiveness and a skewed regard of the city. Another voice was needed. Other histories of violence and wounding had to be inscribed, such that the writing became more dialogic and multistranded, and the thought otherwise.

R. D.

Blues, flights, beginnings . . .

*Wednesday, 19 June 2019*

July 2015. I was on a flight taking me home, from Toronto to Paris. I was leaving with a sense of anticipation, holding within the palm of my hand a psalm, a purpose to write, to document, to participate in the creation of a lived archive for now, for later, of lives past, of lives present. An ethnography that would welcome voices unheard or silenced, and let them emerge on their own terms. With this purpose, I thought, I was going home.

Home? At the time, and still now, something rang untrue about calling *it*—or anywhere else, for that matter—home. I had grown up between France and Canada, between the south of Paris and Toronto, the eldest in a modest household surrounded by my parents' pedagogy manuals. My relationship to rootedness seemed ambivalent. As I balanced my footing between continents I grappled with my sense of history, of memory, of territory.

Was home where memories of childhood resided? Memories of running and playing through the housing block with friends, whose presence had faded although I could still picture their faces and eyes; memories of their jailbird older brothers, police rundowns, and teachers' strikes that my child's tongue could not phrase properly. Or is it where *memory*—the sense of that time immemorial—resides? Memories of ancestors and their learned hands crafting life and land; memories of that land and those crafts being ripped apart; memories of leather suitcases by the seashore, of factories and tired backs aching from the weight of entire lives. There certainly was a mixture of both kinds of memory as I sat down and slid my knapsack under the seat in front of me. I felt I was going back to where exile was at once past, present, and future; where my own experience of diffracted exile might find a place to rest.

As I sat on that flight, effervescent as if all the passengers were embarking on the same journey, the words of poet Gil Scott Heron coursed through my headphones: "Home is where the hatred is." *Pieces of a Man*, 1971. Experiences of rooting oneself in a space, a body, a consciousness, begin with movement, with transience. As we flew closer to Paris I leaned against the small window, peering out through the clouds. I carried with me archives from the year I had spent in the United States, at Oberlin College where I had been introduced—by faculty, but most meaningfully by Black students—to the radical Black traditions in epistemology, social research, and direct political action. I had learned and practiced a method of respect and collective pedagogy, which I hoped would orient me through the urban and political spaces I was going to navigate once I landed in Paris.

Some weeks later, after having moved into an apartment in the 18th arrondissement, I began attending classes at the doctoral school of the Paris Institute of Political Studies. The distant, and sometimes conceited, attitude of my French professors struck me as going against the possibility of creating a shared epistemic community with faculty and students. It appeared, at least, that the institution did not extend its hospitality to all students, nor did it welcome all ideas and methodologies. I remained attached, however, to the project of collective learning and began to work closely with a handful of friends. Some of these relationships faded, others were irremediably broken, some were interrupted and later rekindled. The most meaningful of these relationships has been with Yasmine Harrison. Harrison is an independent researcher, whose work is grounded in ethnographic methods and historiography. She has worked on the interrelations of feminism, French secularism (*laïcité*), Republicanism, and racism. At the time of writing, her research focused on the medical-military complex in French colonial spaces, past and contemporary. In the final months of 2015, we began an intellectual relationship that has since become entangled in our friendship and life partnership. Another one of these relationships, although more distant and intermittent, is with Amandine Bocco, who has worked on the redistribution of state-owned plantation lands (*habitations domaniales*) in French Guyana.[1]

Yasmine and Amandine were there, on a brisk night in November 2015, as we sat around a kitchen-table in the Goutte d'Or. Thursday, 12 November 2015. Or was it Tuesday? The days are blurred, but the scene is crystal clear.

We sat around the table, thinking about our future in France. I was chewing on cold fries, as Yasmine and Amandine articulated with clarity and depth what I kept silent, reticent to let my voice crack open painful truths.

"All they need is another terrorist attack . . ."

Hesitantly reaching for the unfinished kebab sandwich on the table, I stared, silent and attentive, nervously envisioning how things could unravel.

"First, it'll be the police, right?"

"Intensification of what's already there, raids and arrests."

The moon was shining through the window as we looked out at the Basilique du Sacré-Cœur in the distance. Or was it the police helicopter hovering above the neighborhood that was shining a spotlight on the buildings?

"They can always reactivate old laws, like the state of emergency, like they did in 2005."

I felt uneasy: wasn't talking about it somehow a way of invoking it all?

"They already have detention centers for undocumented immigrants," Amandine began.

"But they'll need to find a way to extend that to nationals . . ." Yasmine added incisively.

The police dogs barked in the street below as street vendors packed up their goods and ran away. It was small moments of intimacy like these that gave me the respite and energy to continue learning, documenting, writing—a collective intimacy that could only exist when we felt safe to speak, to express doubt or dread, to embolden ourselves, to reconsider what we thought we did not know, to rest.

"You and I are just different," one student said during a discussion in a political sociology class the week after the attacks. "I'm French. And you're an Arab. That's why you don't relate to these horrible attacks the same way we *all* do."

Our professor nodded awkwardly.

I tried to argue, to explain that in the aftermath of the attacks lay repression and suspicion. "How are parents supposed to explain to their children that the state of emergency has made us—immigrants, Muslims, Arab and Black people, or whatever you call us—all suspects?" I tried to explain that the collective grief—nationalist and Republican—produced borders, reiterations of the antiterrorist police operations that took place, nightly, during the state of emergency. "How uncanny," she seemed to say as her face folded into a confused frown, "he thinks." It was in moments of confrontation like this, contrasted with stolen hours of respite, that I began to situate myself properly. I felt my presence, my body in these spaces, was a question mark: to those who had determined the conditions of accessing elite institutions, but also a question mark to myself.

The sociological outlook that came out of this relatively intimate process relies on a combination of autoethnography and a construction of the "object of study" through collective discussion and collective analysis. I turned to my own family history as a starting point to orient myself in histories of colonial immigration from which my family emerged. I became more familiar with the collective disasters that accompanied our intimate histories; I came to understand more clearly what I had somehow known all along, what I had retained from listening in on hushed conversations between uncles, aunts, and elders. To me, disasters looked like small archives that we had hoarded, transmitted, and received unknowingly.

The events of 13 November 2015 proved that disasters have a way of normalizing their presence. I remember the military bombings in Syria, the police operations on rue du Corbillon in Saint-Denis, the thousands of homes raided by police in French social housing projects all over the country, the hundreds of Muslim families suspected of having ties with "political Islam" and placed under house arrest without judiciary process. I remember the long speeches, claiming civilizational and cultural wars be waged to protect a French way of life. With these came calls for demonstrations of allegiance to the Republic. In the university I attended, students took to the short-lived habit of singing the national anthem, *La Marseillaise,* boisterously solemn or teary-eyed. More often and more discreetly, however, suspicion trickled into friendships. The absence of performed grief or fear became an element for discussion, as phantasms of racial difference blurred what one and the other not only witnessed as disastrous but *felt* and expressed. If it can be safely stated that everyone in France understands the loss of life that took place on 13 November as a disaster, the same cannot be said of the lives lost and caged in figurative and literal prisons. Such differences in what constitutes the real and the imagined would have been anodyne, harmless even, were they not inextricable from their material context: the expansion of the legal domain of security and carceral practices under France's state of emergency (2015–17). In resignifying borders, situating us all in our respective positions in society, the disaster reinscribed normality with hauntings that had never dissipated. Had we not inherited other disasters, which weighed down on the one we were now living in?

It was with all of this buzzing in my mind that I walked into Robert Desjarlais's guest lecture in Alban Bensa's anthropology seminar at the École des hautes études en sciences sociales in March 2017. I was eager to participate in discussion. A professor from New England spoke of archives and traces of violence, thinking and writing about the attacks of 13 November 2015 in a compelling way. His gaze, I thought, contrasted with French common sense. He seemed open to debate and, I sensed, would not be vexed if I formulated a critique. I suggested that were he to reorient his concepts toward a sense of the plural and overlapping histories inscribed in the city of Paris he might be able to tune into the ways in which the materiality of such histories produced plural and overlapping affective realities. In retrospect, this implied walking deliberately toward what Raymond Williams dubbed a structure of feeling, some ways off from the path of unanimous collective grief. Toward something uncertain, and yet to be.

We spoke, and we began walking through the fog together, noticing how the light shone differently from our distinct perspectives; noticing how our partial knowledges formed—not a coherent image—but a mosaic of shadows. After wandering together in the north of Paris, in July 2017, Robert invited me to join him on an ethnographic exploration of traces of violence. Our intellectual relationship relied for a time on my interrupting his thought processes with questions of method and epistemology, with historical facts and ethnographic texts, which I had assembled during fieldwork between 2015 and 2017.

My ethnographic work consisted of formal and chance conversations in the Goutte d'Or, with shopkeepers, young men and boys who hung out in the streets of the neighborhood, as well as undocumented Algerian men between twenty and sixty years old, and immigrant elders from a local café. I also conducted daily observations, focusing my attention on police presence in public space. These observations relied in part on urban drift, sometimes along police patrol routes, and in part on static observation. In both cases, whether by wandering or by staying still, I interacted with police officers—not as a student, but as a suspect, falling into the practical racial and police category of a French North African youth. To put it differently, it was my body as method that worked in contrast with Desjarlais's spectral anthropology.

In order to respond to his work in an informed way I began to integrate critical phenomenology into my work, and I have since used it with Robert to displace the imaginary of war and of foreign and internal threats to the national body politic, which undergirded the sites of the attacks he chose to study. This, in turn, had the unexpected effect of forcing me to reconsider the stability of my position, as I began to feel disquieted by how central my subjectivity had become in our collaborative anthropology. As Robert and I moved together, exchanging and challenging one another to write more, and differently, I began a silent process of recentering my experience of race, gender, memory, and space. Not in light of the shared disaster of Algerians in France, but of my own unaddressed queerness, of the fact of anti-Black racism, and the diasporic African spatialities that make up the palimpsestic history of violence in Paris.

Blues, flights, beginnings.

*K. H.*

———

# ONE

# *Névralgique*

And I have already told you: no works, no language, no words,
  no mind, nothing.
Nothing but a fine Nerve-Meter.
A kind of incomprehensible stopping place in the mind, right in
  the middle of everything.

ANTONIN ARTAUD,
*Le Pèse-nerfs,* "The Nerve-Meter"

## NERVOUS AIR

*Wednesday, 15 June 2016*

A weather-darkened red canopy runs along the side of the building, imprinted with the words, in white, *Le Carillon.* The awning serves in part to block the rain that might fall onto the tables, protecting patrons with its expanse. A sign bearing the words *Hotel Carillon* is fixed into the wall above the awning; by a side door another sign, temporary in appearance, reads *Hotel Closed.* I write these words while seated at one of Le Carillon's tables, set up on the sidewalk running along rue Alibert, a terrace consisting of some ten rows of three tables. It's a relatively quiet street, with cars slowing when they approach the intersection with rue Bichat or rue Marie et Louise, and then progressing further into the city, toward Canal Saint-Martin and place de la République, or northeast toward Belleville and Ménilmontant. "This is the village square," reads a 20 November 2015 article in *Le Monde,* describing that minor intersection of streets and interests in the traditionally working-class, now gentrified 10th arrondissement. "A crossroads of nothing but central to a little hidden corner of bobo Paris popular today and yesterday."[1]

The word translated as "crossroads" here is *névralgique,* the adjectival form of *neuralgia,* a sharp and paroxysmal pain along the course of a damaged nerve. In French the word *névralgique* carries the connotation of a nerve center or strategic point—a personal or collective point that is particularly sensitive. In the article, the sense of "center" or "central" is most dominant;

yet true to the roots of the word, the streets crossing that unnamed space and the buildings there stand like axons within the ganglion of a city in which paroxysmal pains shoot through the interconnected cells of a tense mass of nerves. Look closely and you just might detect the spasmodic pulsations of pleasure and pain that sear through everyday life in contemporary Paris. Or so this is the phantasm of the day.

Night or day, the city terrains, neural firings and misfires, pain in a nerve or a distribution of nerves. The writing here is similarly neuralgic, *une écriture névralgique,* let's say, charged with intermittent intensities and jolt affects, scattershot perceptions—words primed as both nerve damage and diagnostic sensory test.

A man on a motorcycle passes, and then a young woman on a bicycle. A slight breeze rustles. The sun is lighting cumulus clouds within a disparate blue sky.

It's 18:11. People are on their way home from work or school, meeting with friends, shopping for bread and wine for the evening meal. From within the bar emanates the frenetic excitement of a European Championship football match being played between Russia and Slovakia; the rushed cheers from thousands of fans flow like ocean waves churning into a shoreline. In the bar, men stand facing a large screen with drinks in their hands. France is the host country this year, and in Lille, where the game is being held, there must have been a series of security checks for those wanting to enter the stadium. I wonder if fighting will break out, if the Russian "ultras" will rage in the city, if armored police will block their passage in the streets. That the game is going on, elsewhere, and the fan zones are packed with people, implies the idea that less populated areas, bars, cafés, and other "soft targets" are safer now than they might be otherwise; any dark energy will be elsewhere, or so this is the thought.

A bus approaches the intersection, slows, brakes, and continues along rue Bichat. Across that way stands the wall that circles Hôpital Saint-Louis. Fixed above part of the wall is a poster bearing the words, *Ici, vous pouvez donner votre sang!* Further beyond that sign, atop several buildings within the hospital grounds, rest several strands of what appear to be Tibetan prayer flags, frayed and tangled.

The hospital was built at the beginning of the seventeenth century, during a plague epidemic, to serve as a space of quarantine and care for afflicted Parisians. It's said that several people who worked at the hospital were at the bar that night, enjoying drinks with friends. They helped to care for those

FIGURE 1. Le Carillon, rue Bichat and rue Alibert, June 2016. Photo by R. D.

who were injured. The metal cut into the integrity of the body, lacerating muscle and nerve.

Who was there, by chance, that night, and who was not.

Le Carillon was one of the epicenters of the violence the night of 13 November 2015, along with the suicide bombings at the Stade de France in Saint-Denis; the raid of the Bataclan; the shootings at rue de la Fontaine-au-Roi and rue de Charonne; the bombing at boulevard Voltaire; 130 dead in all, another 413 people injured. The first shootings occurred around 21:45, near the crossroads of rues Bichat and Alibert, in front of Le Carillon and the restaurant across the street, Le Petit Cambodge. Fifteen people were killed, ten critically injured. How could this have happened here, in those sudden moments, rupturing what had seemed so calm and peaceful? What happens when violence wracks havoc within a particular place? What sorts of processes and politics of affect, perception, inscription, effacement, image-making, time, archiving, and memorialization emerge in such situations?

It's the end of the workday on this Wednesday evening, in the early turns of summer, when there is still promise of light, and in these dusky hours people are starting to relax after the day's labors. A mother walks along the side of rue Alibert with two girls, each carrying a doll. On the table several yards away, two men are seated. They are talking with one another. Two blonde beers are set on the table, along with a cigarette case that reads in large letters, *FUMER TUE.*

Cell phones. Ashtrays. Chairs. A newspaper. Espresso. Cognac. Perrier with lemon and ice, the low hum of chatter. At a nearby table sits a young man. The glass cover of his cell phone, still intact, is fractured in small pieces. Through the web-like fissures of the crack one can envision the point of contact. The man makes a call with the phone by tapping his fingers to the sheen of broken glass. The glass reflects the light of the sun. Fingertips touch the fractures.

There is no threat of rain just now. This, too, could change with the passing of a new configuration. There has been a lot of stormy weather this summer, turbulent skies shifting from clear to overcast to heavy downpours. The Seine overflowed its banks a couple weeks ago and workers had to excavate artwork from the depths of the Louvre. Politically, in Paris, the atmospherics have been taut, apprehensive, potentially explosive. The air is pressured, tense, uncertain, with flashes of joy and pleasure.

Across the street, close to the hospital, two boys sit on the seats of small bicycles, their hands holding the front bars. One of the boys is carrying a French flag.

There is a small newness in each moment.

I write observations in a notebook. My handwriting, clusters of jottings, cannot be read by others. I enter cafés and bars quietly. My occasional appearance must strike others as insubstantial, diffuse, inarticulate—a passing specter, drifting through history. More phantom than anthropologist, I am nearly imperceptible, not speaking much, not heard well, wandering streets, pushed by obscure forces. If a ghost were to write, what words would he trace out?

One has to wonder what other phantoms might be lurking about this place. There is, for one, the phantasm of the event, the lingering miasma of the violence that devastated this intersection of streets. While a number of people were hit directly by the violence, its effects have settled in the lives of many; the force of the shootings inhabits the streets surrounding Le Carillon and in the bar itself as a haunting, hauntive energy that stirs in places and touches on perceptions like a restless ghost fading in time. You can almost see the damage, you can nearly sense the disaster within the pavement of the road and the light reflecting upon the café windows. You can sense the damage in other *quartiers* of Paris, though there is no apparent damage. Then there is the spectral residue of the attackers that night, who appeared and disappeared like fleeting phantoms. They have remained obscure figures to many. There is also the vivid potential for the shades of the dead and wounded to haunt the memories and perceptions of those who continue to frequent Le Carillon. Also feeding into this phantasmal mix is the sovereign power of the French state, with the historically contingent subject of that sovereignty a "juridicopolitical fiction, a regulative phantasm" that promotes the sense of authoritative, legally justified powers to enact further violence in apparent defense of its citizens and its sovereign rights in times of war.[2] Spectral subjects, all. If *phantasm* can be considered in the variable sense of an "apparition or illusion; a ghost or phantom; an imaginary construct; a fantastical image or vision; a haunting memory; a fanciful idea; or a cohering fantasy, momentary or lifelong, conscious or unconscious," then such phantasmal aspects can be said to course through myriad thoughts, perceptions, and encounters in present-day Paris.[3]

Within much the same phantasmal times and places, some persons might assume the diaphanous look of the phantomic while walking about the streets of Paris, standing and talking with friends, or entering into shops or bars. Clothing, skin color, a certain look about the face, the call of Islam, the mark of geography; spectral imageries such as these might designate such arrivals as apparitions and "fictionalized enemies" to be received with disaffection or suspicion.[4] What phantasms do people read into the appearances of certain figures, woven out of "a thousand details, anecdotes, stories."[5] What imaginings shape a life? Some figures are cast as malevolent others, waiting for the right moment to strike.

In the streets near Le Carillon one might encounter the imagining of one's own death, from the hands of others. I have done as much, when the clouds pass. I phantasmally conceive a body's end that night, alongside hobbled others. This is a doubled death, a death that echoes the perishing of others, an imagined, simulative time of dying, death fantastic, recurrent, a deferred death, disaster still to come.

In filling pages of a notebook I am trying to trace something out. I am trying to write on the everyday, observant of its constitution and possible fractures. A photograph or two would add to the visuals but I am wary of photographing anyone near the site of the wound. I write not so much for those lost in the violence or for those who mourn them but for the world itself, as if writing might be a vigil on life, a vigilant watch of its pulsations of joys and pain and nervous tremblings. This is a kind of witnessing, uncertain and open-ended. I am trying to find a way, a passage, through certain forces

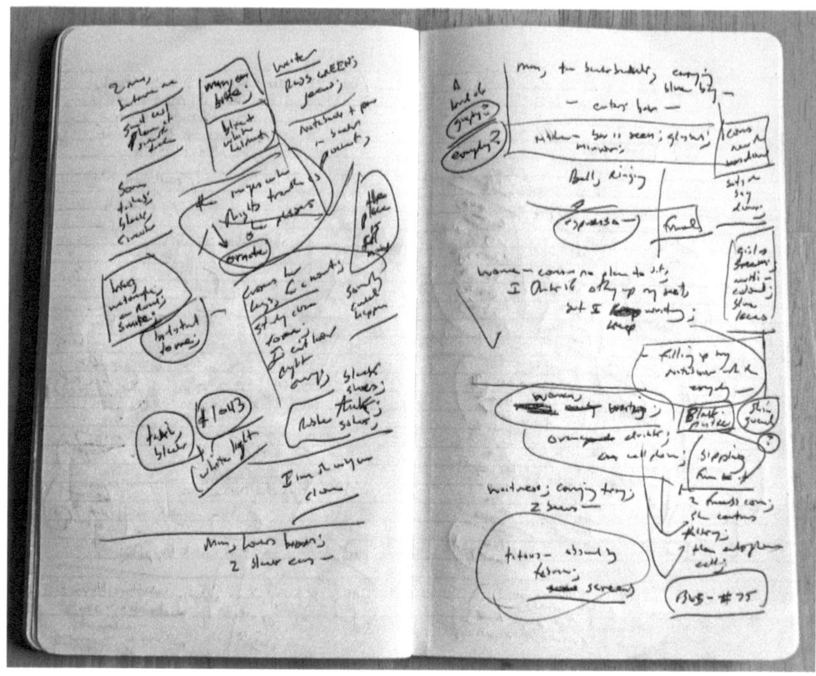

FIGURE 2. Notebook from June 2016. Photo by R.D.

of violence. I am struggling to comprehend its angles, energies and aftermaths, within a taut spool of writing.

EDGING ON DISASTER

To write the everyday is to write the disaster. This is the case, at least, in the sense that Maurice Blanchot gives to the word *disaster*. As conveyed in his difficult and elusive book, *L'écriture du désastre,* disaster is on a par with the collapse of existence, ruin of the self, situations of weakness, passivity and nonpower, the end of a world and a self's relation to it, ruptures in perception and time, dispersion, liquidation of stable meaning and knowledge. Disaster resulted in the concentration camps during World War II and haunts the somber ashes of the Holocaust, "the calm, the burn of the Holocaust, the annihilation of noon—the calm of the disaster."[6] Disaster can be sensed in moments of personal dissolution and unsettling encounters with others—and in the vulnerable intimacy of close friendships. As the site "of an agonizing collapse of the signifying process itself," disaster lies in the breakdown of language and in the limits of knowledge and of writing, the other night beyond night—"white, sleepless night—such is the disaster: the night lacking darkness, but brightened by no light."[7]

Disaster can also course through the tender force of writing. In *writing the disaster* Blanchot sought to express an orientation that attends to the incessant "dying," weakness, passivity, and dissolution that shadows many situations in life. "Dying" for Blanchot (*le mourir*), is, in contrast to "death" (*la mort*), something beyond subjective or temporal horizon, beyond clear-cut meaning and conceptualization, beyond power or possibility. The abstract purity of death, as an idea or ideal in the world, stands in contrast to the jittery, open-ended tracks of dying. The wrenching sharpness of dying is forever wounding, forever cutting into the flesh of life and the cold stillness of death. "It is though there is, in death, something stronger than death: dying itself— the intensity of dying."[8] For Blanchot, death is "power and even potency— and thereby limited." Dying, in contrast, is "absence of power" (*non-pouvoir*). "Interrupting the present, always a crossing of the threshold, excluding all term or end, providing neither release nor shelter. In death, it is possible to find illusory refuge. . . . Dying is the fleeting movement that draws into flight indefinitely: impossible and intensively."[9]

Dying pulls indefinitely. It draws us away from any easy models of life and death and situates us in moments of pain and nonclosure and a terrible, unending openness. Dying tears at the self. Dying tears at the world.

"To think the way one dies: without purpose, without power, without unity, and precisely, without 'the way.'"[10]

For Blanchot, who is in implicit conversation with Hegel and Heidegger, among others, the philosophers' concept of death implies a potential mastery and assuredness, in which a person can search for authenticity in death and, potentially, become master of himself. Death is of a clear formation; within time it appears relatively changeless. It offers an illusory refuge and holds the possibility of transcendence. Dying, in contrast, is passive, impersonal, endless, limited, strangely other. In depicting death and dying in such terms Blanchot is not speaking solely of these forms of cessation. He is also trying to get at a certain dissonant ontology of existence, one that attends to a "strange, insectlike buzzing in the margins."[11] Blanchot seeks to express an orientation through writing that attends to the incessant dying, weakness, passivity, and dissolution that shadows many situations in life. Writing should attend to the inassimilable force of such disasters while working in correlation with the dissolutions involved. Blanchot advocated that one write not simply to destroy, conserve, or transmit, but to write "in the thrall of the impossible real, that share of disaster wherein every reality, safe and sound, sinks."[12]

What I read in these lines is that the flow of time can collapse at any moment; life itself is predicated on ruin. In Paris these days people know of certain realities, seemingly safe and sound, that have collapsed in sudden bursts of violence. They faced these disasters in November 2015, as well as the day of the *Charlie Hebdo* killings in January 2015. The attacks troubled people in ways both collective and personal. The aura of the attacks recurs in the mood and history of the city, which continues on. "The disaster ruins everything, all the while leaving everything intact," Blanchot wrote.[13] "The disaster takes care of everything."[14] The disaster touches on everything; it marks all perceptions and language, memory, coordinates of time and space, the formed and unformed. The idea of France as a place of liberty and fraternity has been undermined. Paris is no longer a realm of "lightness" (*légèreté*) and of carefree, spirited life. The disaster keeps watch. People are living under "the surveillance of the disaster."[15] There is a lingering sense in France that catastrophic violence might happen again, possibly this summer. "We are on the edge of disaster without being able to situate it in the future," wrote Blanchot.[16] On the edge of disaster, in a "wounded space," I write in the thrall of a Parisian summer afternoon, where the actualities of the everyday are nearly, seemingly impossible, given the fragility of their design.[17]

Seated at a table a few feet away are two women. One of the women, prim and dignified in appearance, is holding a cell phone to her left ear. While talking she takes a sip from her beer. She has a small bandage on her right cheek. The bandage, close to the pale color of her skin, is nearly imperceptible. It's a minimal wound, a nerve prick on a stately appearance, yet there is a need to protect and conceal.

Sharp and sudden sounds implode like firecrackers. Excessive speed or slowness. Irregular movement or no movement at all. Hesitation, pauses. Bulky bags. Indistinct vans with tinted windows. A man fidgeting with a parcel in the metro leads you to get off that train and take the next or leave the system altogether. Welcome to the new new materialism, where matter carries imaginal impact and emotional force and pieces of the everyday become sights and sounds of potential harm—violent matter, at times.[18] In this nervous sensorium perceptions easily grow heightened, intensified, skewed, tinged with delirium. *If you see something suspicious.* Every few days one wakes to reports of another mass shooting somewhere in the world. Life carries a temporality of hesitation and interruption. Time itself is jumpy, fraught, tense. In Paris as elsewhere there has been a mutual absorption of the violent and the ordinary.[19]

Soft targets. We are all soft targets. A strange, unsettling sensation occurs when it comes to inhabiting the space of a soft target—thus becoming a target, oneself. The body's flesh is soft and porous, the stomach exposed. The cranium can hardly protect delicate tissue. The woman's arm, with its narrow bone, looks tender, easily bruised, how could she be protected? The mind turns on different possibilities, safety or violence. You cannot let it paralyze you. Like others I count on the percentages. What are the odds that a bomb would go off at this place, at this time, while I am here?

"How many people live in Paris?" asked one man as he watched a football match in a bar. "Over two million," he said, answering his own question. "And how many will die in the next attack? A hundred, maybe, at most? So what are the odds I'll be among the dead?"

This is probability theory at work. Usually, my body is not in the most critical sites, places of extreme and tender softness. Steer clear of the Arc de Triomphe, the Eiffel Tower, stadium concerts. "I try to avoid places where there are lots of people, lots of movement," someone said.

"In France now there is a permanent state of vigilance," one woman related.

"Yesterday," said a resident of Paris, "when I was in a small square by the Centre Pompidou, I realized that if something bad happened a few streets away—like a bomb going off—I wouldn't know about it at all, right then. I would be completely oblivious. I would only know about it once I saw people rushing past."

Any given body of flesh and effort is a potential site of violence. A body can become an agent of violence or the recipient of the harmful malevolence of others—or a troubled combination of different trajectories of violence. Potentialities are apparent in both being-becoming and in violence. These two kinds of potentiality can get caught up in manifold relations, complex entanglements, and feedback loops in life and death. There is a plasticity to violence, it carries metamorphic potential; violence can readily break into new forms and histories in life and death. Violence can turn into a kind of becoming, crystalize in new forms of life death, including forms of becoming-violent, a dark poiesis in line with the potentiality for darkness.[20] There might occur an antibecoming counterviolence; creative seriality in life,

FIGURE 3. Rue Alibert, June 2016. Photo by R. D.

or sequence nodes in a kill-chain. Violence can be world-destroying and or world-building. Acts of violence can quickly go viral. Violence can sheer in many directions, break into self-destroying destruction or revolutionary zeal and the overthrow of oppressive regimes, or provoke the annihilation of lives. Generative fashioning in life can shut down in the midst of violence and aftereffects, fix becoming dead in its tracks. While new forms of life and relation can end a damning tract of violence.

Violence is not just about what happened, that rupture and ballistic debris; it's about what could happen, soon, or later on. It's about what happened elsewhere, years ago, or last year, with other histories of violence.

Some say they do not think about it—it does not faze them. Others say they think about the possibility of violence all the time. Whenever they are out and about they worry over potential harm. It's in the back of a mind; a moment or situation can bring the idea of violence into the fore of consciousness.

"Most people think something will happen soon," said the owner of a café. "There will be another attack, sometime this summer. It's just a matter of when, and where."

Three white minivans proceed smoothly down rue Alibert. Several military soldiers are seated inside each one. Painted onto the front and side of each vehicle are the words *OPERATION SENTINELLE.*

A book never to be written: the lives of the people there, that night. There will be no archive of suffering, no interviews with the wounded, no trauma studies; just a sense of the place through certain vectors of time, perception, image, trace, and graph; minute observations for a spectral anthropology, after the event.

What is involved if one writes within an interval of dying, from a fractured space of weakness and of nonmastery, without power, without unity or determination, without potency and domination, without the strength of a clear way? This writing, I gather, approaches the singularity of the extreme, a fragmentary unstory that bears ruptures, effacement, exposure, excess. Such writing rests on fragile, awkward discourses that are torn, incapable, feverish, violent; the writing transpires in an intermediary between where phantasms are as real and unstable as wounds; in which the phenomenal and the phantasmic are deeply intertwined. This writing, this dying, requires an "exigency of strangeness."[21] It proceeds in relation to alterity, an otherness and non-knowing that exceeds one's grasp; dying is always other. This way of knowing knows faintly of nonknowing, a deprivation of sure truths and clear foresight. The writing reflects and inhabits a wounded space, the hurt of the dying; an unceasing, passive, neutral, inept dying; a deep cut in the possibility of any cut at all.[22] The writing suggests a perilous threshold between being and nonbeing, wherein the subject is not quite there, where words imply less stable subjects than an absence of bounded subjectivity or secure intersubjectivity with no fixed position or truth in consciousness, no sovereignty in being, no singular continuities in time. The name wears away, and words as such cease to be means of action. Words have an air of dissolution, subtraction, passivity.

A boy comes close to the terrace on a scooter. He stands, looks up, gazes at the act of writing, turns away.

A heavyset man, walking with a slight limp, steps toward Le Carillon. He comes close to the entrance and stands near the street. He raises his cell phone and holds it close to his eyes. He takes several photographs of the bar.

Within Le Carillon are mirrors above the bar and trays of glasses of many shapes and sizes. All of this looks fragile. A sharp force could shatter the crystal array.

The engines of the motorcycles that barrel down the street make low, grumbling reverberations dense and rattly. These sounds carry a gravelly track of the ominous. The sounds soon diminish.

The woman with the bandage on her cheek is seated alone at her table. She looks my way though she is not looking at me. The woman looks lost in thought. She suddenly appears alarmed. She reaches with her right hand to touch the bandage on her cheek. Her fingers feel its contours. The fabric is still intact, smooth and flush against her skin. The woman appears set at ease.

"The disaster: stress upon minutiae, sovereignty of the accidental."[23]

The restrooms could be good places to hide. This might not have worked so well. The doors look soft, porous.

On-line reviews of Le Carillon, posted before November 2015, describe the bar as *décontracté* (laid-back), with a rustic décor "fixed in time." A commentary holds that it is "one of the most pleasant bars of Paris, for its ambiance, its terrace." "The wine is always so disgusting, but the atmosphere is always so relaxed." The place is *vrai,* true. After the attacks people left heartfelt messages on Le Carillon's Facebook page. The pain and sorrow were palpable, as was as the show of solidarity.

Who was excluded from these considerations of the aftereffects of violence?

Four youths tall and skinny walk past the terrace, potentialities in motion. They must be heading toward Canal Saint-Martin. Small bands of friends are seated along the quays there. They have brought bottles of wine with them, imported beer, cheese and bread, enjoying the summer night together.

The football match is now over. Slovakia won, 2–1. On this night devout fans roam the streets of Paris, each sporting the colors of their nation's team, Swedish yellows, Portuguese green and reds. Buddies drink and dine together and go carousing in the hills of Montmartre, singing nationalist anthems; fights flare between opposing units; police patrols stand firm near metro stops to block thugs enthralled with conflict and breakage.

The everyday is stitched together through small, concrete actions, fragments little by little, suddenly. These constellations come undone, new strands stitch anew. Each bundled moment is altogether precarious, tender, and fragile. Today everything has remained intact, so far. The recent *attentats* make some think of the bombings in the Paris metros in 1995 and 1996; twelve dead, more than three hundred wounded. Some are wary of entering that remembered underworld. Violence is temporally proximate, and echoic: it happened recently, or long ago, and it could occur again soon.

The everyday contains ghostly threats recalled and imagined, dangers imagined as real. It comprises spectral histories, remnant marks.

At Le Carillon time turns, and turns, slowly. Each moment contains a multitude of possible futures within the open-ended emergence of the world.

A police car speeds down Rue Alibert in the direction of the canal. Its blaring, whining sirens pierce the air. Two or three persons are inside. A few heads turn to watch it pass. After the sirens fade it's as though the air has cleared.

A single bird flies past, its shadow body lighting across the sky.

Sunlight, slanting down.

A group of four women, college-aged, pass along the street near the terrace.

"It was here?" one of them asks, gesturing toward the bar.

"Yes," says another.


## TRACE AND EFFACEMENT

You wouldn't know that something happened here. You wouldn't know of the carnage that occurred that night, just there, by the doorway, unless you knew already, or were told by someone, or looked up addresses on the Internet and undertook a mournful pilgrimage to the sites, one by one; or read of the number of dead at each place. You would not be able to perceive the actions that devastated so many lives. There are few signs of the deaths, few remaining traces left within the materiality of the place.

This, at least, is what I encountered when I arrived in Paris a few weeks back. I took the metro to Oberkampf and walked to several of the sites of the attacks, including the Bataclan theater and the bars and cafés by Canal Saint-Martin. I thought I could observe, in a quiet, respectful way, where the violence took place. I went to the Bataclan and stood before that squat ornate structure; it was surrounded by scaffolding.[24] The concert hall was undergoing revocations. I walked to La Belle Équipe one Sunday afternoon and found families and friends enjoying brunches together, glistening china and glasses lined the mirrored walls. No sign of damage, a pure sign of imminent danger. The café had undergone an extensive renovation to repair the structural damage from the attacks. I passed by À La Bonne Bière, a café seemingly built of glass. There I encountered apéro-goers seated on an asphalt-lined terrace set along busy streets.

In visiting these sites of recent violence I was struck by the fact that there was little to see of the carnage. I thought there might be informal shrines or signs, traces of past violence. That the attacks caused little or no destruction to buildings or within the physical topography of the city—as was the case of the collapse of the Twin Towers in New York on 9/11—had something to do with this, as most traces had to be put there after the event.[25] Yet months later nothing was all that visible. Everything looked so ordinary. It was as if, within less than a year, a fold of the everyday had come to form a strata-like layer over a chasm of violence, with few archaeological traces remaining. This was disconcerting. Traces of the violence were not overtly apparent.

There are many places like this in Paris—sites of battles, martyrs, killings, assassinations, arrests, disappearances—that emit only dim, apparitional auras of past bloodshed. Some streets carry a marker of the violence and deaths that occurred there, as with the plaques around Gare du Nord that detail the number of resistance fighters killed by the Gestapo in May 1941, or the memorial sign bolted into the façade of an apartment building in Montmartre, where Jewish families were taken by the Nazis and deported to concentration camps, never to be seen again. Beyond the nearly forgotten aura of that sign and the wilting flowers placed on the wall below there is little trace of the disappearances. There are countless streets, squares, and bridges in Paris where violent deaths occurred, unsigned and unremembered, and many of those walking about the city know little of those dismal haunts.

In the days and weeks after the attacks in November 2015 a vast number of flowers, candles, and letters were placed at the sites of the attacks. Photographs taken in those first days showed stunned and tearful faces, friends and neighbors quietly looking upon shattered glass, bullet holes, bouquets of flowers, struggling to comprehend.

In the weeks that followed, while the bars and restaurants remained closed and under repair, these makeshift, deeply intentioned memorials became like funereal landscapes. These memorials were similar in form to collective, "grassroots" articulations of mourning and shock in the wake of the 2004 Madrid train bombings, the 2005 London bombings, and 11 September 2001 in New York.[26] "Wild memorials" of a sort, they were not managed or formally condoned by the state, though the Paris government allowed them to exist for a while. The memorials offered a means to mourn the dead, to relate to what had happened, and to communicate a sense of solidarity and continued life. The memorials slowly dissolved, or they were disbanded or cleaned away by street cleaning crews. "We cleared out six trucks' worth of wilted flowers and several kilograms of candles," one cleaner told television network France 24. "We didn't want to get rid of things, but it feels a bit like a cemetery with all the flowers."[27] By the time the bars and restaurants reopened in

December and January of 2016, with new windows and clear pathways, the flowers and messages were gone.

Le Carillon reopened on 13 January 2016, with patrons, neighbors, and journalists attending the festive event. There were streamers in the bar and lines of flags suspended across the intersecting streets. "Welcome! Le Carillon is open. We continue to live," said the senior owner, who in 1957 at age seventeen left his native Kabylia for France, during the Algerian war of independence. He bought the bar with other family members in the early 1970s. A neighbor was relieved that Le Carillon was back. "These last two months, to pass this intersection every day, it was very hard," she said. "There prevailed an atmosphere of death. There were always so many people at Le Carillon that to see it closed through this period, it weighed down the morale and the atmosphere."[28]

The family that owns the bar had sought to preserve the space as it had been, and tried to efface, as much as possible, any marks of the bullets and their impact. A few scratch dents remained on the zinc counter at the bar. "I wanted everything to resume normally," said one of the owners at the reopening. "I don't want this place to become a pilgrimage site. I'm afraid of voyeurism, unhealthy curiosity. We want to become a bar again, like other bars."[29]

Journalists visiting Le Carillon wished to hear from one of the owners. He would not talk with them at first. They saw him crying. Then, later on, he spoke. "I feel guilty," he said, "because thirteen of my clients died, just because they liked to come to my bar. We have always been tolerant in welcoming everyone, young, old, Catholics, Jews, Muslims.... I finished my medical studies two months ago, I'm an emergency physician, but I wasn't prepared for that. Nobody can be prepared for that. We did what we could with a firefighter who was there by chance, because he had been called for an illness. We saw war wounds, horrific, dead people whose eyes continue to fix on you. I could not save anyone, anyone..."[30]

Such is the disaster of wounded self and others wrecked upon this man that night: the helpless inability to save any lives; the specter of eyes locked onto his own. May these painful memories leave this man. May he be soothed and sutured, unfixed.

Some memories of that night are almost too much to bear. There has been a work of repair and healing, of recovering tones of normality within the ordinary. Also in effect have been efforts to remove traces of the event from the bar, to make the place less a site of collective mourning, fixed by disaster,

FIGURE 4. Informal memorial established at the base of a monument, place de la République, June 2016. Photo by R. D.

and return to it a sense that it's an ordinary neighborhood bar; as though the flesh and skin of a body was healing over a deep wound, with scarring apparent. A curative effort in analgesia, the absence of pain, was called for, to counter the *névralgique* wound of that night. As with many situations of loss and mourning, there has been an intricate play between the desire to preserve traces, to remember and retain lost ones, and the need to forget the pain, to banish reminders, remove traces. Complex, contradictory movements of memory and erasure, grief and healing, trace and effacement, mark and unmark the remnant sites of the attacks.

In time, the energy invested in the makeshift memorials established at different sites shifted, in part, to a collective memorial that had taken form at place de la République. This is where tens of thousands of people gathered after the murders at the editorial offices of *Charlie Hebdo* to express their sympathy for the people killed and their defense of French values of liberty and freedom of speech. And this has been where, since early April, thousands of people have been engaged in nocturnal "sit-in" protests associated with the movement *Nuit debout*.[31] In these days, circling one side of the large monument there—below the bronze statue of Marianne, personification of the French Republic—flowers, letters, messages, pronouncements, and names written on placards and pieces of paper have conjoined with mementos left in the wake of the *Charlie Hebdo* attacks of January 2015. The aggregate of words and images—a "shrine to the dead"—include expressions of personal and collective grief and statements of protest and solidarity.[32] Energies of mourning swirl about Paris, and crystallize in specific times and places.

### TIME AT LE CARILLON

It's well past eight now. Still more light to go. The scene has altered, the place is full of people, most of them younger than me. I am getting in the way of the pleasures of others, strangers. Other ghosts are about now, different spectralities, times, and hauntings.

After the attacks some were wary, at first, of sitting on the terraces of cafés and bars in Paris. Yet many patrons soon returned to sitting close to the streets for a coffee in the morning or a drink in late afternoon. There was a sense of defiance, that no one could take away the epicurean pleasures of life in Paris, where its inhabitants should enjoy the company of friends with good food and drink in bars and restaurants. *"Boire en terrasse, fumer, parler de sexe, sans règle ni doctrine. . . . La liberté. . . . La France !!!,"* ran one Facebook comment at the time. When the café À La Bonne Bière reopened a banner ran along its awning, proclaiming *Je Suis En Terrasse* (I am on the terrace). Others voiced the same statement, a proud, defiant spin on that earlier proclamation, *Je Suis Charlie.*

Seeded within such statements were images of patriotism and nationhood in which the terrace came to signify a symbolic space of civil discourse, free thought, global enlightenment, and the pleasures of social life. As President Hollande put it in an address and homage to the victims a few days after the attacks, "These women, these men . . . were in Paris, a city that adorns itself in bright ideas, that vibrates by day and shines at night. They were on café terraces, those open meeting places of encounters and ideas." The open places of encounter and ideas embodied and symbolized by café terraces, the moral and discursive logic went, was under imminent threat of destruction, and they needed to be protected and preserved.[33] One irony in such a discourse is that the French state was then conducting military operations in Syria and Iraq, bombing campaigns that contributed to destructive violence.

Down the way from rue Alibert, past Canal Saint-Martin, along quai de Valmy, stands a shop window that carries the graffitiesque work of the artist

FIGURE 5. Quai de Valmy, June 2016. Photo by R. D.

Jérôme Mesnager. The painted image shows two people seated at a table, clinking wine glasses together, looking out at a reflected view of the city with an élan of pleasure and lightness. Below it are the words *Nous sommes . . . en terrasse* (We are . . . on the terrace). The figures are muscular in form, fit, the compound bodies an athletic image of strength and flexibility. And yet the bodies emit the feel of being exposed, seated alongside the street, their backs turned to passing traffic. The two men are taking a stand, primed for fight or flight. They could flee the terrace, if need be. The chalk-white flesh looks prone to bullets.

A Parisian terrace is a liminal space, betwixt and between the interior of a café or restaurant and the surroundings beyond that structure, a changing threshold between interior and exterior. At any moment someone can approach, looking for a cigarette or a light or spare change; buskers, beggars, drunkards, and newspaper barkers; passing friends stop to say hello. You're right there, on the terrace, singularly exposed to the commerce of the street and the city's thrills and dangers. This phenomenality of the terrace became intensified with the attack of 13 November, for many of those killed at the bars and restaurants attacked were standing or seated on terraces or near doorways. After these events, being *en terrasse,* sitting alone or with friends, became a moral and political act with potentially real or phantasmal consequences.

The terrace at Le Carillon holds sights and specters unseen. Soon after the attacks of 13 November the French comedy duo "Eric et Ramzy" posted online, in homage of Le Carillon, a scene from their 2008 film, *Seuls Two,* which tells the story of a cop and a thief who find themselves in a Paris emptied of all of its inhabitants. The title is a *verlan* inversion of the French phrase *tout seul* (all alone). In commenting on the three-minute clip, one person wrote, "That seems so peaceful . . . hard to imagine the horror that's been caused here . . . thank you for putting a different image on this place."[34] "Too much," wrote another. "This gives me the chills." The filmmakers posted a still image of their filming at Le Carillon, with a caption that read, "We will continue to try to make laughter, and you are going to try to laugh yourselves. It's all that one knows how to do, it's all that one can do today. Carry on."[35]

When shooting the film in 2007, the filmmakers and lead actors, Eric Judor and Ramzy Bedia, found the terrace of Le Carillon a good place for one scene, in which the two men engage in sporadic conversation while seated at tables close to the entrance. "As for the terrace," explained the director, Eric Judor, "one normally places oneself there to watch the people pass. The scene is all the more absurd since the guys have nothing to contemplate."[36] The aesthetics of the intersection also motivated the filming of the scene. "There are beautiful lines of flight, from the perspective of cinema. It's a very graphic place."

The scene begins with the sound of a man's voice and the camera's steady pan across columns of austere Haussmannian buildings set along long, empty urban corridors. Soon apparent was a deserted rue Alibert, leading toward the canal. The man who has been speaking comes into view. He is seated at a table just before the doorway to Le Carillon, talking on the phone, " . . . *Ich bin disparu. Ich bin kaput.*" The camera comes closer, moving from the street toward the tables by the entrance. The bar is unmanned. It's a different time, a space unpeopled and quiet. Another man approaches from the left and takes a seat at a nearby table. He whistles to the first man to get his attention. The two engage in a testy conversation, shifting from table to table, with the second man trying to get the first to talk and the first resistant to these efforts. With no one else about, they have little to see or to contemplate beyond their own relation. The scene appears like the sequence of a dream, with the two men attending a strange and ghostly apparition of Le Carillon, silent, empty of others. As with film in general, the sequence appears as a hallucination, a material ghost.[37]

Watching the three-minute scene invokes a strange, uncanny sensation—*unheimlich, étrange.*[38] The setting is directly where the shootings occurred, the camera approaches (possibly) much as the men did that night, but the actors in the scene, the filmmakers, and the viewers of the film had, until recently, no knowledge of that, and now, in watching the scene, one is eerily aware of the catastrophe that awaits, and of the killings that recently occurred. The attacks have happened and the attacks will happen and the attacks will never happen.[39] The scene carries—at a minimum—a double temporality; appearing both anterior to the event of violence, and after the tear of that calamity. The scene is fused with remnants of the present (and, now, remnants of the future). The absence of other people within the scene adds to the unreal mood. It's as if the patrons, workers, clients, and pedestrians are now absent, somewhere far away, removed from vital existence. These absent personages haunt the screen like unseen ghosts, looking upon the scene, much as the camera and viewers are, or any phantom visitors.

To watch the scene brings into awareness the dying that lies in the shadows of everyday life. The absence of others at the tables set along the terrace, in the dark interior, in the fragile loneliness of space, time edging toward devastation, streams through the clip. I doubt that a few years back anyone would have noticed the shadows much in any viewing of the film. But because of certain events, and marks left on the place, the moments of dying are right there. It's not death so much as it is an interminable dying within a space of everyday life. Once you have in mind this unending fragility of life, you start to sense it in other places. The disaster is already there. You just need to notice it to bring out its vast potential.

Such an awareness can get painful. And so there can be a need to erase, rewind; maintain a screen that does not get too close to the real.

The scene carries the form of a ghostly observance. The film clip is haunted by a hauntology of spectral images, times, and reverberations.[40] The temporality of the place provoked by the scene is multiple and refractive. There is, nearly coterminous:

1. Le Carillon the day or days of the film shooting, *le tournage,* the streets clear of people early one morning, circa 2007, the film crew out of sight, the actors the ghosts of their later, less young selves;

2. Le Carillon within the virtual, cinematic time and "universe" of the film, two men seated on a vacant terrace, cop and thief;

3. Le Carillon in its normal hours, with many people about;

4. Le Carillon the night of the attack, bodies on the ground;

5.  Le Carillon of the mournful days afterward, flowers and candles on the sidewalks;

6.  Le Carillon of the present day, with most overt traces removed though the place remains phantasmatic, rich with specters.

7.  Le Carillon in any future, possible day, when things are quiet once again, the phantoms linger, the specters of past days;

8.  as well as all those Carillons that mean something to someone within the temporal flow and vital imaginaries and remembrances of a life.

There is also the unsettling possibility that the men responsible for the attacks sat one day at Le Carillon, much as the men do in the film, and observed meticulously, through a cinematography of their own—producing an unseen script and film, damning and damaging. These temporalities emerge, connect, interrelate, combine, clash, displace, unsettle, and unwork, temporal folds veer in and out of appearance and consciousness as the spool of film plays on. In one brief strand of film there is the time of the past, the time of dying, time of killing and death, a time of mourning and memory, of forgetting, healing, and future possibilities. Within this palimpsest of shifting virtualities each time haunts another. Each scenario stands in spectral relation with others, with no scene more original or authentic than another. Each temporal fold is a trace of others. The film is an anterior graph of the violent event, of that wounded time. It's also a trace of a future, possible time; of what already has occurred and will occur in the future.

Each scene keeps tearing back to the night of the attacks, cutting incision of the disaster. The temporality of that night is a crease in time that draws other folds of time toward its sphere of wounded time and space.

It's like that every day around here. Fluctuations of time and space are multiple, refractive, shape-shifting, intercutting, interhaunting. Any moment one's consciousness can go to the temporality of that night, and then consciousness flits back to the scene at hand. So many lives have intersected within this space, memories fixed in time; the structure has taken in countless looks and stares, along with the glare of photographs, video recordings, news reports, media posts, graphs, traces, effacements, all those images swirling about, haunting, soothing, emerging, fading. Spliced is a convergence of time; a collectivity of memories; lines of interest and affection, histories of suffered lives.

Time inhabits Le Carillon, bothers the place. Complex interwoven folds of past, present, and future flow through the materials, persons, images, and histories here. It's tempting to say that violence screws with time, fractures it into countless shards, amplifies time, or freezes temporal strands into fixed and unchanging memories. Violence creates echoes of time, trips up time into wounded multiplicities. Can violence wound time itself?

A blue van slows, to let another vehicle pass.

A man is wearing a black T-shirt with letters stamped in white, PRIDE OR DIE. FIGHT CLUB.

A young boy helps his mother push a baby carriage that holds his infant brother, who is sleeping. The boy touches a folded umbrella hanging from the side of the carriage.

"*C'est parapluie, là?*" he asks.

"*Oui, c'est le parapluie,*" his mother answers.

The everyday is delicate, ephemeral. Perhaps it takes a spectral outsider to see that the everyday constantly forms and reforms in series of endless, fleeting inscriptions that might shift at any moment or break into something else.

All of this writing, pages of ink now, is, I fear, for nothing. Incessant vigil. Still, there is a need to find a way, and trace a passage through the concerns involved. And so one writes of phantasms and the impossible real. The writing weighs the tension, like a fine nerve-meter right in the middle of Paris.

A woman and two girls approach along rue Alibert, from the direction of Canal Saint-Martin. The three walk with leisurely purpose, the elder in the lead. I take them to be a mother and her two daughters, perhaps from the States. They look up toward the awning above the bar and see the white letters inscribed. The older of the two girls is carrying a light green plastic camera in her hands. The three enter the bar. Minutes later they walk past the terrace, toward the canal. The girl holds the camera in one hand and a sheet of waxy paper within the fingers of another. She lightly flaps the paper, a Polaroid photograph, it seems, which bears a picture of the bar's interior or front façade. The image, unseen, develops in the night air.[41]

R. D.

## INTERRUPTION: NEURALGIA IN THE GOUTTE D'OR

*Monday, 8 May 2017*

As you leave Le Carillon, walk east toward the Canal Saint-Martin. Cross the bridge from the quai de Jemmapes to the quai de Valmy and onto rue Dieu. Stay on the left and continue down rue Beaurepaire, to the place de la

République. There, walk toward the statue, then around it, and down the stairs at the center of the plaza. Enter the metro station, find your way to line 5, the orange one—noting the two men getting searched, hands on the wall, in the fluorescently lit corridor—and hop on a train heading north to Bobigny/Pablo Picasso. Wait a few stops and get off at Gare du Nord. Get out through the RER B exit on rue de Maubeuge. You'll see taxis lined up, a large arch; walk the opposite way, north toward the boulevard de la Chapelle. On your right, you'll notice security guards and Border Police (Police aux frontières; PAF). You might see vans lined up, officers of the Antiriot Police (Compagnie républicaine de sécurité; CRS) eating sandwiches, their rifles on the ground, standing upright or leaning against the door of the van. A small white car might join them. Notice the civilian dress officers coming out: Anticrime Squad officers (Brigade anticriminalité; BAC), guns on their belts and bright orange armbands as markers of their profession. You'll notice a crowd and thunderous commotion as you get closer to the boulevard. It's ten o'clock on a bright Saturday morning. The Marché de Barbès is crowded and lively, stands filled with vegetables, fruits, meat and fish, clothes and cloth; the *maraîchers* advertise their products to a dense crowd, some yell out the name of their city: Mascara, Annaba, Wahran. Around the market, near the entrance of the metro and on place de la Charbonnière, the market continues, with cardboard stands: from clothes and cigarettes, to electronics and fresh bouquets of cilantro, mint, and parsley. As you make your way through the market walk up to rue Caplat, by the music stores blasting Algerian *chaabi* and *Raï*. The cobbled street you reach then is rue de la Goutte d'Or. Note on your left the police station, then continue straight on rue des Gardes and into the square Léon. Continue walking north, throughout the streets of Château Rouge—Léon, Myrha, Suez, Panama—until you find the Marché Dejean. From one *névralgique* center to another.

Neuralgia, in my writing, refers to the changing intensities with which phenomena of violence circulate through space and body-subjects. It is, however, more than a sensorial metaphor; I attempt to ground neuralgia in historical, political, and social realities. If neuralgic indicates a sometimes-imperceptible wound, neuralgia grounds us in the conditions of wounding.

Before the French Revolution, the Goutte d'Or (Golden Drop) was a small hamlet known mainly for its production of white wine and its cabarets.[42] What was still a rural space in the outskirts of Paris already attracted travelers and seasonal workers, who would spend their nights in the cabarets and hostels, as they transited in and out of the capital. Starting in the 1830s, the

FIGURE 6. View of the Basilique du Sacré-Cœur, rue de Chartre and boulevard de la Chapelle, January 2020. Photo by K. H.

hamlet was progressively urbanized, as the contemporary urban geography of what would eventually become the 18th arrondissement slowly took shape. From 1830 to 1860, blueprints were drawn up under the various monarchical, republican, and imperial regimes that took root and then collapsed in Paris; the urbanization of the Goutte d'Or, however, remained hasty and chaotic. Baron Haussmann's "great works" under Napoléon III's Second Empire, and the annexation of the Goutte d'Or and la Chapelle into Paris in 1860, would only affect the borders of the neighborhoods, where the construction of steel structures and large boulevards took place. The interior of the Goutte d'Or, meanwhile, continued to develop through the rhythms of the workers coming and going, building homes with wood, plaster, and brick.

Following the annexation of the hamlets north of Paris, the Goutte d'Or progressively found its place within the political economy of industrial Paris. The Gare du Nord shaped it, both as an enclave of working-class poverty and a dynamic space of transience. With the reconstruction of the train station (1860–66) by architect Jacques Ignace Hittorff, the neighborhood was simultaneously sectioned off and inserted into the rhythms of industrial Paris. The boulevards and the station demarcate it, while the train tracks rip through the neighborhood; a "spatial laceration" in the words of sociogeographers

FIGURE 7. *Terrain vague* (wasteland), rue Ordener, May 2020. Photo by K. H.

FIGURE 8. Looking north onto the Gare du Nord train tracks, boulevard de la Chapelle, April 2020. Photo by K. H.

Jean-Claude Toubon and Khelifa Messamah.[43] The Second Empire's state capitalism, the one described in Walter Benjamin's *Paris, Capital of the 19th Century,* ripped through the Goutte d'Or, inserting the area within the production of everyday Parisian life.

With industrialization, the Goutte d'Or also became an object of study and phantasm. Throughout the 1870s, naturalist writer Émile Zola would base his monographies of working-class Parisian life on a corpus of observations and notes on the Goutte d'Or. "Working classes, dangerous classes," as French historian and sociologist Louis Chevalier would later write, peoples prone to alcoholism, violence, and premature death. For some, the Goutte d'Or is an enclave, surrounded by an aura of fear as it fixes people, captures them and stops them, like Gervaise Macquart in Zola's *L'assommoir.*[44] But the Goutte d'Or was, and is, more than a space of crime, dereliction, and danger.[45]

Coming from the French provinces to work in the factories of greater Paris, bringing with them their languages and rural knowledge, the Auvergnats, Savoyards, Picards, and Belgians were the first inhabitants of the Goutte d'Or. Between the 1890s and the 1920s, the neighborhood progressively became a multiethnic European space, with Spanish, Italian, and

Eastern European Jewish immigrants. Some had fled persecution, others poverty. Most came to fill the ranks of the Parisian working classes, in factories, workshops, or small storefronts.

The Jewish shop owners, by settling through craft and local commerce, participated in the "constitution of the historical core of the communities of foreigners in the Goutte d'Or."[46] The contemporary commercial and social fabric of the neighborhood, what Toubon and Messamah describe as an immigrant and commercial centrality, rests on these historical cornerstones of Jewish immigration. The craftsmanship and commerce of textiles still exist today, more than a century later, inherited by North African Jewish and West African Muslim shopkeepers.[47]

After the First World War, the Goutte d'Or progressively became a central knot of sociability for Algerian workers who had been employed in factories during the war and had managed to remain in France. From the 1920s on, Algerian shopkeepers, café owners, and workers began to shape the south end of the neighborhood. The Algerian history of the Goutte d'Or is made up of shops and hotels, of cafés and bars. Places of (almost) public intimacy saw the burgeoning of Algerian nationalism in the emigrant community—on rue de Chartres, the North African Star was founded in a small café in 1926. Later, the neighborhood also witnessed the emergence of a new genre of music, *Raï*, whose singers were part of the North African community in France. Algerians, Moroccans, Tunisians, Senegalese, Malian, Ivorian, and Congolese immigrants continue to shape the neighborhood, assembling a space negotiated at the intersection of lands of exile and lands of origins. New spaces are invented, as French youth, descendants of immigrants from the 1950s through the 1980s, appropriate and transform culture, fashion, sociability. As asylum seekers, regularized and unregularized immigrants reformulate contemporary experiences of exile and diaspora. By the 1990s and the early 2000s, the Goutte d'Or had become an African cosmopolitan neighborhood. The plurality of cultures, nationalities, spiritualities, commerce, and craftsmanship paralleled the plurality of statuses within communities—and between family members—living between citizenship and undocumented (criminalized) status.

Sociogeographers Khelifa Messamah and Jean-Claude Toubon describe the Goutte d'Or as an immigrant and commercial centrality, meaning that despite its symbolic marginality within dominant collective representations, the neighborhood has a force of attraction that stretches over all of Paris and its suburbs, to London and Brussels, and well beyond Europe. The notion of

FIGURE 9. Looking north onto the Gare du Nord train tracks and a photograph of the Cinéma Debussy of Algiers, boulevard de la Chapelle, April 2020. Photo by K. H.

*centrality* may suggest that the Goutte d'Or occupies a position of exceptionality. The immigrant and commercial centrality, however, can only be understood when we place it within a larger geography of immigration in Europe.

As the twentieth century unfolded, a vast geography of exile—of spatialized, sociopolitical othering—constituted itself in France : in street camps (*camps de rue*), shantytowns (*bidonvilles*), camping areas for Roma travelers (*aires d'accueil pour les Gens du voyage*), furnished rooms rented out by slum landlords (*chambres louées par des marchands de sommeil*), immigrant workers' housing (*foyers pour travailleurs immigrés*), temporary housing projects (*cités de transit*), and social housing blocks (*grands ensembles*).[48] This urban geography of exile continues to shape the Goutte d'Or, within as well as immediately outside the administrative borders of the neighborhood and the 18th arrondissement. The immigrant centrality is a space of circulation, where social fixation and mobility weave contrapuntal experiences of exile. Each community that has left its collective mark on the neighborhood, in the form of local commercial culture, for instance, has also been the object of state intervention—in the form of administrative scrutiny, police surveillance, incarceration, or deportation.

At the turn of the twentieth century, the 18th arrondissement was a place of asylum for Russian Jewish ragpickers (*chiffonniers*), textile workers, and shopkeepers, followed by Jewish exiles from Poland and Romania. By the 1940s, after a decade of fascist agitation and the "rupture" of German occupation, racist restrictions to public places for Jewish persons, expropriations (through the state-enforced transfer of property from Jewish owners to non-Jewish French citizens, known as *aryanization*), surveillance and compulsory registration, targeted and mass arrests, and mass deportations altered the form of Russian and Eastern European Jewish diaspora in the Goutte d'Or. The most striking of these alterations, as memorialized by plaques throughout the 18th arrondissement, is the deliberate targeting of children; children continue to shape much of the public life and sociability in contemporary north Paris.[49]

It is in this ruinous landscape of Paris that, a decade later, the neighborhood began to take on a particular Mediterranean and North African inflection, with Muslim and Jewish Algerians and Tunisians, *pieds-noirs* settlers from Algeria, and Corsicans setting up shop in cafés, cabarets, storefronts, hostels, and brothels. Anticolonial activity in the Algerian Muslim community became more organized, and rigorously criminalized by French authorities. By the late 1950s and until Algerian independence in 1962, the Goutte d'Or was a central locus of *la bataille de Paris,* with the police torture cellars on rue de la Goutte d'Or, home raids, and roundups (*rafles*) in the street; practices of colonial warfare, policing, and torture were imported and applied in the imperial capital.[50]

Part of this period was recorded in the form of testimonies and transcriptions of court sessions by journalists Paulette Péju and Marcel Péju. In their account, the Algerian men interviewed describe the abusive police raids of their homes and harassment in the street. As they recount the screams of cellmates or the executions of Algerian prisoners, they also convey their experience of the arbitrary and discretionary power of police officers—and particularly of the Auxiliary Police Force (Forces de police auxiliaires; FPA).[51] This police contingent, mostly composed of colonized Algerian Muslims known as the Harki, was sent to Paris to participate in a wider effort of racist policing of North African colonial workers, overseen by Paris police prefect Maurice Papon. The prefecture confronted the immigrant cultural and commercial life of the neighborhood with state surveillance, torture, arrests, and summary executions. The normative imperative of the Algerian community, which at the time revolved around the ability to work but also to express a commitment—practical, financial, or ideological—to anticolonial revolution, was altered with the deliberate imposition of a distinct French Republican and colonial imperative.

A spatiality of exile relies on these dual processes: on the one hand, it has been maintained through time with the production of a commercial and cultural centrality; on the other, that centrality and the normative script it generated have been forced to negotiate with considerable state mechanisms. In other words, and following Ruth Gilmore's definition of racism, the Goutte d'Or is a space in which the cultural, political, memorialized, and normative production of immigrant communities has been consistently mediated by the "state-sanctioned or extralegal production and exploitation of group-differentiated vulnerability to premature death."[52]

With the 1970s (a period of low economic growth, inflation, and mass unemployment) came new ways of producing and managing otherness. The symbolic charge that resided in the colonial status of "natives" (*indigènes*) was progressively shifted into the administrative categories of immigration and exteriority, categories that had been fortified during prior restrictions on Jewish and Spanish immigration in the 1930s.

With the end of the postwar economic boom, mass unemployment began to loom over the French industrial economy. The first workers to be laid off, starting in 1972, were Portuguese, Algerian, Moroccan, Tunisian, and Senegalese. In 1973, the ministerial circulars Marcellin-Fontanet, named after the minister of the interior and the minister of labor and population, began a cycle of restrictive immigration policy. The legal *circulaire,* overturned by the French High Court (Conseil d'État), made the deliverance of a regular immigrant status contingent on a work contract and home address. For laid-off workers, over half of whom lived in shantytowns, these conditions meant that they were now irregular laborers and forced into a form of clandestine administrative existence.[53] This clandestinity, fabricated by bureaucratic maneuvers, made immigrants the objects of suspicion, potential delinquents in violation of immigration legislation.

Those who were arrested were held indefinitely, awaiting deportation. In 1964, the Marseille police started to hold undocumented migrants who had been arrested during patrols in an unused factory in Arenc, a neighborhood in the 2nd arrondissement of Marseille. The Arenc holding cells were unknown to the public until 1974, when a press scandal forced the authorities to address the living conditions of the detainees and the overall absence of a legal framework. The 1981 law drafted by minister of the interior and

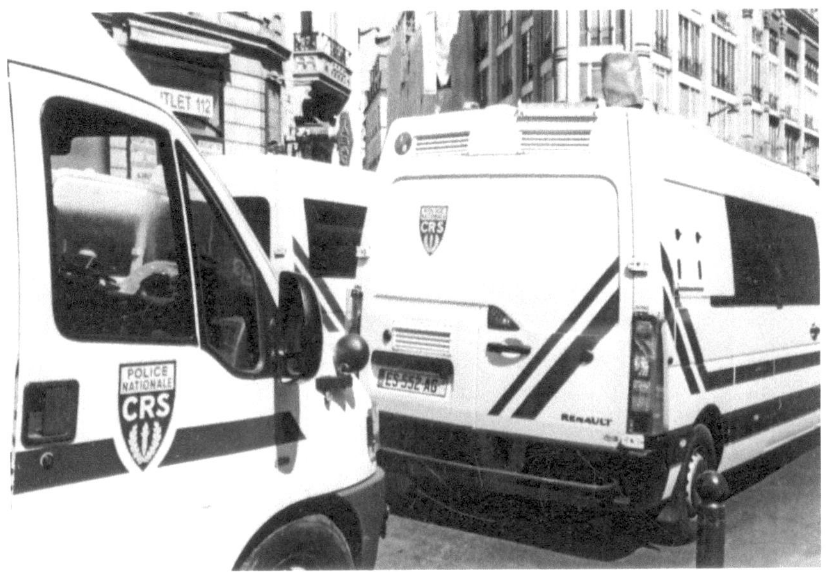

FIGURE 10. CRS (Antiriot Police) vans parked near place de la République, March 2020. Photo by K. H.

mayor of Marseille, Gaston Defferre, ended the scandal and posed a legal framework for the detention of undocumented migrants and the police procedures for their deportation. The clandestine holding center in Arenc and the Defferre Law of 1981 can be seen as cornerstones of the contemporary archipelago of immigrant detention centers that make up the national border of the French carceral geography in the twenty-first century.[54]

In the Goutte d'Or, these laws were territorialized and applied to the neighborhood. They affected the economic, social, and cultural fabric of Maghrebi and—especially—of West African immigrant communities. On 23 August 1996 several hundred Black African undocumented immigrants, mostly women and children, were evicted from the Saint-Bernard Church where they had taken refuge after being faced with potential deportations. On that Friday morning, around 7:30am, some 1,500 officers of the national police, the CRS, and the gendarmerie entered the Goutte d'Or and surrounded the church. They started by disaggregating the human chain that had been set up around Saint-Bernard. Then, with hatchets, officers broke down the church's wooden doors.[55] Like the police order against the occupation of Sainte-Ambroise church in the 11th arrondissement that same year, the French government decided to "evacuate" these humanitarian and political occupiers.

Around the same time, the set of laws drafted by minister of the interior Charles Pasqua, in 1986 and 1993, formalized the legal framework within which police ID checks and stop-and-frisk tactics could take place. Namely, they established the link between identification checks and the policing of irregular immigration. In parallel, earlier legislation criminalizing drug trade—the 1970 Mazeaud Law—put the dismantling of drug trafficking networks at the forefront of police work and reoriented that work toward the policing of "users-resellers" (*usagers-revendeurs*). ID checks thus became tools to make immigration or drug arrests; both actions often targeting the same groups. In line with the reorientation of police work, the penal procedure was reformed, relying progressively on summary trials (or immediate appearances, *comparutions immédiates*) to accelerate the judiciary process and increase the mass of arrests leading to convictions and prison sentences.

Part of this legal and penal expansion relied on police officers' practical interpretation of the racial subtext of immigration and antidrug discourse. Police work in France has always found itself in a peculiar position. Police officers are expected to put into practice the spirit of the law; however, in doing so, and therefore in applying the racist selection implied in immigration and drug legislation, they find themselves at once enforcing Republican order and suspending legality.[56]

Some researchers, like sociologist Dominique Monjardet, have studied this question in terms of police officers' professional identity and their quest for autonomy. Analytically oriented toward institutional reform, Monjardet's findings are useful in describing the internal configuration of French police bureaucracy, but they offer little help in understanding how this autonomy plays out in public space.[57] In contrast, police sociologist Jérémie Gauthier interrogates police autonomy by focusing on officers' discretionary practices. Through an analysis of his fieldwork with patrols and during arrests, Gauthier explains that officers indeed mobilize a register of racialized practices—that is, police practices that rely on racial representations and administrative typologies.[58]

Based on a detailed typology created in 1950 by Marseille police inspector René Canonge, the Infraction Treatment System (*Système de traitements des infractions constatées,* STIC) lists twelve racial types to qualify victims and offenders:

- White Caucasian
- Mediterranean

- Gypsy
- Middle Eastern
- North African Maghrebi
- Asiatic Eurasian
- American Indian (*Amérindien*)
- Indian (*Indien d'Inde*)
- Mixed (*Métis Mulâtre*)
- Black
- Pacific Islander (*Polynésien, Melanésien, Canaque*)

These categories are still in use. Given a racial typology to categorize their target population, and afforded a certain discretionary power meant to guarantee the enforcement of the law, police officers come to know the spaces they invest in through their institution's racial imaginary—as well as their own personal prejudice. The autonomy that police officers claim as constitutive of their practices may rest outside the bounds of legality, but it remains well within the imperatives of state reason.

The concept of (urban and cultural) insecurity became a leitmotif of the late-1990s moral panic around the presence of so-called zones of ethnic settlement (*zones de peuplement ethnique*) in French urban landscapes.[59] As the coded vocabulary of racial threat circulated from the fascist right to the socialist left and back again, policing of low-income, majority "immigrant" neighborhoods became a panacea to quell fears—and feed them.

The proliferation of new police weaponry and squads and the escalation in methods of intervention worked alongside the emergence of new territorial categories designating specific urban spaces as territories of police intervention. This has meant, on the one hand, that new police squads were created—like the Specialized Field Squad (Brigade spécialisée de terrain; BST) or the Securitization and Intervention Squad (Compagnie de sécurisation et d'intervention; CSI)—operating on the basis of aggressive, fluctuating, and polymorphous presence in public space. This has also meant, on the other hand, that public-private partnerships have been developed in order to articulate locality-specific surveillance assemblages. These local security contracts coordinate the efforts of police prefectures and precincts, school administrations, hospitals, social welfare and tax collection, local sociocultural residents' associations, and—most notably—of private security companies.[60]

Policing constitutes a central aspect of public life in the streets and housing blocks of the neighborhood. As I began to work on state violence,

FIGURE 11. A police car parked under a metro viaduct, at the intersection of boulevard de la Chapelle, rue de Chartres, and rue de Maubeuge, January 2020. Static police presence marks the borders of the ZSP and the entrances of the neighborhood. Photo by K. H.

racialization, and histories of immigration in the Goutte d'Or, the administrative category that oversees local policing and public-private surveillance imposed itself as an object of study. Since 2012, police operations in the Goutte d'Or have been coordinated by the Priority Security Zone (Zone de sécurité prioritaire; ZSP). The ZSP is an administrative zone created by the ministries of the interior (policing) and of justice. The explicit mission of the ZSP is for police to "reconquer territory" and "occupy public space" in order to ensure the proper respect of Republican order. Part of the novel aspect of this administrative apparatus is the police-penal cooperation that structures it: more police, more controls, more resolute prosecution, and more systematic incarcerations are the institutional, short-term objectives of the new zone.

The territorialization of this police-penal administrative zone manifests itself, first and foremost, through the concentration of police capacities, with officers, squads, vehicles, equipment, and weaponry. A number of police squads, in addition to the national police of the local precinct, intervene in the zone, namely: the Paris 18th arrondissement's surveillance agents (*agents de surveillance de Paris du 18e arrondissement*); the Antigraffiti Squad (Brigade anti-tag); the Railroad Squad (Brigade ferrovière); the K9 Squad (Brigade canine); the Paris Nighttime Anticrime Squad (Brigade anti-criminalité parisienne de nuit; BAC-N); the Antipimping Squad (Brigade de répression du proxénétisme); the Drug Squad (Brigade des stupéfiants); the CRS; the CSI; and the 2nd district of judicial police, in charge of relaying suspects to the judiciary.

Police squads alternate their presence in public space and deploy their squad-specific methods of intervention. Some, like the BAC, are particularly aggressive and operate using undercover cars and civilian dress, while CSI patrols are meant to be visible.[61] In fact, the CSI patrol in dark blue uniforms, with assault weapons held by their chests and various arrest and wounding equipment dangling from their belts. The visibility and variety of police activity in the zone is conceived, on the one hand, as a way to "strengthen the links" between denizens, shopkeepers, and police, on the basis of proximity and repeated contact. On the other hand, police activity is meant to be dissuasive and catch offenders red-handed. Any suspect caught red-handed (*en flagrance*), arrested and charged in the ZSP—especially for drug charges, sex work, or theft or dealing in stolen goods—is funneled into a penal-carceral pathway. The coordination of policing with the Paris prosecution allows for "extremely strong penal responses . . . with [the prosecution's] petition for summary hearings [*comparution immédiate*] and, at stake, immediate incarceration," explained Abdelakim Mahi, vice-prosecutor at the Paris high court, in the public notebooks of the Paris Prefecture.[62] Police interventions thus participate in expanding penal geographies. But they are not alone in this expansion.

The ZSP relies on additional apparatuses such as the Parisian Prevention and Security Contract (Contrat Parisien de prevention et de sécurité; CPPS). This local security contract, signed by similar actors as the ZSP agreement, coordinates police patrols with the work of a local Social Housing Surveillance Group (Groupement parisien inter-bailleurs de securité; GPIS).[63] Similarly, the Barbès-Château Rouge ZSP "benefited" from the additional resources of the 2016 BAC-PSIG Plan. This plan consisted in upgrading the Gendarmerie Surveillance and Intervention Platoons (PSIG) with several million euros of weapons and new training. Specifically, they were trained alongside anticrime squads in various ZSPs in metropolitan France and the overseas departments. Adopting the more aggressive policing techniques of the BAC, these platoons were given the label PSIG *Sabre*. These contracts, administrative categories, and evolutions in police weaponry and modes of operation are not simply abstract metaphors. They constitute practical realities that can be documented.

August 2016, dawn. Yasmine and I are walking home to place de la Charbonnière, as the sound of barking dogs gets louder and louder. Rue Caplat is completely occupied by dozens of police officers and GPIS security guards: an agent is posted every six feet, police officers with their right hand on their assault rifle, security guards with their arms crossed high up on their chest and their legs spread out. I ask one of them for information. The police officer maintains a blank stare and ignores me. As we walk up the street toward what looks like a group of high-ranking officers, we notice parked GPIS vans; uninterrupted, loud barks jet out of their open trunks and echo through the nearby streets and courtyards. The security guards seated in their vans converse nonchalantly, smoking cigarettes. Their composure contrasts with the other officers' military-style formation, creating a strange atmosphere where the silence echoes the barks, the laughs, and the orders being shouted. As we reach rue de la Goutte d'Or, we understand that the police operation is centered on a group of twelve young Black men from one of the housing projects in Barbès. The boys, most of them still teenagers from the looks of it, are lined up, hands against a wall. A police officer walks back and forth with a hand on his rifle. He shouts and kicks someone in the shins when he hears one of the boys whisper. Another crouches and pats them down. The high-ranking officers are grouped together and engaged in a hushed, animated discussion. An officer turns toward us; Yasmine asks him if, and why, they are making arrests. The officer is looking at me, scanning my body from head to feet, when he replies: "Go home, *madame*." What looks like a serious drug bust, however, is probably nothing more than a noise-complaint. The vans and cars fill up with officers, before driving off without making an arrest.

Police presence in the Goutte d'Or has varied over time, as contracts are renewed or modified, as police and security squads are given new training, as policies are voted into law and enforced. It varies according to institutional time and police officers' practice of their profession. In this way, police operations are tied to the state, to its crises, and the orientations of state reason. Understood as a process of territorialization of the state, police presence also

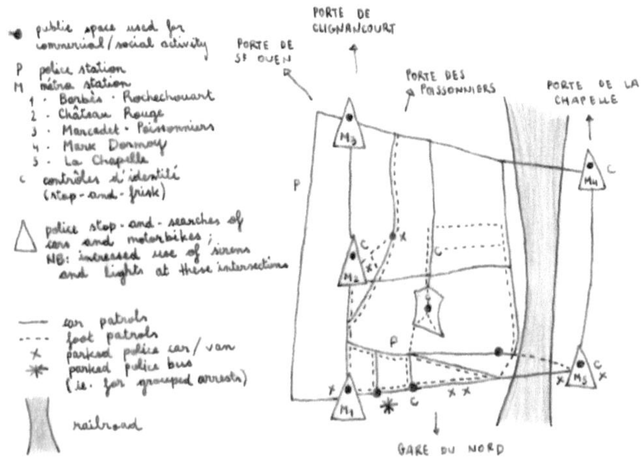


FIGURE 12. Map of daytime police activity in public spaces in the Goutte d'Or. Based on a series of maps made during the state of emergency (2015–17), December 2020. Sketch by K. H.

varies in reaction to the neighborhood's sociocultural, religious, and commercial life; patrols increase in frequency and aggressiveness during market days and the month of Ramadan.[64]

As an ethnography of the ZSP as an administrative category that plays out in space and in people's lives in the Goutte d'Or, my work initially consisted in documenting police presence by being attentive to the variety of brigades and methods of intervention. I went on walks and quickly identified the routes that police patrols took. I noted the street corners, alleys, and boulevards where ID checks took place. I noticed how certain patrols tightened their perimeters and intensified stop-and-frisk actions along two or three streets.[65] Often these week-long operations were followed by arrests of street vendors and the closing of shops. Slow processes of eviction contrasted considerably with more intense, spectacular police operations. Somedays, the police presence was quiet, with vans lined up on the boulevard; sometimes the streets smelled of pepper spray and tear gas, echoing the shooting of rubber bullets.

As I read studies on police work—such as the ones I reference in this text—I noticed that sociologists, anthropologists, and historians often wrote from within the institution. Whether their work is inflected by critical, reformist, or managerial concerns, authors like Fassin, Gauthier, Jobard, and Monjardet study the police from within the precinct, in the backseat of the patrol van, in a police academy classroom, or by overlooking the desk of the judiciary police officer processing an arrest. I wanted to ground my methodology outside the institution; to study police officers by looking at them from the position of the targeted population, in one of their priority zones of intervention. I began by soliciting shopkeepers.

June 2017. Storefronts are opening in the streets of Château Rouge and Barbès. I walk about, stopping by each shop and presenting my research project to the person inside. Most of the employees and shopkeepers have little time to afford me.

In a small Algerian-owned textile shop, an older man folds his accounting sheet on his lap as I greet him. He turns and looks at me with interest as I explain that I want to work on policing in the neighborhood without talking to police officers, but rather by building an analysis that would emerge from the residents and shopkeepers of the neighborhood. He stares for an instant and then blurts out, "I'm working over here. The boss is about to get here, the shop isn't ready. I have to do the inventory; we just got a delivery. No, I'm sorry, chief, I can't sit down for an interview. Come back tomorrow, *in cha Allah.*"

Like most people working in the shops, he is busy and has little time to talk at length.

"It's injustice!" he tells me, before I leave.

In another Algerian textile store the shopkeeper nods as I introduce myself.

"It's total injustice. They kill, they control. They are always here! But I don't have time for you."

I walk on to a small restaurant, where the cashier greets me and laughs.

"There's a lot to say, that's for sure!" he says. "But I'm working, chief. And then I go straight home. I don't have time to talk about this. Come back, *in cha Allah* the boss will be here. He'll be able to sit down with you. The police here, they behave like hoodlums. They stop and frisk our clients and then they walk in to buy their kebab dinner. Nah, come back later."

I walk up to rue des Gardes, cross square Léon, and turn onto rue Myrha. I walk into a Malian haberdashery, where an older woman greets me holding a box of wool rolls balanced on her hip. She nods and quickly answers, "Yes, we see the police all the time here, they patrol this street. They also control people's IDs [through stop-and-frisk efforts]. If you want to know, go talk to the children who hang out at the square Léon. They get beatings from police officers."

She pauses. "Listen, I've got clients coming in all day and I have to work on my orders."

She calls out to the back of the shop and a younger woman walks in and takes the box of wool rolls. She looks at me and concludes, "I can tell you that we see the police, all the time, by foot, by car with their blue lights. But that's it."

I walk into another grocery shop. The owner, a large Algerian man, interrupts me when I introduce myself as a student.

"You, you're studying? All right, that's good."

He doesn't look too convinced.

"Listen," he interrupts me again. "You can't go up to people like this. Act like a sociologist *shouya* [a little bit], you look like you want to talk around a coffee."

He laughs loudly before smacking his hand on my shoulder.

"All right, tell me what you're researching again."

I repeat my pitch.

"Yes, well it's injustice, eh, you know it well enough, no? *Enta 3arbi oula la?*"

"Are you an Arab?" he asks. I nod.

"So, you very well know that it's injustice, what more do you want me to tell you? If you really want to understand what the police do here, go see the kids at the square Léon. They'll tell you how things happen. Or talk to the owner of ———— [a restaurant in the north end of the neighborhood], he knows the history." I nod. He continues, "Why do you want to talk about all this, though? What are you trying to achieve?"

"I'm trying to do a sociology of the police that doesn't center on the police's perspective. I want to talk to the people that experience police work directly, and contribute to changing the way racism, police, insecurity, and so on, are discussed."

The shopkeeper nods tentatively. I pause, and then add, "Also, I think it's important to put our perspectives into writing. For future generations, so that there's more to go on than what we have now about the generations that preceded us."

He looks at me, his face suddenly heavy. As he wipes his hands on his apron, he says in a serious tone, "Our voices will never change anything. They don't listen to us, to the things we say. And when they do, they find it exotic or interesting. But it won't change how they see us because they won't understand what we mean, they won't have an *intimate* understanding of it. So, why talk about it, huh?"

He pauses. I stay silent. He rubs his hands together and continues. "Yes, yes, I understand continuing your education is important. So, first off, people work hard here, all right, so you have to find people who have time and that won't be easy. Then you need a place to meet with them, any café is good. And, I don't know, man, put on a shirt or something, you look like ghetto youth [*jeune de cité*] right now."

He laughs heartily, grabbing my shoulder warmly as he wishes me good luck.

I continued to meet with shopkeepers, asking more precise questions about their experiences with police officers while at work. I also took note of the persistent reorientation that these conversations suggested: if I wanted to study police work, to understand how it interlocked with processes of racialization, I needed to speak with the "youth of the neighborhood," the young men and boys who live out part of their social life in public places like the courtyards, shops, plazas, and parks of the neighborhood. The shopkeepers had indicated a very specific group of people: Black children and men, citizens, sons of West African immigrants.

At that time, the beginning of June 2017, I spent my mornings walking as shops opened and market stalls were set up; I introduced myself, the research, and mentioned to my interlocutors how I had thought to come speak to them. I often felt it necessary to explain that I did not speak with police officers and that their anonymity—in name, appearance, and the place, date, and time of our meeting—would be respected in my writing. With some, often young men my age, I met alone and we spoke more at length over several days. With most though, especially with the children, I introduced myself to groups and met with three or four people at a time. Doing so meant that I inserted myself in existing groups, shook everyone's hand before sitting down, and intervened only when it seemed appropriate and generative. I was received with respect, which I earnestly returned. And while it appeared that I prompted interesting and nuanced conversations on the impact of policing on their lives, with time I came to understand that police violence and its material and emotional effects on their lives was a permanent topic of conversation. The less loquacious boys and men described the police in two words: *humiliation* and *corruption*. Others went from anecdotes to analyses, describing patrol routes, weapons, brigades, as well as ID checks, beatings, and arrests.

The metaphor of neuralgia extends to the Goutte d'Or. *Centre névralgique* to the history of immigration in France, *centre névralgique* of the history of working-class Paris. Neuralgic, too, as the Goutte d'Or is itself made up of knots of activity, markets, and places of public sociability; knots of receding intensities. The Goutte d'Or is neuralgic as well in the place it occupies in the cartography of the Republic's police and penal apparatus; a neuralgia onto itself, one that produces its own twitches, nervous movements, difficulties speaking or breathing, palsies.

From one center of neuralgia to another.

And a question penned by Édouard Glissant lingers: "Would it be ridiculous to consider our lived history as a steadily advancing neurosis?"[66]

*K. H.*

## TWO

————————

# *Graffs*



Living means leaving traces.

WALTER BENJAMIN,
*The Arcades Project*


TERRORGRAPHY

*Friday, 22 July 2016*

Some mornings I wake at sunrise and venture into quiet morning streets with a camera in my hand. The light is good then, and there are few people about. Walking sleepily toward their destinations, they pay little attention to my efforts. One day I photographed Le Carillon before it opened for the day. The place looks silent, as if asleep. The curtains are drawn. There are no tables or chairs on the terrace. No one is around.

I have photographed À La Bonne Bière in much the same manner, silent, still. The spirit of these early morning ventures and the resulting photographs (if not their mediocre quality) bring to mind the work of Eugène Atget, the revered Parisian photographer—largely unknown in his time—who in the early 1900s would wake at four in the morning and lug heavy photographic equipment and plates on his back to diverse locations in Paris where he would photograph buildings, palaces, unpeopled avenues, sunlight slanting through trees in parks—beautiful, haunting images, some of which Atget would sell as "documents" to artists, used as studies for their creative work. I think of Atget when I wake before sunrise, as a ghost might reflect on an earlier apparition. In 1931 Walter Benjamin remarked in his "little history" of photography, "Not for nothing were the pictures of Atget compared with those of the scene of a crime. But is not every spot of our cities the scene of a crime? Every passer-by a perpetrator? Does not the photographer—descendent of augurers and haruspices—uncover guilt in his pictures?"[1]

FIGURE 13. Le Carillon, rue Alibert, July 2016. Photo by R. D.

It's not lost on me that I photograph crime scenes. A stealer of images, *photos volées,* I take pictures and use them for spectral purposes. At night I look at the photos and try to imagine what happened, and why.

I roam a city of specters. My thoughts move from haunt to haunt and dwell within pools of energy and fragment perceptions found along the sides of streets or the edges of buildings. No one seems to mind much while I am photographing marks on cement.

I return often to Le Carillon. To the left of the bar, on the cement fixtures of the building facing the street and sidewalk of rue Bichat, stand a few images and inscriptions etched into concrete, trace-marks from different kinds of ink, no names attached.

One graph reads, in pink-red ink, *MAINTENANT VOUS ETES TOUS DES ANGES.* "Now you are all angels." The words suggest a conversion of form and spirit, an alchemy into newfound identities, conceivably better than the lives and sufferings of mortals.

Another inscription, below an aura of blue, penned in small words of black ink, is a statement in Italian: *mi basta immaginarti per averti qua . . .* The import of these words can be translated into themes of imagining:

FIGURE 14. Words inscribed on building surfaces near Le Carillon, rue Bichat, July 2016. Photo by R. D.

> It's enough for me to imagine you here.
> It's enough for me to imagine you to have you here.
> I just need to think of you to have you here.
> *Il me suffit de t'imaginer pour que tu sois ici.*

The fantasy is so vivid that it's as if you were here. "This is someone," said a woman from Milan, "who has come to accept that the person is no longer there in actuality . . . That absent person has a life in the imagination."

One might imagine a traveler from Italy who came one day to this place to observe and take in where a close friend had died that night. This person left this thoughtful, poetic homage to absence and the lingering presence of a life within the vitality of imagination.

So much of life takes place within realms of the imaginary. It's enough to imagine the violence. ("Why would you *want* to imagine the violence?" someone asks.) I cannot but imagine; the images come of their own volition, vague and spectral wounding. I imagine the lost lives, precise biographies remain opaque. I imagine the men there, a mind nearly pieces it together. It's like trying to recover a lost strand of film that holds obscure forms of movement and action, a dreadful haunting of a film that plays and loops incessantly, without resolution, without a secure and final end, until the reel burns out from its own cindering heat. It's a mild November evening, autumnal night illuminated by the city's lights. Around 21:45 a black Seat with Belgian plates approaches from rue Bichat, the men get out, like phantoms, they shoot "indiscriminately" into the crowd. They wield Kalashnikovs like professional killers, turning left and right, bursts of gunfire. Bodies fall. Thirty-second blasts seem like a long time. The car tears off. Silence, afterward, and the stunned response. It's not just a bar anymore, no longer another night of the everyday. I can almost imagine the violence, not quite. I can nearly trace it. It's almost there, a soft image, compared to what happened. That imaginary of violence does not match the actual injury.

Imagining has an *almost* quality to it. It's there, not quite. If only it were just a figment of my imagination. Are such shards of violent imagining related to a mourner's compulsive drive to repeat, reenact, and reimagine— here in ways spectral, indirect, and incomplete?[2] I appear to imagine the life deaths of others, for others, in a supplemental mourning and prosthetic trauma, on the sidelines of violence.

What did they see when they came here, before? What processes of affect and reasoning led them to choose this place? A statement released by ISIL after the attacks noted that the locations of the killings were "meticulously chosen in advance at the heart of the French capital."[3] It's unclear that the organizers of the attacks did in fact meticulously choose their intended locations—ISIL says a lot of provocative, unnerving things in its public dispatches. Still, it's unsettling to think that the arts of the meticulous, the work of a scholar or engineer, can be integral to acts of violence. The men might have taken notes and photographs, looked at Google maps, sat in a delirium of hatred and planning on the terrace.

With the attacks of 13 November 2015, it could be argued that there was an indirect and relatively unseen agency motivating the creation of devastating marks and wounds within the streets of Paris. In acts contributing to what might be called *terrorgraphy,* the writing and inscription of terror, the grafting of fear and violence within the world, the gunmen inscribed a sense of death and violence in the lives and bodies and histories of a city. They wrote on the city, leaving lasting marks and wounds in specific sites that, in time, work spectrally to mark other places and time.

"We come every day to this bar because it is friendly, it is simple," said a woman the day after the attack. Two of her friends died at the bar. "Coming here is normal for us, so we have no idea why they [the attackers] were touching this kind of place. This is horrible. It is touching a neighborhood."[4]

The act of "touching" here can be said to carry a sense of physical contact, affect, contamination, existential disturbance; one realm of life touched (*touché*), "hit," affected, another. The skin and corpus of a neighborhood, a way of life, was disturbed by a violent hand, irruption of otherness, "the outside drawing near."[5]

A force from the outside hits against and "pierces" the envelope of a self-sustaining organism, shattering that organism's integrity: this "effraction," this wounding, is a trauma of a certain kind.[6] Another way to comprehend such violent "touching" of a neighborhood is through Jacques Lacan's concept of *tuché*, "the encounter with the real," "the real as encounter," the sudden—traumatizing—intrusion of the real (*réel*) into the symbolic.[7] The raw, incomprehensible force of the attacks intruded into the symbolic structure in which certain residents lived their lives and felt at home. The attacks broke open these structures, leaving many confused, dismayed, out of sorts; some were broken. What emerged from this were efforts, from different hands, of various positions, to rebuild the structures of lives—to remake worlds.

An absolute alterity brought violence and death that night into the space of a bar and a neighborhood and other places like it in Paris. In "hitting" these places, the attackers touched all of Paris, for their actions introduced the imminent possibility of the same deadly force in other bars and restaurants. "They attacked only a few places, but they marked every place in Paris," said a resident of France. The attackers touched on the fabric of everyday life, the integrity of which can no longer be taken for granted. They seeded violence into space and time through a spectral dissemination of damage—a kind of phantom touching. The sudden acts of violence left a silent, spectral trace in other public places in Paris—and, more distantly, potentially, within other cities in Western Europe. The attackers left a graphic trace of their perceived otherness. Their actions put into place a "phantom territoriality" in Paris and its outskirts, and in much of Europe, to use the words of anthropologist Dejan Lukić, in speaking of a dimension of space "which is contiguous with terror, exhaustion, survival, that is with bare passions."[8]

Violence in a flash seizes hold of a multitude of signs and imaginative scenarios. Acts of violence reach into an environment and shape what is encountered there; a neighbor, a parked van, trash bins lining the street. In Paris, recent histories of violence trace possibilities of harm around every street corner. That radiance sustains fear.

Spaces look different now. Street, entrance, pavement, terrace, chair, table, glass, foot soldier, military patrol; words like these have acquired new

FIGURE 15. Place Fréhel, June 2016. Photo by R. D.

valences. The grammar of everyday life has gotten entangled with a lexicon of violence, suspicion, and fear.

In Belleville stands the faux or real matter of a hand grenade fixed into a wall, apparently the work of an unknown street artist, a "vandal." Like so many scattered explosions, images of violence are seeded into the architecture of Paris, absorbed within a topography of marks, wounds, cuts, scratches, traces, erasures.

There used to be bullet holes from that night in the wall facing the intersection near Le Carillon, with police identification markers posted close to them. The fractures have since been patched and painted over.

One theory is that the attackers chose this part of Paris for their actions because, in other neighborhoods, such as on the Left Bank, they might have been stopped by police officers while driving toward their destinations, whereas in the "mixed" 10th arrondissement, they would go relatively unnoticed.

The idea is, ISIL sought to destroy the "grey zone"—*la zone grise* of peaceful coexistence between Muslims and non-Muslims—and the institutions attacked—bars, a music hall, a sports stadium—symbolized places within that perceived zone. "One thing is clear," said a lifelong resident of Paris. "Those who didn't know that France was at war, and had soldiers fighting in

Syria and Iraq and elsewhere, well, now they know. We are at war. Everyone knows this now."

A scholar of war might argue that violent attacks on 13 November 2015 were in direct response to France's anti-ISIL bombing campaign in Syria, and that correlation in violence, strike for strike, was both anticipated and occluded by the French government. Anthropologist Allen Feldman puts the matter starkly:

> Consider how François Hollande politically and perceptually severed the random killing of Parisians on November 13, 2015, from the proceeding damage of his bombing campaign in Syria. Hollande, under the ceremonial innocence of retribution and resecuritization, effectively escalated France's greyed-out anti-ISIS bombing campaign whose collateral damage provisioned tit for tat legitimacy for domestic terror. The killing, mutilation, and displacement of, not only ISIS, but of contiguous and expendable Syrian noncombatants, drove the future anterior of the 2015 Paris attacks as the catastrophe *that will have been*. Hollande and his advisors recursively calculated the civic sacrifice of collateral domestic deaths at a temporal distance as corollary to vertical killing at a geographical distance in Syria. Bombing Syria was the temporal prepossibility of the Bataclan and other deaths and of the contrived accidentalization of the "random" Parisian victims cordoned off by Hollande as absolutely external to his already in-place arbitrary Syrian deaths. The "surprise" catastrophe in Paris already happened before it happened as a node of the kill-chain preassembled by the French aerial assault on Syria.[9]

The bombings authorized by President Hollande contributed to a violent temporality of retaliation, a ricocheting return-effect seriality in which the killings in Syria provoked the subsequent killings in Paris, with collateral damage all around. On 14 November 2015, ISIL claimed that the attacks were in retaliation for Opération Chammal, France's military efforts to contain ISIL in Syria and Iraq.[10] In response, French forces increased their attacks against ISIL in Syria, perpetuating the kill-chain. The code of counter-retaliation snakes back onto itself. The French government cast the November 2015 attacks as an unprovoked assault on French values and lifeways and portrayed the resulting deaths and injuries as random, accidental catastrophes unrelated to the military's violent operations in the Middle East. It then capitalized on this national trauma to revitalize its bombing campaign in Syria and augment its coercive state of emergency efforts at home. The French government shaped the disaster to suit its interests; arguably, its representatives anticipated, provoked, framed, and foreclosed the violent events and their recurrence. Yet other temporalities and trace-effects of violence have been at work, and other catastrophes are at hand.

France is haunted by its colonial past. It's haunted by the negated, neglected, nearly forgotten. The recent violence implies the spectral, hauntological return of atrocities committed in the name of imperialism, colonial order, dominance, exploitation, and the presumption of superiority graveled into *la mission civilisatrice.*

It's unclear why Le Carillon and Le Petit Cambodge were attacked, specifically, as well as the other bars and restaurants, while other places went unharmed. One aspect noticed in visiting the sites of the attacks is that each of the establishments hit is set along a wide and open intersection of streets, which would make it relatively easy for someone to approach with a vehicle, get out of it, and then return to the car and leave in a hurry.

This, too, one imagines. Clear roadways, before and after. Enough space to maneuver. The planning for this; the quiet scoping out of places and boulevards; the determination of a route; realization of meticulous plans; the mind returns to the specter of that night and other nights in trying to piece together a sequence of events.


DO NOT ARCHIVE

The structures around Le Carillon carry remnant marks of the violence and its aftermath. At the modest, off-to-the-side wall where the writings in ink are found, along the horizontal slab of concrete, there was once an informal, makeshift memorial for those who died in the attacks. There are photographs of this on Facebook, from late November and December on into January 2016. Mourners had placed flowers, cards, candles, messages, and a set of photographs of the deceased beneath the shuttered window, as though the fixture was an altar that emerged spontaneously from the sense of shocking loss and grief felt by many.

Now only the words and images painted onto the concrete surfaces remain, like a museum emptied of its holdings. The makeshift memorial did not last for long, a month or two at most. The substrate of the concrete slab was cleared free of the most overt signs. (Were the items and inscriptions removed by the city? By the owners of Le Carillon? By *les conservateurs du patrimoine*

FIGURE 16. Words inscribed near Le Carillon, on rue Bichat, June 2016. Photo by R. D.

working for the Archives of Paris?) The statements imprinted onto the surfaces of the wall proved less easily effaced. The ink resists erasure.

The largest statement here is sketched in black ink and underlined by an unknown hand. Presently the most visible trace of the transient memorial that once stood there, it reads as *NE PAS ARCHIVER*. "Do Not Archive." The meaning of this negative imperative is unclear. Do not create an archive of the lost lives? Do not let the French government maintain control of such an archive? Do not dwell endlessly in a catacomb of painful remembrances, where memories and material reminders remain in a fixed and codified formation?

When an anthropologist from France heard about this cryptic inscription she read the statement as a cautionary warning to any unknown but anticipated representatives of the state: do not archive this site of remembrance. Do not take the items here, the mementos of letters and photographs, and store them in a museum or in the city's archives. Do not archive our sorrows. Do not scoop up our correspondences with the dead for the sake of your national agendas. Viewed in these terms, the statement *ne pas archiver* was an anticipatory command to representatives of the state not to remove the materials of the shrine and take them for their own purposes of political commemoration and archiving.

In effect here is a politics of traces. Derrida wrote of the politics of the archive, particularly in terms of how the work of an archive selects certain items for preservation, for interpretation, and neglects, overlooks, passes on, and destroys, even, other traces. "The archive begins with selection, and this selection is a violence. There is no archive without violence."[11] There is also the violence of preservation, of appropriation and transformation, such as the displacement of words and images and materials set upon a cement wall to a storage room in a city's official archives.

At times I read the statement differently. It's possible that someone came along in the weeks after the attacks and felt compelled to critique, in lasting ink, the memorial shrine that was forming there. In this rendering, the statement writes against the formal memorialization of the dead, of the inscription and fixed instantiation of the dead within archival memory. Do not worship at the site of the dead, do not construct a fixed altar of remembrance. Indeed, the gathering of signs that occurred along this cement wall could be understood as an archive. The mnemonics of the recently dead were organized, set within a specific place, a *topos* of trace memories, an arch-house accessible to the public, put into order, set within a stable substrate, situated in a tense, unsettled play between vestiges of appearance and absence, life and death. This fits within the thematics of an archive, the meaning of which comes from the Greek *arkheîon:* "initially a house, a domicile, an address, the residence of the superior magistrates, the *archons,* those who commanded."[12]

The specific intent of the inscription "do not archive" remains unclear. The multiple ways that a simple yet complicated graff can be sensed and interpreted points to the uncertainty and ambiguity of most graphic inscriptions in the city. The graffs and images are usually left anonymously, often at night, by "writers" largely unperceived by others. In the full light of day there is no one around to say what is meant or intended by the words or images; much is left to the viewer's imagination and circuits of interpretive reasoning. What did the author of the statement "do not archive" mean? There is a measure of undecidability within such graffs, and an element of *destinerrance,* to use a neologism of Derrida's; there can be an erring or wandering when something or someone embarks on a destination, there is the potential for a message to get lost or displaced within correspondence or on the way toward its intended destination.[13] There is no guarantee of a full and direct arrival of sense and significance. This often adds to the mysterious tones of graffs.

*Ne pas archiver.* The *pas,* the "not," in the middle of the statement is doubly underscored in the words inscribed in the concrete, as if to accentuate the negative, nay-saying command. One might take this anarchivist statement to cut against the state's proposed archival work. In his 1995 book *Mal d'archive* (translated as *Archive Fever*), Derrida writes of the feverish "sickness" (*mal, mal de*) that troubles contemporary efforts to archive aspects of the world. "We are *en mal d'archive:* in need of archives," he writes.[14] To be *en mal de* is "to burn with a passion."

> It is never to rest, interminably, from searching for the archive right where it slips away. It is to run after the archive, even if there's too much of it, right where something in it anarchives itself. It is to have a compulsion, repetitive, and nostalgic desire for the archive, an irrepressible desire to return to the origin, a homesickness, a nostalgia for the return to the most archaic place of absolute commencement. No desire, no passion, no drive, no compulsion, indeed no repetition compulsion, no "*mal-de*" can arise for a person who is not already, in one way or another, *en mal d'archive.*[15]

The statement *ne pas archiver* appears to anticipate and criticize the state's passionate, nearly feverish desire to collect and retain traces of the pain, grief, sorrow, and rites of mourning that emerged in the days after the attacks— and then use those traces for the purposes of national memorialization.

Within the economy of words and marks in and around Le Carillon there are (at least) two energies that work at times against the force and flow of the other. There is a movement toward inscription and remembrance, toward maintaining traces or generating new marks that register traces on the traces, a tracking of traces in life or after the end of a life; *ne pas oublier,* do not forget. There is also a movement toward forgetting, toward erasure and effacement, of holding off on acts of retracing and preservation; *ne pas archiver.* It could be that any minds and bodies or collective efforts milling about Le Carillon are involved with a similar field of forces, charged and complicated and multivalent, forces contrary to one another, tied to rounds of inscription and erasure, forgetting and archiving. Do not forget the violence; do not efface the lost lives of the dead; remember the dead, mourn for them; preserve traces of violence and mourning. Do not memorialize the dead, do not systematize memories of them. Do not archive death and loss and memory in life and body or within the structure of the city. Remove the trace of images that weigh on places and thoughts, sensations. Do not archive the archive. Do not allow life to become a mausoleum of memories such that you cannot move on to other images and acts of writing within the charged flow of signs and pulsions within life death.

When I first came round to Le Carillon I was struck by the absence of any significant indications of the recent violence. Little was noticeable near the materiality of the bar or within it. I returned a few days later. I walked around and sat at one of the tables on the terrace, along a sidewalk where there were once flowers. I ordered a beer. While drinking the cool liquor, I came to like the ease of the terrace, the flux of the streets, passing conversations. Space, I found, was oddly doubled. Time was fractured, multiple. Emergent was a double consciousness linked to two perceptions that could not be reconciled: Le Carillon was a place of leisured pleasures, friends chatting over rounds of drinks; the bar was a site of violence and death, men killing others.

Others faced similar perplexities. There was a blunt visceral sense of an absence of sense. *"Je ne comprends pas"* was a statement that recurred in newspaper accounts of the attacks. "I do not understand."

"I go there to hang out with my friends," said a seventeen-year-old girl of the Casa Nostra, a pizzeria where five people were killed by a gunman. "I don't understand it. I am in shock."

"I just need to come here and look," said a young woman of the same restaurant. "I ate in that restaurant with my parents before the attack. I pass in front of it every day. It is a shock. I don't understand. I can't stop crying."

"It was really shocking," said a woman who lived above the pizzeria. "It was the first time in my life I saw someone dying in front of me. I mean people there were just sitting outside having a drink. They were not politicians, they were not particularly engaged. They were just enjoying the beginning of the weekend. So, why?"

Related to such incomprehension, Mayanthi Fernando and Catherine Raissiguier write of the 13 November 2015 violence in the context of the aftermath of the January 2015 attacks at the Charlie Hebdo offices and a Hyper Cacher kosher supermarket in Paris:

> The November violence rekindled the fear and outrage as well as the calls for national unity that emerged in the wake of the *Charlie Hebdo*/Hyper Cacher events. However, unlike the January murders, the November attacks did not seem to target anyone because of their ideas or their religion; they were seemingly meant to stun and terrorize, and they did. Indeed, many had difficulty making sense of the November violence, since the majority of people killed—racially mixed cosmopolitans who frequent the bars and music venues of *bobo* Paris—are precisely the kind who are critical of the military

adventures propagated by the "War on Terror" that have created the conditions of possibility for terrorist groups like ISIS and al-Qaeda.[16]

A similar perplexity troubled me when I observed the sites of violence, months later, and looked upon the same impossible subject. And now, in coming to Le Carillon and returning there, without end, I have been trying to reflect on certain aporias of violence here and elsewhere, though reflection might not be the best word for that vague, diffuse brain squash that occurs when trying to think on the possibilities and impossibilities of violence. Aporia is a good word for the situation at hand, in any event, for in that word is the sense of an impasse, a paradox, a contradiction or puzzle.

Aporia implies the absence of a passage; an inability to proceed; impassable. This modern word stems from what the ancient Greeks called *aporiai.* Aporia literally, etymologically, means "lacking a path" (*a-poros,* "without passage"). It designates a situation that is absolutely impassable, without solution. Put another way, an aporia is "an antinomy arising through the simultaneous existence of mutually exclusive entities, each irreducible to the terms of the other."[17] The mutually exclusive phenomena that simultaneously exist, irreducible to one another, within the times and spaces of Le Carillon are, bluntly, moments of the everyday, and a time of violence. There is no easy passage from one to the other. This brings the haunting sense of an impasse, a paradox. A mind gets lost in the transition. It's a murky thing, this translation; a vague nonspace, unclear, ill-perceived. It's like trying to know a ghost well.

The aporetic state here is not a problem to be solved, or a contradiction or antiphony to be managed and transcended through logic and dialectical reasoning. The aporias of violence remain insolvable, unfixable, untamed, and not in a way that settle into any kind of calm stasis of knowing or not knowing.[18] As Sarah Kofman observes, "There can be no aporia, in the true sense of the word, without a transition from a familiar state which affords one every security to a new, and therefore harrowing, state."[19]

Transfixed by the gaps and paradoxes involved, the endless, unstilled remainders, I have been trying to write out the dimensions of such incomprehension, striving, apparently, to clarify what remains unclear. Give a word to it, *aporia.* Give it a name, a concept; define it. Draw a frame around it, a canopy that might protect. Assign a plurality to the field of sensation, *aporias*—for when it comes to such acts of violence there appears to be a labyrinth of multiple nonpassages, which relate to and haunt one another.

(a) How is the impossibility of violence possible? How could it be that someone killed several people a few feet away from where I am sitting? How can the everyday become a scene of violence?

(b) How could some people kill others? How could the men bring themselves to pull the triggers on their weapons that night? How could they shoot so indiscriminantly, without care, without knowing even who they were killing?

(c) How could others want those men to kill? How could certain men have drawn up plans, looked at maps, found motor vehicles to use, planned entry points and escape routes, prepared weapons, communicated with each other, all with the intent of orchestrating the deaths of others?

(d) How could some people want this, encourage it among others? How could some want the death of others?

(e) How could some celebrate such a horrific event? How could they applaud it from afar? How can they post on social media sites expressions of their delight in the deaths, signaled through smiley face emoticons and an image of the Eiffel Tower burning to the ground?

(f) What kinds of violence, unperceived, untracked, brought on this violence? It's difficult to find passage into the conditions from which violence arises.

(g) The randomness of the violence presents an impasse. Why did it happen at Le Carillon, Le Petit Cambodge, and the other bars and restaurants that night and not others? Why there, then? Why did those people die, and not others? Why were some injured and others killed?

(h) How could the ordinary suddenly become extraordinary? What transformative potentialities are invested in the ordinary? How can an object of everyday life, such as a piece of shaped metal, or a truck, glass, be used to hurt others? How can the newness emergent in each passing moment be violent? How can time open into devastation?

(i) How could a situation of violence return to a condition of the ordinary? How can there not be clear signs of the carnage in and around this bar? How can an act of violence not always leave a mark? How can perceptions shift back to the tasks and consciousness of everyday life? How could the time of killing go away?

(j) How can a past scene of violence still be ongoing within the present? How can a past wound—or the past more generally—exist within the present?

Such are the paradoxes of thought, time, and perception that fire through the axons of a body seated *en terrasse* at Le Carillon, watching figures pass. These quandaries might be subjective concerns, of one uncomprehending mind only, which some might consider naïve or unknowing; though my guess is that others can relate to the inability to comprehend. Any act of violence, I would wager, is aporetic: implicitly or explicitly, there is a gap in understanding—how could this happen? The violence at hand, a few months back, still here, not quite here, lends itself to a strange void of understanding. A vehicle of mind and language wishes to comprehend how such violence is possible, how deadly wounding came about—and will come about, again, no doubt—but this effort does not come easily.[20] In trying to perceive, something gives way. Nothing is clear; one is left unable to proceed into a situation or perspective that makes sense. With such disastrous nonperceptions there is not knowledge of the disaster so much as knowledge as disaster and knowing disastrously.[21] Disaster lies as well in noncomprehension or incomprehension, the inability, or unwillingness, to comprehend the reasons and motives of those who kill.

With an act of violence something *turns;* something changes; there is a mutation within the lineaments of ordinary life. This turn can be difficult to fathom or picture at all. The aporetic domain of violence, if a domain at all, is vague, nearly imperceptible. Engaging with the aporias involved is not simply a question of philosophical thought and reasoning or of thinking through a paradox of logic to be solved. The engagements are at once perceptual, experiential, ethical, and this in intertwisting ways. It's a lived aporia, which makes living rather aporetic. The impasses lie on the edges of consciousness and at the limits of one's imagination. The disaster lies at the limit of writing and comprehension.

> The disaster: unexperienced. It is what escapes the very possibility of experience—it is the limit of writing. This must be repeated: the disaster de-scribes [*dé-crit*]. Which does not mean that the disaster, as the force of writing, is excluded from it, is beyond the pale of writing or extratextual.
>
> *It is dark disaster that brings the light.*[22]

There is no experiential passage into or though the impassable. Have I been trying to comprehend something that cannot be comprehended? Is the writing on the subject of deadly violence the artifact of a mind striving, ceaselessly, helplessly, for some sort of clarity in a situation that cannot offer resolution? One lies singularly exposed, without solution, without recourse or possible substitution, without theory, or any sure way of acting or sensing.[23] There is a fascination with this nonpassage, of "not knowing where to go."[24] A complex of body and mind is drawn to what it cannot comprehend, lies caught within the force of the incomprehensible. And these words, drawn from a letter I received from someone visiting Paris in April 2016:

> And when I met with C., who had a friend killed that night in the Bataclan, there was no mention, not the most tacit one, of the tragedy. But there is no doubt that the suffering is there. I think the extremity of the event, the unimaginable atrociousness, fills people with a sort of aversion. But still, I can't quite explain it.

Like others I face the impossibility of comprehending or explaining fully. I face the impossibility of forgetting or resolving or fleeing from the encounter with that impossibility. It's unclear what one is to do with this encounter with aporetic impossibility and its interminable remainder, tears, traces, effacements. How does one proceed in thought or action, or in writing? How might one write on the impossible? How does one describe that which de-scribes, how does one portray that which breaks language and comprehension?

Perhaps one needs to endure the aporias without trying to solve or banish them, or extinguish or efface the paradoxes and paroxysms involved, even if one comes to be haunted by them. Writing can be a means to respond to the impossible without effacing it. Is it possible to live with and within the impossible? Can one cultivate a certain passion for the impossible, for hesitation and uncertainty, and the many hauntings spurred by violent jarring? Perhaps one needs to accept the haunting, write the haunting—passionately, vitally—and sustain and salute the many phantoms in life. To the point, perhaps, that one becomes phantasmal oneself.

R. D.

## INTERRUPTION: GRAFFITI, TRACES, AND DISAPPEARANCE

*Wednesday, 23 August 2017*

To graff or to tag is a practice of leaving traces, of leaving marks—such as signatures or "flops" in the form of acid engravings, paint or marker, key scratches, or more expansive collages and murals. These marks are always simultaneously writing over and written over by the changing landscape of the city. In refashioning urban and postindustrial landscapes, graffiti—and the cultures of hip hop that have been its contemporary aesthetic backdrop— interrupts representations of the city as a sanitized, straight, and disciplined space. From dirty, messy tags to detailed murals, graffiti reminds us that that which is being contained, hidden, or expelled from the city streets does not disappear; rather, it leaves traces in space.

Graffiti is an ephemeral testimony of an artistic performance, of a particular presence, of an individual or collective memory. And since the 1970s and 1980s in France it has brought the presence of those kept at a distance back into the centers of economic activity, wealth, and patrimony. Sprayed on commuter trains, graffiti brought the Bronx to lower Manhattan; it brought Saint-Denis to the Île de la Cité. Graffiti and street art in north Paris are lodged within rhythms of urban renewal, graphed onto walls, in wastelands, later built over by housing projects or private apartment buildings. Graffiti emerges out of erasure, out of a dialogue with state processes of urbanization that then submerge it.[25]

A brief sociohistory of contemporary urban planning and urbanization may be helpful here. From the 1950s through the 1970s, France entered a period of economic growth known as *les trentes glorieuses*—the thirty glorious [years]. This boom relied on state intervention—in the form of social security as well as close ties between state actors and industrialists, known as *dirigisme*—and rested on the underpaid, mobile, and malleable labor of immigrants living in shantytowns around industrial hubs. As urbanization accompanied industrial expansion, the shantytowns were progressively destroyed and families relocated in transit housing (*cités de transit*) and social projects (*grands ensembles*). The *grands ensembles,* although poorly conceived and hastily built, were represented as symbols of progress and French modern urbanity.[26]

As the 1970s unfolded, the combined effects of the economic crisis, the precaritization and criminalization of undocumented workers, the penalization of cross-border drug trade, and the continued rehousing of North African, West African, and Caribbean working families in projects participated in reshaping the collective representations of neighborhoods like the Goutte d'Or. Under the bureaucratic designations of *quartiers prioritaires* (priority neighborhoods, categorized in terms of housing conditions and rates of poverty, delinquency, criminality), spatialities of exile became "symbol[s] of a bleak urban environment, deviant youth, and segregated minorities."[27]

By the end of the 1980s, these racialized representations came to orient the state doctrine of urban planning known as *politique de la ville.* As sociologist Sylvie Tissot explains, administrative categories such as *quartiers* or *zones* partook in a "growing but disguised racialization of discussions of poverty, with territorial categories functioning as euphemized racial categories."[28] This rearticulation of racial categories through urban planning worked hand-in-hand with the expansion of the penal state. Geographer Mustafa Dikeç writes that the shift from welfare to penal management of urban poverty took a particular "republican twist, and shifted emphasis from prevention to repression through a legitimizing discourse organized around 'the republic' under threat by allegedly incompatible cultural differences and the formation of 'communities' unacceptable under the 'one and indivisible' republic."[29]

This particular penal orientation of urban planning in France serves a more general and multifaceted phenomenon of "territorial stigmatization." Formulated by sociologist Loïc Wacquant, the concept of territorial stigmatization refers to the dual process of naming spaces—the symbolic power of bureaucracies—and of producing stigmata reliant on race, religion, and nation. Territorial stigmatization denotes a process of racialized spatial ascription that operates around the production and circulation of "spatial taints" stretching from stigmatized urban spaces to the stigmatized inhabitants, and conversely.[30] This process rests on the reproduction of stigma. Stigmatization is ensured by penal institutions and the territorialization of penality in priority zones, which in turn produces "pathways of incarceration."[31]

Often, scholarship stresses the metropolitan historicity of urban policy. Concepts like race or colonialism are mentioned either as discursive categories or as succinct qualifiers of the "problem population." *Politique de la ville,* however, is a reiteration of the old, colonial, and postenslavement problem of social separation and spatial proximity between racialized and hierarchized collectivities. For instance, the considerations of racial government implied in Tissot's description of territorial categories and Dikeç's analysis of the "republican penal state" echo the racial, military, and police imperatives of colonial urbanization in 1950s Algeria. As architect and historian Samia Henni explains, counterrevolutionary war in Algeria invested territory not only as space to be occupied but also as something that could be weaponized. In other words, shaping the built environment within which Algerians lived partook in the dual process of shaping Algeria in the image of modern France and furthering the psychological and the corporeal control over the "native" population.[32]

FIGURE 17. Paris High Court, avenue de la Porte de Clichy, April 2020. Photo by K. H.

The French military invested Algeria through rhythms of urban destruction and production. Rhythms of the demolitions of homes, of the scorching of fields and villages, administrative and military operations to relocate hundreds of thousands of uprooted Algerian peasants in surveilled military camps known as "regroupment centers" (*centres de regroupement*). Complete with the construction of vast segregated housing projects, all together this made up the moving landscape of French urbanization in post-WWII Algeria. In their 1964 work *Le déracinement,* sociologists Pierre

FIGURE 18. Building set for demolition, boulevard de la Chapelle, January 2020. Photo by K. H.

Bourdieu and Abdelmalek Sayad argued that the concentration of over two million Algerians in regroupment centers had actualized and, in many ways, finished the colonial process of uprooting begun during the conquest of Algeria and continued throughout the settler-colonial project that ensued. In uprooting agrarian communities, military zoning and segregative architecture also participated in inserting Algerians within industrial modes of production, making landless agricultural workers salaried employees (in grape, orange, wheat, and oat plantations, etc.). Algerian working-class immigration to France was a consequence of this colonial *déracinement,* "uprooting."[33]

As Sayad continued to work on the lived experiences of Algerian immigrants and their children in France, cycles of uprooting and fixation, displacement and relocation, became motifs of Algerian exile to France. Exile reflected the relationship to the country of emigration that had been left behind. Exile also prolonged itself into the country of immigration in residential segregation and controlled access to education, labor, and property. This, Sayad argues, produced the immigrant as a "colonized [subject] beyond colonization."[34] The subject positions of immigrants, of racialized and spatially constrained citizens, are continually inscribed in processes of spatial fixation and uprooting.

Thinking about one's inscription in processes that shape our relationships to space and time can be difficult. A way of approaching it is to think of segregation and displacement in terms of rhythms. For instance, the ZSP cannot exist without being actively enforced by the actors that it coordinates; in other words, in order for the ZSP to exist (in terms of arrests made, sentences served, etc.) it needs to be put into practice in the territory it designates as such. The territorialization of administrative categories is processual and happens in rhythms such as the changing intensity of police patrols, the extension and retraction of police operations around particular perimeters. When Henri Lefebvre mobilized the notion of rhythmanalysis to study urban space, he used it to capture the discontinuous and antagonistic rhythms that make up the city. Tuning in to a particular cacophony allows one to listen to an overall orchestration.[35] And yet one necessarily perceives the city from a particular position, with a particular way of standing and moving in space.

In my case, this meant walking about and staying attentive to the movements I could see—or rather the movements that I could sense, meaning that one also smells, hears, and tastes what makes up the atmosphere of a place. I formulated a method that resembles what situationists like Abdelhafid Khatib defined as the mapping of urban psychogeographies through individual or collective urban drift (*dérive urbaine*).[36] I was inspired by Khatib's work, which he had undertaken during the 1958 curfew imposed on North-Africans in Paris. But I moved beyond the "sensorial" method of the situationists. I traced out rhythms that were informed by the history I was learning about at the same time: reading, but also speaking with people in public and private places, oriented what I looked for and how I understood it.

Looking for certain rhythms rather than others also leads one to trace certain histories.

February 2017. Evening. The sun has set and the lampposts light up the streets of Château Rouge. The market on rue Dejean is still bustling and stretches out into rue des Poissonniers. Four young Black men, leaning against the entrance of a small barber shop, call out to me as I walk past them. They are in the middle of a debate and one of them wants me to back him up.

"Fam', how do *you* pronounce *soixante* [sixty]?" He explains that they can't agree on the pronunciation. I accentuate the first syllable of the word, the way he just did. He nods and starts boasting.

One of the young men interrupts him, asking me, "Who are you colonized by though?"

"By the French."

"Well, all right, then, that's why you say it like him. He's colonized by the French too. Us, it's the Belgians. That's why we say it like that."

History can manifest itself in surprising ways. Sometimes traces of it appear as one looks to the state's rhythms of spatial and symbolic separation. Sometimes it is by listening and by letting oneself be called into conversations. Traces of exile and colonial history emerge from residents' own social rhythms and their appropriation of urban space.

Because displacement takes place over time, rhythms that we could understand as historical in their span also play out in the everyday, scattered into timed repetitions. In the Goutte d'Or, the administrative rhythms of police patrols unsettle the social fabric of the neighborhood—its public manifestation in parks, plazas, and outside shops—daily, through raids, ID checks, and the constant presence of officers in the streets. Officers walk with the sense of reconquering territory and orient their actions toward the social, commercial, and cultural rhythms that have taken root in the neighborhood. And so, understanding the city as made of rhythms and knots of neuralgia not only refers to the intensity of police operations, but also sketches out a way of making sense of the localized social rhythms of its inhabitants.

The daily rhythms of the markets, the symphony of metal bars smacking against one another as the stands are set up, the slow buildup of the bass notes and thundering drums as the trucks arrive and the clients begin to

FIGURE 19. Ephemeral renaming of rue de Tanger as avenue Lalla Fadma N'Soumer, who led an anticolonial tribal coalition in 1854 in Algeria, June 2020. Photo by K. H.

fill the streets, the diminuendo that follows the uninterrupted climax as the leftover fruits and vegetables are sold at half-price . . . Daily rhythms of shops opening and cigarette vendors lining up to sell their goods, the hourly rhythms of street markets gathering and dispersing with the arrival of police patrols.

The spaces within which graffiti was born, the spaces and communities that propelled and transformed hip-hop culture—from the boroughs of New York City to the industrial wastelands of Paris and its *banlieues*—are spaces

FIGURE 20.  Construction site on rue Étex, May 2020. Photo by K. H.

of localized violence. The violence of evictions, of police raids; the violence of prison sentences and deportations; the violence of a young man taking the life of another. Graffiti emerges out of that social and affective materiality. If architecture is frozen music, as German poet Goethe may have once said, then graffiti constitutes a frozen rhythm; a glimpse of social and administrative rhythms that oppose and submerge one another.

The walls of the square Léon in the Goutte d'Or are a testament to those experiences of violence, with its murals, its memorials. And through these acts of remembrance, through these ephemeral imprints on public space, on its infrastructure, graffiti participates in shaping collective memory. The public practice of grief works as a symbolic space for congregation.

> Never again.
> RIP.
> *Allah yrhamh* (God grant him mercy).
> *Que justice soit faite* (May justice be done).
> *Nique la BAC* (Fuck the Anticrime Squad).

Statements like these are echoed throughout demonstrations, invoked in speeches, and more often inscribed on the walls of the city. As both singular and collective expressions of artists' styles and visions, graffiti participates in the production of the spatiality of north Paris. Graffiti aestheticizes spatial constraint, but it does not hide it or undo it. The wall remains, as does the barbed wire that crowns it.[37] It remains, as a physical prefiguration of what may come yet; and as a memory of what has passed, too. It clothes the brutality of daily, banal catastrophe with visual metaphors—but graffiti does not do away with its canvas.

Sociologist Maurice Halbwachs argued that collective memory is constructed and maintained through space. By appropriating and shaping space, social groups construct a spatiality that holds the sociosymbolic and material traces of their existence.[38] The spatiality of the Goutte d'Or does not "fit" the definition given by Halbwachs. A look at the history of the neighborhood allows us to see that the spatialities constructed by immigrant communities have consistently had to negotiate—and often fight for—their claims to space. As postcolonial immigrant communities construct their own spatiality, born out of exile, the Republic—in this case via policing and urban planning—attempts to uproot, displace, erase, or shape it into an image it can control and reproduce. In doing so, the interweaving of rhythms in urban space actualizes a dialogical process of erasure and colonial sovereignty.[39]

Spatialities of exile are particular in that they exist between rhythms of territorial state intervention. Like graffiti, the symbolic traces of the immigrant spatialities in the Goutte d'Or appear ephemeral. Identifying such traces becomes a work of seeing them dissipate, written over, and of remembering their shape and changing forms. But these ephemeral traces do not indicate the disappearance of the immigrant collectivity. They indicate the considerable efforts invested by the state to shape urban space and, conversely, to shape sociabilities, spatialities, and the symbolic traces that constitute col-

FIGURE 21. Graffiti piece in the square Léon, spray-painted over tags expressing collective grief, January 2020. Photo by K. H.

lective memory. It is a work of erasure that the state undertakes but never achieves nor ends.

A portrait, an image of intimacy and humility; the trace of a worker who toiled in shantytowns and factories, staying upright. The will to graph the presence of these silent elders who held within them the memory of *la coloniale.* And perhaps there is a similar urge in my writing, in my will to engage in ethnography. I am moved in fact by a will to graph onto blank paper the existence of people whose presence remains locked in rhythms of fixation and displacement that surpass them. It is in a sense a *mal d'archive,* a feverish, almost nervous urge to put my *anamnèse* into writing, so that *we may not forget that we remembered.*

This fever leaves a bitter aftertaste of unease. I am disquieted by the possibility that I may have written the wrong word and left out what was important. A question remains, then: in my urge to write my anamnesis, what do I graph over? What have I erased in turn?

*K. H.*

# THREE

# Operation vigilance

Our sentinels were gaining in experience: they were learning to distinguish the footsteps and voices of the Arabs from the sounds made by the wild beasts that prowled around the camp in the dark.

AUGUSTE BARCHOU DE PENHOËN,
*Expedition to Africa,* 1835

We are not sufficiently awake. We have to wake beyond wakefulness; then vigilance is the night, wakeful.

MAURICE BLANCHOT,
*The Writing of the Disaster*

## MILITARIZED SENTINELS

*Thursday, 11 August 2016*

A band of military soldiers approaches with semiautomatic rifles in their hands. This is a platoon of men and women on patrol, strolling through the neighborhood with an air of leisurely vigilance. A few of the soldiers look toward the terrace. The platoon crosses the intersection of streets and turns toward rue Alibert.

The approaching unit is a multieyed, multiped assemblage of consciousness and weaponry. The soldiers wear berets, brown leather boots, and khaki camouflage fatigues fixed to weighty box-like backpacks. Helmets hang from their belts, omens of a future street battle. In their arms the men hold semiautomatic rifles nestled like babies. The guns point down, toward the ground; safeties on; they can be raised at sudden notice. Fingers stay close to the triggers, close to serious damage. The metal looks dangerously real.

The soldiers are on the alert for specters of terror. They pass like phantom apparitions, images from a strange dream. For lingering moments their mobile presence disrupts the everyday; the street takes on an ominous tone, dangers lurk, curtains are drawn, imagined threats of violence are sensed vaguely. When a patrol passes the space becomes different; one becomes aware of the potentiality invested in hidden spaces, cardboard boxes, capacities of men and women. The atmosphere changes and suddenly there is a different affective space.

The soldiers' vigilance is founded on the uneven anticipation of perceptions yet to be perceived. Their movements and perceptions work in relation to the obscurities, opacities, and changing sightlines in the city, in calibrated rhythm with the unperceived actions of anticipated enemies. This anticipatory stance is in accord with Foucault's observation that the specific space of security in modern nation-states refers to "a series of possible events; it refers to the temporal and the uncertain."[1] The threat of terrorism relates to the uncertain possibilities within the securitized space of the nation-state. "Security is a potentiality. It is future oriented and preemptive."[2]

The soldiers pass out of sight and soon the everyday returns; motorbikes, children playing, glasses of Côtes du Rhône. Watching this, I am left again with the sense of a tense and awkward schism between the banal pleasures of everyday life and its potential disintegration at a moment's notice.

The military patrols appear to have increased in the streets of Paris. This is in line with the actions of Opération Sentinelle, launched by President Hollande and the French government and military after the *Charlie Hebdo* attacks in January 2015. The operation is part of the broader Vigipirate program in effect in France, in which a number of security measures are employed to encourage vigilance against potential terrorist attacks at both the collective and individual level. President Valéry Giscard d'Estaing created this national security alert system in 1978, at a time when France and other nation-states in Europe were faced with waves of terrorist attacks carried out by extremist groups or internal national separatist organizations (Basque and Corsican, notably) and Catholic sectarian fundamentalism, alongside other social and political movements. The government organized a centralized alert system allowing the rapid alert of administrative authorities and cultivating a policy of vigilance in the Republic. Vigipirate, an acronym of "Vigilance et protection des installations contre les risques d'attentats terroristes à l'explosif," has since been updated three times. The first was in 1995—following a series of bombings in the Paris metro, attributed to the Armed Islamic Group (GIA)—and then again in 2000 and 2004, with revamped systems and retooled devices replacing obsolete ones, to adjust to new and pressing realities and terroristic threats. With each incarnation a distinct alert code has been set in place, with logos visible in public spaces denoting levels of vigilance and attack alerts—signs of imminent danger within intercalibrated surges of terror, violence, media coverage, surveillance systems, and security protocols, a fiery, governmentalized dance of terror and alarm.

There is a complex history to the ever-emergent vigilance, one that dates back at least to the first days of the Republic and its Reign of Terror, criminological theories and practices, military police systems of surveillance and arrest employed during the First and Second World Wars, colonial apparatuses of control and surveillance, the police tracking of migrants in the twentieth century, ethnographic studies of colonized peoples conducted by the French military, and the state's management of "anomaly detection."[3] Written into the history of modern France are genealogies of human beings being followed, tracked, typified, studied, confined; populations surveyed, surveilled, rounded up, killed; behaviors coded and predicted. In recent years, other countries in Europe have encountered similar kinds of terrorism, from armed Islamic fundamentalist groups as well as other forms of political violence, prompting parallel kinds of collective consternation and state systems of surveillance and vigilance. All of this ties into broader geopolitical configurations, including political engagements and conflicts in the Middle East, Africa, and Europe, such as the Lebanon civil war, Israel-Palestine armed conflicts, international anti-imperialist movements, the deployment of European military troops and weapons in the Middle East and Africa, separatist and independence movements, and turbulent colonial and postcolonial legacies. Yet another political-security-military formation involved has been the global war on terror, catalyzed by the United States government after the 9/11 attacks, "with its military authoritarian legalities, culture of manufactured fear, offshore carceral complex, and imperial pretensions"; a war of infinite time and space, perhaps best described as "the relentless diffusion of cruelty."[4]

Tying as well into concerns and practices of vigilance in France, and an often lingering atmosphere of fear and suspicion of others in its towns and cities, are discourses and sentiments associated with what has been called a "new Islamophobia," which Vincent Geisser identifies as "a process of stigmatization that combines an ethnic reference (Arab) and a religious referent (Muslim)."[5] Such stigmatization has been layered onto a European image of Islam as an "obscurantist, archaic, and despotic phenomenon."[6] As Mayanthi Fernando writes, "The new Islamophobia, which draws on much older tropes of Islam and Muslims, emerged after the 1979 Revolution in Iran, picking up traction with the Algerian civil war, 9/11, and the ensuring global War on

Terror. Often morphing into a defense of Western secularism, the new Islamophobia regards Islam as a civilizational threat. The problem with Islam, according to this discourse, is that it cannot separate religious and political life and be merely a religion—hence its supposed existential threat to the secular West."[7] Anti-Islamic racism can come of such phobic, anxious regard of Islam and its practitioners, and this can translate into suspicious concern of persons perceived as Muslim—or possibly "radicalized" fundamentalist Muslims, opposed to the values of the Republic—as encountered in the streets and neighborhoods of Paris, Marseilles, Nantes. Apparent Islamic "others" can be construed as potential threats and engaged with through cautious vigilance.

As elsewhere in Europe, the French state is concerned with the protection of its citizens, economic and welfare systems, and its sovereignty and political influence from threats perceived or unanticipated, and it has sought to do so through a combination of security, police, and military apparatuses. Dating back to at least 1978—while carrying vestiges of intensified police and military surveillance during the war years—the vigilant police state has affected all French public institutions, from schools and airports to public space. Diverse experiences of security and safety, comfort, anxious nervousness or trauma, or police harassment and house searches tie into such acts of police and state vigilance. In response to earlier terroristic attacks and bombings, from the 1970s on, soldiers were employed to patrol sensitive sites in Paris and other cities in France, including synagogues and mass transportation systems. Echoes of such deployments are found in the current patrols, with some residents of France recalling scenes of past violence and trauma, militarized responses, and jittery, nervous dispositions of everyday life. Others have felt the brunt of the surveillance state.

Opération Sentinelle is a step further into militarized vigilance and surveillance, an expansion of vigilance that, for years, has been intermittently in effect. The state has convened and mobilized the energies and combat skills of the military and deployed them on the streets of its cities. With this effort, some ten thousand troops "are engaged on the national territory to defend and protect the French."[8] As of 20 November 2015, some 6,500 troops are stationed in Paris. It's an operation, not a state of war; temporary, for as long as needed. The state of emergency might last for decades, the emergency state might become the norm, not the exception, continued vigilance for intensity warfare. The soldiers' mission is "to protect, dissuade, and reassure." Some citizens are concerned that the military is being used not to protect the country at its borders, and beyond, as has traditionally been the case, but within the territory of France itself.

The territory of the French Republic is becoming militarized. Such operations echo the ways in which, as Michel Foucault posits it, starting in the seventeenth century, modern politics in Europe and elsewhere have been underwritten by the discourses and logistics of warfare.[9] The designs of civil society stem from military logics and campaigns; the civil order came to be known as "an order of battle."[10] With the implementation of military and security systems in France, civil society is being further colonized by military practices and epistemologies. The intensified police apparatuses in contemporary France relate, in part, to a sense that the attacks of November 2015 were a breach of the state's security systems; additionally called for was a soldier-based, real-time vigilance. The mobilization of a sentinel army is in line with increased efforts of security and securitization in modern nation-states, in which national governments—like the United States—employ projects of counterterror that "mobilize affects (fear, terror, and anger) via imaginary processes (worry, precarity, threat) to constitute an unlimited space and time horizon for military state action."[11]

As a key apparatus of the French security regime, the military patrols in Paris are a correlative of the state of emergency (*l'état d'urgence*) in effect in France, which gives the police and the military the right to enter homes and conduct searches without search warrants. These actions and policies have the effect of disturbing and discriminating against the lives of certain residents of France, particularly those who risk being conceived as possible threats against the Republic and its peoples. As anthropologist Didier Fassin observed in March 2016,

> The state of emergency, in general terms, gives the executive branch of government extraordinary powers over the mobilization of the army, control of the borders, limitation of movement, and setting of curfews. But in practice it has four main concrete consequences. The police can conduct searches in private and public spaces at any time without judicial warrant. The minister of the interior can put anyone considered a threat to public security under house arrest. State authorities can ban demonstrations and gatherings on the same grounds. Law enforcement officers can stop and search anyone without specific justification. . . . Stop and search is now regularly and arbitrarily carried out in public spaces, particularly in train and metro stations, manifestly targeting people on the basis of their physical appearance. Racial profiling, which is common though illegal most of the time, has become licit and even encouraged by the authorities.[12]

Fassin points out that such governmental measures and policing efforts are supported by most of the public in France, and this for two apparent reasons: "First, they are widely thought to be effective in countering terrorism; second, most of the population never gets to see the negative consequences."[13] The government's response to the threat of further terroristic violence, and its surveillant policing of marginalized residents, situates the nation and its peoples in differential and divisive ways. "The terrorist attacks, it seems, have served as a pretext to expand the lawful extent of the use of state force.... The politics of fear, which all parties seem to deem profitable in electoral terms, have made these exceptional measures more than acceptable to most people, since only a stigmatized and marginalized section of the population is affected."[14]

The word *sentinelle* has roots in the Latin *sentire,* "to feel, to perceive by the senses." The new recruits learn how to perceive by the senses in order to ward off acts of violence. The urban military cultivates a "high-strung sensuous apprehension" of its environment, to draw from Dejan Lukić writings on the sensory alertness of hostage takers in the contemporary Islamicate world.[15] An animal is "a being fundamentally on the lookout," Gilles Deleuze once observed.[16] The military sentinels are beings on the lookout, land-based sensor operators. They metonymically signal the eyes and ears of the vast animal formation of the state, sensitive to vibrations, signs, movements, and incidents that might portend danger. A prosthetic of the sovereign state, in all its imagined powers and perceptive acumen, they embody at gunpoint its sovereign right to kill, if need be.

"Being on the lookout," Lukić suggests, "means being in tension, being intense and without rest, always looking over one's shoulder.... Being on the lookout intensifies the place it occupies, which can be any place."[17]

The patrols walk irregular routes through the streets of Paris. Microassemblages of sentinel alert, with limited and fragile scopic powers, the soldiers drift through urban terrains, looking for perturbations, advancing a state-manufactured critical phenomenology of potential threats and dangers. The soldiers territorialize neighborhoods for a few minutes at a time, command a visual field, and then tread on. The soldiers walk slowly, taking time to see, look, look again—into that passageway, at a car parked unevenly on the curb. Their training has given them calibrated teamwork in threat perception—a hermeneutics of suspicion in the time of ISIL. Within the flow of nomadic surveillance they scan for signs of weaponry, bombs, unclaimed bags, anxious eyes and determined faces, desperate migrants, hateful militants willing to sacrifice lives for the cause. The soldiers proceed with shifting thresholds of apprehension, concentration, threat, danger, distraction, rest, boredom, fatigue. Several pairs of eyes move in tandem through a complexly shifting terrain. Within this network of vigilant sight, slight but significant shifts in perspective bring new perceptions; a compound eye lights upon bodies, alleyways, trash bins, fleeting shadows, a thousand intensities of urban sensing.

The eyes look and look, and in that steady show of regard the soldiers make themselves seen while looking. The visuals go both ways; the soldiers look for signs of imminent terrorism while simultaneously commanding a visual display of military potential, vigilance in the flesh. This is a political theater of looking, of showing that one knows how to look. Through acts of visual and embodied performativity the soldiers demonstrate that they know how to spot danger. The state's sensorium of power and nonpower is at times spectacularly on display—much as the construction and patrolling of border walls can limn into spectacular theater, a show of sovereign might has emerged in times and places when that potency is altogether uncertain and insecure.[18] Paris is one of the main theaters of operations of the French state, and in its central arrondissements the soldiers foot a scenic affirmation of military power and vigilance at a time when such powers radiate as fractured, questioned, undermined. The sentinel patrols are just as neuralgic, porous, protean, indeterminate, insecure, and stressed as France's military and security regime. With their limited optical powers in an assemblage multiplicity, in a shifting dramaturgy of seeing and not seeing, threat perception and threat enactment on the cusp of violence, the soldiers reflect the state's anxious powers.

Through such a militarized optics, secured and financed by the French state, the foot soldiers articulate a vision of safety, violence, threat, and danger—much as the French state does. In brandishing select military, political, legal, and media deployments the state cultivates a certain "distribution of the sensible," an arrangement of the perceptible that makes some violent threats seem apparent, altogether real and possible, while shifting attention away from or not realizing or underscoring the perceptions of other forms of violence, including swaths of violence enacted by the state itself.[19] The soldiers scan for terroristic devices in the streets and structures of Paris, yet little is seen or said about the violent terror inflicted by the French state and other military-security regimes on various peoples through armed warfare, covert operations, smart bombs, signature drone strikes, detention camps, black sites, and ghost prisons. As Allen Feldman puts it, "Governmentality in the war on terror resides in archival control over the apparition of threat. The powers of threat revealability are self-referential idioms of government; traversing the state, the media, and public culture; sovereignty itself is containerized in select scenic affirmations through its visible presentation, timing, and spaces of peril. This providential scenography determines not only what and how danger may appear, but also what threats will never be allowed to come before the public gaze, including the political formation of that gaze."[20] The forces of Opération Sentinelle entail a scenic affirmation of a war against terror, which makes apparent certain threats and instills a politically shaped gaze while other kinds of visions go unmentioned and unheeded. It's like a magic trick in which members of an audience are encouraged to look at one kind of potential violence while other tracts of violence go unnoticed. Misdirection is the magician's word for that art: *look here, not there.* The guns point in a certain direction.

Most people do not seem to mind the mobile, machine-gun presence much, nor do they engage with the soldiers. There is little verbal interchange, yet much watching on both sides. Some Parisians say they find themselves comforted by the presence of the soldiers in their everyday lives. Others say it's all a joke, that there's no way the soldiers could prevent violent attacks. "The intelligence work is very important," said one man. "The police who are working on the surveillance of certain groups and individuals, and telephone and internet communications, they're doing a good job of keeping track of people. But the military patrols are not effective. It's to make people feel protected, safer."

"It's doubled-edged," another man said. The soldiers are both reassuring and disturbing.

"Ah, the soldiers, they look at nothing," said a man with a dismissive wave of his hand when he heard mention of the patrols.

"*C'est pour la galerie,*" said one woman. It's all a show, for the onlookers. Yet what are the effects of such displays?[21]

The soldiers tend to be young men in their twenties, early thirties; a few women; no aged faces. Some must join the military because of the promise of a steady income in a nation struggling with high rates of unemployment. Many want to serve their country. The soldiers come from different parts of France. Many do not know Paris well. What instructions on surveillance do their superiors give them at their military bases? What archival traces of training missions and militant battles fuel their actions and cognitions? Do

FIGURE 22. French soldiers on patrol, Basilique du Sacré-Cœur, June 2016. Photo by R. D.

the men patrol the main concourses in Paris, soft targets where bodies are most vulnerable? Do their superiors map out coverage of the entire city, from Notre Dame and the Eiffel Tower on to the far reaches of the banlieue?

I once watched a video posted on a government website of a military command center, the visuals of which showed a medal-decorated general and his uniformed assistants monitoring a vortex of video and info-tracking systems aligned in Paris, cybernetic signals of threat and deterrence feeding into and out of the sentinel base. So goes the sovereign state's imaginary of terrorist threats and security fortifications. Also in play, we are led to grasp obscurely, are matrices of international and multicorporation networks of information circuits, technoscience devices, cybersecurity strongholds, biometrics imaging and database systems, visual-behavioral mappings and facial recognition systems on the lookout for "malintent," with all of these wired intensities constantly being tweaked and fine-tuned by experts and trained practitioners in points of emergence and creative guesswork.[22] The specter of the state looms over the city's passagework.

I want to learn how they see. One night I was seated on the steps of the Basilique de Sacré-Cœur in Montmartre, within a crowd of tourists, when a unit of three men and one woman walked slowly past. Each soldier held a single index finger close to the trigger of the gun carried. The woman made quick incidental eye contact with me and kept walking. I decided to follow. The group walked down a cobbled lane leading away from the basilica. I left the steps and stood a way's away. One of the soldiers turned quickly, to see what was behind him, and then turned back around. Another young man turned in much the same way, swirling his gun around, as if to make sure no enemy combatants were following. I sensed their cautious nervousness on a pleasant summer evening. I followed in their wake. The soldiers walked onto another street, unpopulated with people. One person, alone, trailing behind—I grew too nervous to follow. I feared bodily harm.

I switched to other methods. In mimetic desire I walked the streets of Paris slowly, vigilantly, trying to see as the soldiers did, crave as they craved, palpate the generalized fear. I kept an eye out for anything suspicious in the shadows in the ordinary. I did not see all that much. I sensed palely, through my own private *opération vigilance.* Through a sensuous apprenticeship I wished to learn how to perceive potentialities of death and violence. For a few days I kept a vigilance log in which I noted perceptions of possible harm. The notebooks hold fragments of subjective vigilance:

Three men, walking past; carrying a cart.

A man on a cellphone, standing on a street corner, looking about.

The woman, dressed in black, walking along the bike path.

Police, on bicycles.

I hear sirens often, now.

While in the studio apartment, on the sixth floor of the building, I hear the sirens of police cars. At times they go on for several minutes at a time—a rush of alert, alarms, vigilance. I hear the alarms but I can't know what's going on. I'm tempted to go out onto the streets to see what is happening. I've turned on the television, to see if some new attack has recently happened. The television stations are calm.

Two men leave the metro car quickly, at the same time.

A man lingers at a street corner at midnight. He sees me looking his way. He shifts his feet, lights a cigarette.

Men, talking last night, in the apartment across the way, until three or four in the morning. The language is not French. Arabic, most likely. Silence, quiet, and then I hear the voices again.

I gave up on the effort. In stepping into phantasms of anxious vigilance I was starting to detect death and injury in the words and faces of strangers and that acuity troubled me. It was not that I thought the violence was necessarily there but that I had come to imagine the violence to be there, threats real or unreal on a warm summer night. That kind of imagining was dangerous. Perceptions soon grew violent, looks carried a knife's edge. The mind-wired vigilance, of looking suspiciously at a cardboard box lying in the street or sensing threats in the talk of others, created phantasms of violence. Paris was morphing into a phantasmagoria of imminent violence in which a shifting and complex succession of optical effects and illusions, images seen or imagined, fused and turned in fantastic dreamlike ways as I walked through a maze of narrow streets. I shied away from such fearful imaginings. From dreams to nightmares, specters of alarm nervously haunt me.

Presently I observe the soldiers' vigilance with a keen vigilance of my own. I have become a being on the lookout. My neuro-optics exert a phenomenology critical of the state's optical imperatives and militarized phenomenology. One evening I watched a band of soldiers pass a few feet from where I sat along a sloping sidewalk at a Moroccan restaurant in Montmartre. The soldiers passed inches from my right elbow; I could have touched the cold metal of their rifles. I tried to make eye contact with one or two of the soldiers, to see how they saw. No one caught my eye. Without missing a step one youth looked up and undertook a quick study of the blue awning above the restaurant shifting in a slight wind, his eyes darting there, there. What phantom threats and eruptive possibilities was he trained and training to see? His eyes showed their dexterity, quickness, speed, and their youth. Perhaps the young man's detailed looking just then was for my benefit, as well as for others seated in the restaurant, and, in extension, other residents and visitors of Paris. We can dine at ease in a summer breeze and rest assured that skilled others are on the lookout. We might be reassured by this. But the sudden sight of soldiers carrying deadly guns is unnerving, in all its implications. We learn to fear our neighbors. The vigilance can demarcate divisions between an "us" and a "them," and spawn paranoias of self and other.

If I looked otherwise to the police, if my appearance was coded differently, as suspect "other" to them, then my person and my watching would be watched right off, with suspicion.

There is a weird Kafkaesque irreality in watching soldiers walk through the social intimacies of everyday life. After a while, after several platoons pass through daily consciousness, one comes to see space and time differently, and the nature of sociality. Daily life is peaceful, light, calm, fun; yet a deadly war is going on.

"*Ils font tache,*" said one woman of the military patrols in Paris. "They stain." The soldiers are like a stain on the fabric of everyday life. They stick out, they're out of place, unsettling. The sudden perception of a team of soldiers walking past shops and cafés is jarring, disjunctive. Rupturing the everyday, they are a reminder of the possible explosion of violence at any moment. "In reading a novel on a terrace, enjoying a coffee with friends on a pleasant afternoon, you might forget for a while. The soldiers bring it all back."

The soldiers, too, mark the city. They leave traces of their weapons and their vigilant regard in the streets of Paris. They inscribe fear and violence into sideway glances, body outlines, tomorrow's expectations. This is another form of terrorgraphy, a writing of fear and terror into the world.

### AN ETHOS OF VIGILANCE

Emergent through time is an ethos of vigilance—modes of perception, affect, evaluation, and trace-inscription in which visceral modes of appraisal keep one alert to potentialities of violence.[23] This is an *ethos,* I'd say, because the vigilance entails cultural and affective sensibilities, moods, and dispositions at work in the lives of an individual, a group, or within particular spheres of activity. With this, the ethos largely ties into modes of sensing in the world as well as affective sensibilities that are not necessarily conscious or reflected on or reasoned about in ordinary life.

The vigilance is rooted not simply in psychological or perceptual processes, or in individual consciousnesses or cultural sensibilities, though the vigilance is there, too. The vigilance is seeded within an environment—within, that is, in this particular circumstance, the complex, heterogeneous, and ever-shifting material, sensorial, and affective dimensions of urban life in Paris, in a time of recent and potential violence. The vigilance operates through certain forms of looking, listening, and diffuse sensing. It courses through particular sounds and sights and the media of eyes and ears. The vigilance is evident in the transparent bags in the trash receptacles that line the city's streets. It's embedded in traces and nontraces of violence, past and present. It's sensed in the sounds and digital words of a news service that alerts people through their smart phones apps to events relevant to the French Republic, including any recent terrorist activities. It's in the rumor talk of a suitcase bomb detonated by the police outside a café one day. It's in the recordings voiced over the intercom systems in metro stations, with travelers alerted to keep an eye out for any unattended packages or suspicious activities, one message ending with the statement, *"Merci pour votre vigilance"*: thank you for your watchfulness.

An ethos of vigilance is distributed within the sensescape of a city in ways that go beyond any individual agency or subject positions or singular or collective efforts. It's built into perceptions and engagements in space and time. Certain technologies and practices of the self are involved in vigilant thoughts and actions, but so are sensate bodies and forms of matter, styles of architecture, media technologies, encounters with strangers, email correspondences, social media postings, newspaper articles and television reports, pieces of writing, governmental decrees, police surveillance, and military procedures and strategies. Vigilance works through materiality, biology, affect, sensation, talk, writing, images, sounds, media, imaginative phantasy, political subjectivities and intersubjectivities, and processes of governmentality, time, and memory. Perhaps one could speak of an assemblage of vigilance in present-day Paris, in which disparate elements work together in a pervasive, multimodal, indeterminate, ever-emergent sense of nervous alarm and watchful vigilance.[24]

Anyone engaged in such a vigilant sensorium for any length of time can be subtly encouraged to perceive watchfully, attentively, either in moments of acute alertness or while standing on a train platform, lost in thought. A good citizen of the Republic should learn, through momentary and sustained cultivation of the senses, to keep an eye out for anything suspicious or tinged with potential danger. In a society of vigilance alert watchfulness is part of the social contact, or it should be, they say. This is one component of collective living in secular, securitized France these days; a necessary corrective to fear and violent disorder. Any cultivation of the senses in play occurs through sporadic and happenstance perceptions, oblique sensing, low intensity fear, traces and memories of past violence, and a general atmosphere of vigilant regard. Statecraft subjectivity: vigilance works in calibration with the aims and procedures of a vigilant state.

This vigilance is doubled-edged, to say the least. It offers the possibility of watchful looking and listening, the protection of the state and military, and the significant hope of relative safety in Paris. But it also provokes nervousness and feeds fears and phantasies of imminent danger. Alert and sentient watchfulness contributes to specific phantasms of threat and violence within sensory terrains in which the perceived and the imagined are entangled in murky, complicated ways. Given the spectral and phantasmal dimensions of such vigilance, and how such vigilance reverberates through an urban landscape charged with spectral traces of violence, what is called for is less an ontology of life and vigilant being in Paris than a hauntology of vigilance and traumatic wounding, and the ghostly potentiality of any future violence.[25] Each sentinel patrol resuscitates ghosts of colonialism, armed soldiers overseeing the streets of Hanoi, Algiers, Guadeloupe, as well as past histories of *attentats* in the Hexagon. The ethos of vigilance proceeds as much through a spectral sense of potential dangers and possible violence as it does through concrete signs of actual threats or explosive devices. Any ethos of vigilance implies phantasias of terror and alarm. A phantasmography of violence, wounding, and vigilance—a writing of the phantasmal qualities of such—is called for as much as any direct ethnographies on these subjects.[26]

Vigilance—like violence, in its way—is multiple, shape-shifting, creatively emergent, open to time and potentiality, and fused with complex political valences. Each moment of watchful sensing is charged with looks and counter-looks as well as looks upon those looks; it's also charged with a performance of looking and a critical hermeneutics of looking. There can be a rhetoric of vigilance and countervigilance as well as a critique of persuasive vigilance. Vigilant looking requires training; one learns to look warily through specific modifications of the senses, the body, and subject positions and power relations in the world.

An ethos of vigilance is rooted in time. The temporality of vigilance is crucial here. Acts of vigilance build on previous acts of vigilance, as well as trace memories of past acts of violence. There is also the long *durée* of camp sentinels, occupying armies, colonial warfare and administration, biosocial typification, panopticonic structures, carceral and security regimes, border checkpoints, drone surveillance, retinal scans, ghost prisons, black sites. Vigilant perception can also entail a vague anticipatory sense of events that *could* happen in the next minute, hour, or day. Vigilance carries a keen sense of potentialities. Attentive states of vigilance take form in particular moments; they can linger for a while, and then fade away, with acts of intense and concerned alertness shifting into moments of ease and lightness shared among friends seated on a terrace; or the inverse.

With an ethos of vigilance comes certain phantasms of religion. In a vigilant city it's possible to become intensively and irrationally alert to the signs, appearances, and apparitions of a religion, such as Islam, or Christianity, and be on vigilant watch for what the followers of that religious tradition might be up to in their lives and deaths. The vigilance brings to mind other fearful epochs in Paris and elsewhere, times when persons had to be on the alert against pressing dangers. Jewish families of Paris had to be vigilantly on guard against the threat of arrest, deportation, and death during the Nazi occupation of France during World War II. Algerian residents of *bidonvilles* on the city's outskirts were wary of oppressive violence wielded by French police officers and auxiliary officers during the French colonial era.

In other neighborhoods in and around Paris the vigilance can take different forms, with myriad coefficients of visibility, invisibility, and security and insecurity at work in everyday political life. In areas north of Gare du Nord, particularly the Barbès–Château Rouge *quartier*, which the government of Paris has designated as a Priority Security Zone (ZSP), boys and young men are on watchful alert for the actions and movements of police officers. The police try to deter what they perceive as illegal activities by frequently stopping, frisking, and questioning youths and demanding that they show their identification cards. Through these police tactics and "security apparatuses" bodies are racialized, coarsely coded, marginalized, rendered suspect. The same goes for instances of *délit de faciès*—literally, "face offense"—such as being stopped by police because of one's physical appearance (similar to "walking while Black" in the United States). These recurrent encounters with the police lead youth to be vigilantly mindful of the unwanted presence of the police on the streets of their neighborhoods and to fear the ever-present possibility of humiliating searches, physical and political harassment, and possible arrest and incarceration. The forceful actions of the police and the vigilant regard of those actions becomes a banal part of everyday life for many youths in these security priority zones, such that they are warily vigilant toward the watchful agents of a vigilant state. At the same time, the policing techniques of stopping young men and frisking them and asking for their IDs echo in spectral, haunting ways the treatment of Algerian men and women in France in the late 1950s and early 1960s. The embodied, affective sense of police harassment and vigilance in this current postcolonial time is similar to the embodied, affective sense of political and military oppression in the post–World War II colonial era. So as to cipher such correlates, one keeps watch on, and in, time and history.

Writing itself is a vigilant practice, at once observant, attentive, exploratory. Its sensate vigilance is not unlike the weary alertness of an insomniac alert through the night, unable to sleep, though here the insomnia is of daytime.[27]

I watch myself and my watching, track with suspicion my tracings. In walking and writing the city one comes to carry a weaponized consciousness. And then vigilance is the night, wakeful.

"And you lie awake, a watchman, aware of the next one over from the flickering flames of the brushwood fire. Why are you awake? Custom prescribes that someone must stand watch. Someone must always keep his eyes open."[28]

Printed repetitively along the steps of the footbridges crossing Canal Saint-Martin are the words INSOMNIA RIOT.

R.D.

## INTERRUPTION: "VIGILANCE IS DOUBLE-EDGED, TO SAY THE LEAST"

*Wednesday, 1 November 2017*

December 2015, boulevard de la Chapelle. It's almost ten o'clock, the shops are nearly all closed and the street vendors are beginning to pack their goods. I leave a kebab restaurant, my dinner in a plastic bag, and walk along the boulevard. A young man leans against the wall whispering the brands of the contraband cigarettes he sells: "*mboro, légendes, shoum alblad.*" I greet him and ask for two packs of Algerian Marlboro cigarettes. As I open a pack to light a cigarette we begin talking.

"How've you been holding up?" he asks, mechanically.

"Good, *hamdullah* [thank God]."

I ask him if the police checks have gotten more frequent since the state of emergency was put in place a month before.

"Yes, they have," he answers.

"But," I reply, "it doesn't stop you from working."

He shakes his head.

"Nah, nah, they're busy looking for the terrorists now, just like they did in Saint-Denis," during the 18 November 2015 police operation on rue du Corbillon.

"They don't bother us when we sell," he continues. "But the problem isn't when we're working, *it's the rest of the time.* It's because *they can't tell the difference between a terrorist and an Arab!*"

He gestures towards the police station, one street north of where we stand.

"Whereas us," he says, pointing to me, "we fled terrorism. We know what terrorism is!"

He thumps his chest with a closed fist every time he says *we know.*

"Us. We know," he continues, "but they think we're all terrorists. They haven't understood what's actually happening."

He pauses.

"*Ma3lech* [whatever]," he concludes, "they don't need us to burn down their country, they'll do it all on their own." With a short movement of the head, he gestures for me to leave, so as not to attract attention from the police patrol rolling by. I nod and wish him peace.

"Peace," he replies as I walk away.

Something certainly changed after the attacks of 13 November 2015. And, somehow, it felt as if that change had already occurred. The state of emergency, declared on the night of the attacks and maintained for two consecutive years, allowed for antiterrorist policing to target Muslim and immigrant communities. In renewing some of its tools of surveillance—such as deploying thousands of home raids and putting hundreds of people under house arrest without judicial oversight—the French Republic also actualized and deepened the stigmatization, racialization, and *othering* of the collectives it targeted.

The "law instituting a state of emergency and declaring its application in Algeria" was voted into effect in 1955, as a means of repressing the Algerian nationalists as combatants without transferring governmental powers to the army. In the later years of the war of independence, it was used against the terrorist attacks of the Organisation de l'armée secrète.[29] Since then, the state of emergency has continued to stand at a particular junction of the French colonial Republic.

Intermittently, from 1985 to 1988, the state of emergency was declared in the Pacific island of Kanaky (Nouvelle-Calédonie) where an independence movement had been forming, with demonstrations, blockades, and the targeting of police and military officers. This anticolonial militancy was effectively quashed after the massacre of the cave of Ouvéa, when military police gendarmes killed eighteen militants. In 1986 and 1987, a state of emergency was declared and used to police antinuclear organizations in the Pacific islands of Wallis and Futuna. In 2005, finally, the state of emergency was declared in Paris and in twenty cities where uprisings had taken place following the deaths of two children, Zyed Benna and Bouna Traoré, who died as they were chased by police officers in Clichy-sous-Bois (Seine-Saint-Denis, 93).

As we carried this in our sensibilities and familial histories, we were neither surprised by the attack nor by the bellicose reaction of the French state and French "public opinion." *We?* Perhaps the change that it brought, as we stood looking through the screens of these phantasmagorias, was a cementing of the "we" that lived through us, of the "they" that lived through them.

As the names of the attackers were plastered on newspapers and television newsreels, the words *barbarians* and *Islam* became commonplace associations. Things changed; in institutional settings, between friends of various social and geographic backgrounds, in public spaces. People—tourists from other parts of France, from various confines of the world, as well as mundane well-to-do Parisians—stared in the streets, on the subway platforms, in the train stations. And so the phantasmagorias of national threats and vigilance played out, between fugitive looks and gaping stares, in the streets of Paris. One gray afternoon, on place Jules Joffrin in the 18th arrondissement, I witnessed a strange scene. A young man, a five-o'clock shadow on his cheeks, wearing a leather jacket, washed-out jeans, and Stan Smith tennis shoes, sped up the stairs exiting the metro station. He looked exhausted, with black circles under his eyes. His head, which was crowned with tight curls and faded around the ears in a military fashion, moved nervously, as if he were trying to look over his shoulder. He turned around suddenly, his hands in his pockets in a protective posture, to face two women, perhaps a mother and daughter. "What's wrong, huh? What's the problem?" he yelled in distress. "Stop looking at me!" Feeling watched, knowing that you are watched; not just by the state and its sentinel soldiers but by everyone who sees you as "them."

The state of emergency relies on geographies of *otherness;* it relies on the figure of an "internal enemy," an undeclared combatant threatening the political order of the Republic and against which the latter can direct surveillance and legalized violence. The state of emergency allows for the re*tracing* of national sociopolitical borders, between Republican citizens and their *others.*

"They don't need us to burn down their country, they'll do it all on their own."

Incisive albeit offhandedly, the cigarette vendor evoked the vast phantasmagoria of racial and urban otherness that plays out in France and its media representations, political discourses, and scholarship. Since the first sociological studies on "French immigrant youth" in the 1980s, social science practitioners have transferred "common sense" cultural racism, sometimes unwittingly, into their work.[30] Sociologists, anthropologists, and semiologists, reiterated and reinforced the dominant collective representations of "urban ghettos" as spaces of anomy reliant on violence as a semicultural "neo-tribal" normative imperative; zones where youth produce "counter-worlds" as manifestations of spatialized and embodied Republican *otherness*.[31]

As a discursive apparatus, the state of emergency relies on the scientific legitimacy of crime statistics, surveys, polls, and qualitative studies. Unthought and yet hypervisible in criminologically inflected socioanthropology and semiotic anthropology, phantasms of religious, cultural, and racial otherness suffuse scholarship pertaining to the lives of French youth of Caribbean and West and North African descent living in the social housing projects of France's *quartiers populaires*. Such scholarship becomes dangerous once it puts the burden of representation on the groups represented rather than the state, institutional, or political-economic processes through which representation in fact takes place. Constituting sociosymbolic categories and imaginaries as scientific truths, social sciences then run the risk of feeding into national mythologies of threat, internal enemies, and war.[32]

A burning bus, red flames by a gray housing estate.
A hooded figure running in the street.
Stop-and-frisk on the way home from school; police banging on the door.
Young people in traditional garb; an elder reciting a prayer.
A gas cylinder; explosive youth.
But,
"They don't need us to burn down their country, they'll do it all on their own."

Phantasms can circulate as expertise. Yet they rely on lights, screens, and shadows that obscure collective perceptions. Complex social lives and collectivities come to be submerged by phantasmagorias—a multitude of phantasms reified by police protocols; phantasms that lodge themselves in subjectivities. The state of emergency, and the subsequent incorporation of its principles into the French civil code, thus relies on more than state-declared exceptions to due process. It also articulates itself in fearful citizens' collective affective commitment to surveillance, to an ethos of vigilance, and to a more-or-less systematic participation in the "surveillant assemblages."

"Whereas us, we fled terrorism. We know what terrorism is!"

Those who have experienced war and terrorism firsthand, incoherent and absurd, are then, here in the Republic, the objects of surveillance: we are watched. But the phantasms that the surveillant gaze projects blur over the plurality of experiences of war, transience, and movements that make this *we* hard to grasp in the first place. I had fled neither civil war nor terrorist

FIGURE 23. Tags on rue de Maubeuge, near boulevard de la Chapelle. It reads, in English, "Free Syria" and, in Arabic, "All of us with Idlib," January 2020. Photo by K. H.

attacks, but this phantasm created a sense of common understanding between the cigarette vendor and myself. We are not, and that is perhaps one of the fundamental paradoxes of otherness.

"Peace," he replied as I walked away.

July 2016, on rue Caplat and rue de Chartres: I exit my apartment building and greet two neighbors sitting on the steps outside. The sky is blue and the streets are crowded with people who have come for the weekly market on the boulevard. As we exchange greetings, a group of soldiers from the Opération Sentinelle walk down from rue de Chartres toward the small plaza where we stand. The crowd separates in two, letting the soldiers walk through.

"Ah, they patrol by foot now?" I ask. "I've only ever seen them in their cars around here."

I'm surprised they would patrol here, there are no monuments to defend, no religious institutions to protect; no tourists, either. Just working-class immigrants, some with French papers, some without any papers at all.

One of the neighbors says, "They patrol like it's Gaza. They come take a good look so they'll know where to get us when they want to put us in camps."

The second neighbor adds, "Or maybe to put in checkpoints, just like during the war [of Algerian independence]."

As the soldiers pass and leave, continuing their patrol toward the metro station, the crowd gravitates back to the place de la Charbonnière. We change the subject, and express gratitude for the beautiful weather we've had all week.

It is indeed peculiar to see oneself through the peering gaze of another: understanding and becoming oneself by looking inward and outward simultaneously, seeing oneself "darkly as through a veil."[33] "This vigilant ethos is double-edged, to say the least." It settles in behaviors: the civilian partakes in the vigilance of the state, diffusing the work of surveillance that the sentinels undertake. The surveillant assemblage becomes an embodied infrastructure.[34] As vigilance is put into practice in the everyday, it produces phantasms of threats. These phantasms, however, are not mere fictional projections: that is, they produce practical realities. The military units of Opération Sentinelle are in a sense both a product of the phantasm, a continuation of it, and what allows it to subsist in the material world.

But what lies beyond the phantasm? The people who are seen—crept on— as threats are not repositories of violence. Existing through a sort of phantasmagoria making their presence a threatening one, they must engage in vigilance in different ways. A vigilance turned toward the state, a vigilance that understands the implications of antiterrorism as a battle waged on the body and in spaces of sociability and intimacy. A vigilance that does not allow us to put our trust in military patrols. It rests upon the evocation of troubled lives, evoked as if in proximity despite their distance in time—the Algerian war of independence—and in space—the Israeli blockade of Gaza. In the Goutte d'Or, police squads are numerous, and officers patrol the streets in densely coordinated and ever-changing patrols. My neighbors have become subjects on the lookout. They are wary of the actions and movements of police officers. Others, some of them still children, have incorporated the fear of the ever-present possibility of humiliating searches, physical and political harassment, and possible arrest and incarceration.

Ghosts of colonial occupation that the soldiers bring with them as they patrol; ghosts of political terrorism that they project unto the streets of the Goutte d'Or as they make their way to the boulevard Barbès. All-too-real ghosts, when some have had to lay their open palms on a cement wall, spread their legs, and wait for the unusually routine genital pat down to end. A dialogue of phantasmagoria? As the sentinels advance, *we* haunt *them;* and they haunt us as they project phantasms of what we are not and remind us of what they may do. Ghosts that linger and dissipate as we look to a kinder sky.

*K. H.*

FOUR

———

# *Learning with the body*

The reason why all those who are stigmatized—i.e., all those who occupy stigmatized positions within social space—experience the body as the geometric locus for all the stigmas that can be inflicted upon them, is no doubt that the body, which is both a physical individuality and a social product, is both, on the one hand, the most difficult thing of all to modify and, on the other, the very thing that has been most worked upon, polished, and cultivated, and that is most amenable to modification when social pressures demand it . . . the body is the bearer of social identity: it is that identity.

ABDELMALEK SAYAD,
*The Suffering of the Immigrant*

ESSAI AND ESQUISSES

*Thursday, 13 November 2017*

The body is constrained, although it does not let itself be constrained easily. It is grasped and captured by the social forces that seek to transform it into the phantasm that hovers around it. And yet it is constantly, as if a fugitive, escaping that grasp, undoing the grip of its captors, and making itself anew. It is a generative product. Caught within the social configuration that gives it its legitimacy, or, conversely, bombards it with stigma, the body nonetheless generates phenomena that unsettle the very forces that seek to mold it.

This chapter is about bodies. About my own body, to a certain extent. This chapter is about bodies that resemble mine, not because we look alike but because we undergo analogous socializations through racism, sexism, and spatial ascriptions. What brings semblance is a common relationship to historical moments and institutions. This chapter is also about history. And, since the way spaces are shaped and the way bodies inhabit spaces are in constant dialogue, this chapter is also about how bodies are shaped by histories. In writing about the specificity of bodies that are made to inhabit colonial and racial representations, I want to offer an insight into a world that we all inhabit.

89

As we are socialized, through family, through school, through the labor market, the street, and our relationship to state institutions, the body is trained. In learning one's social position within a given society's hierarchy, in incorporating aspirations and ambitions, we begin to use our bodies to move around social fields. Bodies are in a sense a passport that may open ports, just as it may seal and close off whole coasts. Bourdieu uses the concept of *habitus* to describe *acquired dispositions*; that is, all the habits in speech, thought, gestures, perception, and demeanor that are inscribed in a socialized subject. The *hexis* is the corporeal aspect of that habitus.[1] The concepts of habitus and hexis emerge from the epistemology and heuristic of phenomenology; it is toward this genealogy of Bourdieu's work that I etch my reflection.[2]

Police officers, for instance, have acquired a professional habitus. Officers patrol the streets and read them through a lens riddled with socioracial categories. Their reading is not only expressed through discourse—which we could then access through interviews or institutional ethnography—it is also explicit in their hexis: how they walk the streets of low-income immigrant neighborhoods; who they choose to stop, check, and frisk; the way they pat down a body and how they address the person they have momentarily seized.

In his sociology of Algerian immigration, Abdelmalek Sayad located the experience of social death within the material world of exile (*ghorba*) and racism; in Sayad's work, the daily catastrophe of social death emerges out of the process of subjects being made into objects of state reason. Throughout his career, Sayad never stopped to highlight how immigrants were symbolically and materially lodged in structures that withhold, that limit, that delegitimize immigrants' presence in France; veiling the complex personhood of immigrants with phantasms of state efficiency. Hexis, habitus, and the vocabulary of phenomenology serve a conceptual ground to understand the ways in which the body becomes a conduit—in the sense of electrical currents punctuated by conductive nodes—for social structures to actualize themselves in subjectivities. The body makes the social corpo*real*. How do we account for the individual (or rather, the intimate) struggles of one's body against the way that body may be seen, captured, and wounded?


## THINKING THE PROCESS OF INCORPORATION

In his 1934 essay on techniques of the body, anthropologist Marcel Mauss understood the body as an instrument: a "technical object" and a "technical means" shaped through tradition and individual acquisition.[3] His outlook was embedded in the colonial common sense of his time: a "technique," he writes, is "an action which is *effective* and *traditional*."[4] In light of the colonial destruction of such techniques, of the ways colonial sovereignty worked to apply itself not only on territory but also on bodies, one could understand the unsettling of traditional techniques as the application of a distinct technique of the body. That is, racist and colonial projects insert captured bodies in new configurations of constraint and dispossession, and enforce new techniques specific to new forms of discipline and sovereign power. My body, then, is not a pristine vessel of traditional techniques. Rather, it is sculpted by antagonistic social forces. The researcher's body, then, becomes a resource for reflexive sociology: it is at once an instrument for analysis and a topic of study.[5]

In expanding Mauss's theory, I move closer to historian Michel Foucault's work on discipline and subjectivation. Institutions of constraint impose corporeal movements, postures, and a particular distribution of bodies within space.[6] Rather than read into Foucault a form of causality between social structures and the subjectivities that constitute its outgrowth, we could understand the prison—or the city—as spaces that produce specific subject *positions,* which are more or less successfully applied and incorporated in the dispositions of the bodies held captive. This aspect allows to read Foucault's analysis of total institutions as dynamic, rather than as a bleak and deterministic monography.

In his *Anthropology of Ethics,* James Faubion writes that subjectivation, in the sense of constructing and inhabiting one's "subject position," is "not merely [a matter] of wearing the shoe that fits but also—and crucially—the converse: actors must always also adapt themselves to fit the styles and sizes available to them."[7] It is a work of *praxis*—in the sense of doing—as we make do with what has been given to us. In that sense, we are received in the world as already historically constituted, bombarded with representations that prefigure what we may be able to aspire to and which we will need to struggle against. But, in what can seem like a paradox, we must also learn that position and inhabit it as learned and practiced. In other words, we inherit not only a social position, but also the historical conditions that have produced it. This means, on the one hand, that we must learn to live in our bodies and in the position carved out for them. On the other hand, though, the work we unknowingly undertake to become "ethical subjects" is a work of *poiesis:* of creation. We make ourselves new and construct the way we appear to and inhabit the world. While one can be caught within institutions that are oriented toward breaking one's will to live and love, there is always a potential to mold that which one is being molded into. As I consider what a praxis and poiesis of the self may be in my life, I must face the histories I may have forgotten, and understand what my body appears to be, what it absorbs, what it repulses, and how it is welcomed in various spaces.

Philosopher Sara Ahmed writes that "bodies remember such histories, even when we forget them. Such histories, we might say, surface on the body, or even shape how bodies surface."[8] She continues, "In a way, then, race does become a social as well as bodily given, or what we *receive* from others as an inheritance of this history."[9] In producing race as a *practical* category, colonial conquest and enslavement shaped both social structures and how these structures are incorporated. In other words, the invention of race and the histories of colonial occupation have left their trace. "The embodiment of racial memory is not a metaphor," writes anthropologist Didier Fassin.[10] That is to say, we inherit historically constructed social positions, positions that are as subjective as they are material.

But that history would have no actuality were it not for the bodies that work as its conduit. Bodies are inscribed in the spatiality of the neighborhood. They navigate the rhythms of the city, take timed steps within that orchestration, and improvise a choreography of their own. In inscribing oneself within the movements of the neighborhood, all the while inheriting the history of colonialism—through immigration status, socioeconomic condition in the form of access to dignified labor, housing, schooling, and so on—subjects come to embody the histories and the racial and geographic categories that these histories produced.

"For bodies that are not extended by the skin of the social," philosopher Sara Ahmed writes, "bodily movement is not so easy. Such bodies are stopped, where the stopping is an action that creates its own impressions. Who are you? Why are you here? What are you doing? Each question, when asked, is a kind of *stopping device:* you are stopped by being asked the question, just as asking the question requires you to be stopped."[11] In focusing the sociological gaze on police practices of stopping, and remaining within the subjective space of those stopped—rather than in the institutional space of those who do the stopping—what starts to emerge is a form of "fieldwork in philosophy"[12] or a sociological methodology for a "phenomenology of 'being stopped.'"[13] Investigating regimes of mobility then consists in a phenomenology of how bodies are allowed to inhabit space, of racialization as such a regime of spatial extension and subsequent limitation of the body.

FIGURE 24. Gendarmerie helicopter patrol above the 18th arrondissement, heading to the Goutte D'Or, April 2020. Photo by K. H.

The work of human geographers, and their attention to spatial structures, mobility, and corporeality, is particularly helpful in bridging philosophy and ethnographic sociology. In *Spatializing Blackness,* Rashad Shabazz offers a multidisciplinary analysis of the constitution of Black masculinities in Chicago.[14] This critical geographer focuses on legal transformations—federal, state, and city by-laws—and the ways particular architectures shaped urban life for Black communities after the Second Great Migration. Shabazz plays with scales, moving from a bird's-eye view of the projects to the intimacies of kitchenette apartments, in order to understand how masculinities were shaped by and expressed themselves in such spaces.

Shabazz focuses on the negative impacts of the expansion of carceral geographies within urban spaces of sociability. He nonetheless ends his work with an opening on the contemporary reformulation of relationships (to oneself, to one another, and to space) through local projects of urban farming and reappropriation of space by grassroots organizations led by Black residents. Shabazz works with the complexity of subjectivation, with the dialogue between *poiesis* and *praxis.* Making do with what is given, often falling within the cracks that cement fodder traps us in, the potential lies in that communities may yet create space and self anew.

For me, Shabazz's study offers a method. He helps me think about the effects of long-term rhythms of state intervention on the sociopolitical, cultural and spiritual rhythms of the communities targeted. More specifically, Shabazz allows me to consider how state intervention enters intimacy, graphing itself on and within young Black people's masculinities. In a neighborhood like the Goutte d'Or, the immigrant centrality interacts with and is shaped by the rhythms of police, labor, hygiene, and penal zoning. The spatiality of exile that emerges from these long-term processes then rests on a history of competing normative imperatives. The ones I experienced firsthand and studied were, on the one hand, the racial and gendered imperatives of police surveillance and, on the other, the gendered norms proper to the neighborhood as I experienced and internalized them. The question that emerges from my reading of *Spatializing Blackness* is: how do I inhabit this spatiality? How do I interact with these competing normative imperatives?

### BEING STOPPED

A phenomenology of stop-and-frisk requires a lot of persistence, often punctuated by moments of self-doubt or instances of clarity before a new fog and new questions come to replace those that had just begun to dissipate. As a personal process, it requires revisiting familial history and developing a method of introspection that allows for all these moments of doubt to further self-questioning rather than weaken it. As a sociological undertaking, looking into the ways these histories manifest in the present, how policing inscribes itself on bodies requires one to take into account both material realities and affective ones. As a method, which involves intersubjectivity, a phenomenology of being stopped requires one to nurture similar forms of introspection with the people that agree to participate in ethnography.[15]

In the Goutte d'Or, ID checks are a daily—in fact, commonplace—event. They are part of the urban landscape of the neighborhood and they participate in the territorialization of the police-penal ZSP (Zone de sécurité prioritaire) administrative category. ID checks are the work of stopping bodies *as well as* that of extending sovereignty and carceral geography into the city and its streets, alleys, buildings, and hallways. A young man is stopped by police officers on the boulevard Barbès after making a transaction on rue de la Chapelle. Before the officer says anything, the young man turns around, extends his arms and rests open palms on the cement wall, spreading his legs

FIGURE 25. Stop-and-frisk in Paris, December 2020. Sketch by K. H.

as the officer bends to pat him down. The officer finds a pack of contraband cigarettes, which he slices open with a knife. The young man is sent on his way. The movements are learned and repeated, so much so that they become seamless, almost effortless. Open your hands, look down, don't speak a word. Small gestures that allow for a smooth police check. In accepting and incorporating the rules of police checks, one escapes their grasp, slips through their hands, and maintains a certain distance between self and the prison walls that police officers carry into public space.

Like a student learning a lesson and putting it into practice, interacting with police officers requires work. It requires self-control and shutting out the electric shocks of neuralgia that police sovereignty sends coursing through the stopped body. *J'ai les nerfs qui montent.* I can feel my nerves tensing as the police officer slides his hands over a body made bare and exposed in public space. Fear of what they might do if I were to react instinctively; the will to appear as dignified as possible given the situation; or—simply—a friend, a woman, a passerby, a lover reclaiming me as their kin. It is such small, insignificant moments that make one's path differ, from continuing with your errands that day to entering a fast-track path to a shared prison cell. Refusing to submit oneself to an ID check and insulting an officer can be filed as charges of *outrage* and *rebellion,* which can amount to three months in jail. Better, then, to shut up and open my hands.

Personal and collective biographies are profoundly affected by these jolt reactions. The proximity with penal institutions, a proximity that police officers actualize every time they stop and frisk a young Black or Arab man in the Goutte d'Or, is exemplary of the historicity of colonial and racial categories. And while not all racialized bodies are captured in such a way, all may be captured. We inhabit spaces of potential incarceration. Inheriting colonial history in the particular position of the Republic's racial others, we stand at the center of the scenic order: as objects of discourse, policy, cultural production, and subjective fears. National sovereignty then appears as oriented toward keeping "internal foreigners" in check and "external foreigners" out.[16] The "illegitimate children" of immigrants in France, Abdelmalek Sayad writes, are then constantly assigned to a symbolic and material position in the borderlands of the Republic or, in other words, they are never allowed to "feel to be truly at home where they are."[17]

December 2015. Dusk. Porte de la Villette. The road is slick and humid from recent rainfall and oil stains. Yasmine and I are walking toward the boulevard Périphérique, heading to a concert in an old factory converted into an artists' squat. A voice yells *"Contrôle!"* I can't see where the voice is coming from; unassuming, I continue walking. From behind us, a police officer yells again—this time grabbing me by the elbow—*"Contrôle d'identité.* Your papers. Now!" The officer, a young five-foot-five blond man, pulls me into an empty lot, where a white-red-and-blue police car is parked. Two other officers stand there, legs spread out and hands on their hips. One is a tall grey-haired man, with striking blue eyes and a bushy beard, the other is a clean-shaven man that I take to be Kabyle. Yasmine follows us into the lot as I hand my ID to the older, bearded officer.

"What gives you the right to stop me? I'm walking, going about my business," I say.

Yasmine grabs my hand. I take it as encouragement. Wrong. She starts pinching me.

"Shut your mouth," she whispers.

"It's the state of emergency, honey [*mon petit*]," the blond cop replies, laughing. "We have *no* justification to give to citizens."

'"Oh yeah? So this is antiterrorism? Singling me out like this?" I ask, my upper lip curled in anger and arrogance. Yasmine looks at me with round eyes and pinches me harder. I feel ashamed that she is seeing and reading through me like this. The officers are in a good mood and smirk at our joined hands.

The Kabyle officer pulls Yasmine aside. He checks her immigration papers. Asks her to wait. Walks into the crowd in the street and picks out a young white man. He turns to her and says, "Random check, you see."

At the exact same time, the blond officer pushes my arms up, slipping his fingers in my collar, my sleeves, and patting my chest, back and arms. He then crouches and frisks my legs in a similar fashion. He grabs me by the waist and tries to turn me around. I resist. He grabs me harder and pushes me against the wall.

"Don't worry honey," he says, smiling. "It won't hurt if you don't move."

Crouched behind me, he slips his hand inside my pants and squeeze my genitals with his hand. He mimics a moaning sound and laughs. I flinch and try to turn around to look at him.

"You're trying to hide something," he says confidently. "You got drugs? Hash? A knife? Tell me now 'cause I'll find it and that'll be a whole lot worse for you."

There is nothing suspicious in my pockets that evening. The blond officer looks disappointed. The Kabyle officer looks satisfied. The grey-haired officer returns with my ID. "He's got nothing on his file," he tells his colleagues.

"Fuck off, then," the blond officer tells Yasmine and I as we leave and shake our shoulders loose. We get back on track to the concert we are set to attend.


May 2017. Warm, sunny Sunday afternoon. Place de la Chapelle. A group of teenagers, around ten Black and North African boys and two Black girls, are standing on the rue Pajol. They're screaming at police officers standing across from them on the plaza. The officers are in a strange formation, surrounding a police van as if they were hiding it from view.

"You have no right to do this! You have no right!" The children are screaming high pitched screams of scared children. Yasmine and I walk toward the group of children.

"What's going on?" Yasmine asks them.

"They told us we weren't allowed to cross this line," one of the boys answers, as he traces a line separating the rue Pajol from the place de la Chapelle. "And then they took our friend."

We turn around to the van; the figure of a tall skinny teenager appears and disappears between the officers interlocked elbows. His friends continue to scream, staying behind the imaginary line drawn by the police patrol.

Two officers come out of the van carrying the teenager by the belt. They throw him out and a third officer catches him. The child is scared. He looks around, terrified. He tries to get out of their grip and slips a lanky arm out of his sweater. The officers get more aggressive. One grabs his elbows. Another his belt. A third slides a baton between the boys' legs and starts pushing up. The teenager lets out a scream of surprise and pain.

"Film, sister! Film them! Or they're going to do crazy shit to him! Please, film. He didn't do anything wrong."

Yasmine hands me her phone and I start to film, reaching high so as to film above the wall of police officers hiding the beating. One of the officers nudges his colleagues and points to me. An officer reaches into the van and pulls out a camera; he walks to me and films. Two officers walk with him.

"Your papers, now!"

The officer is a short and stocky man, with a long beard and arms covered in tattoos; I recognize him as the officer that some in the community call "Le Portugais" (The Portuguese). He grabs Yasmine by the arm and pushes her against the fence of the place de la Chapelle park. I reach to her to help her up—"Are you all right?"—but the officer pushes on my chest with his flat hand and holds me against the fence.

"You're not allowed to film policemen, you're aware [of that]?"

"What? No, we're allowed to film police officers when they're performing their duties. It's in the 2013 legal *circulaire*."

"And what if we find these images on the internet, without my authorization," he replies. "I have the right to sue you."

The police officers that surrounded the van are now walking toward us. As they loosen their grip, the teenager slips out and runs back to his friends. "Thank you," he says as he runs past us.

Pat down. Sexual jibes. Brisk movements around my genitals. I've gotten used to it.

An officer reaches to frisk Yasmine.

"Male officers aren't allowed to search women," she says calmly.

The officers laugh, visibly excited.

"Marine!" they yell in concert, calling to the woman in their squad. "Marine, we have a pat down for you!"

A young blond woman walks out of the van, where she had apparently been sitting this whole time. She does not and will not touch Yasmine at any time. But while I have my legs spread out and my arms up, she engages in a moral and political discussion with her.

"We're here to protect you, you know? Women aren't safe in this neighborhood and we're here to protect you."

"So, beating up a child and frisking my partner is how you protect women? And your colleague here, he put his hands on me and pushed me. You're telling me I'm meant to feel safe."

The woman officer is perplexed. "Do you people really have to insult [*outrage*] everyone all the time, huh? We can't even talk with you. I'm being respectful, I'm trying to understand. And you, all you have to say is 'No, no, no.' Nah, we can't talk with you ghetto people [*gens de quartiers*]. You're always confrontational. Dialogue is impossible."

Another officer adds, "It's no use with these people."

Yasmine turns to the woman officer and answers, "If you want to have a conversation, it has to be equal to equal, not in this context, all right? You stop and frisk us and you want to have a conversation?"

"But we are on equal footing, miss," she answers. "You're the one who's being arrogant."

The back and forth continues. Yasmine walks the fine line of saying what she thinks while staying within the bounds of what is and is not acceptable in a police interaction. I try to interject. Yasmine pinches my hand when she senses I am about to say something. The tattooed officer, arms crossed, a smile wide on his face, looks at me—at my beard, my crotch—waiting for me to move too quickly or speak too loudly. They comment on where we live. They look through our wallets, comment on what they find. Waiting to provoke something. The woman officer tries to continue her sermon but the other officers speak over her, in jibes and insults.

Neither one of us has committed a crime or an infraction, however, and the police cannot hold us indefinitely. Once the officers who took our papers come back from the ID verification in the van, we will be free to go. An officer walks back toward us—"Nothing on their file," he says—but the tattooed officer grabs our papers out of his hand. He spits at my feet as he flips through the pages of Yasmine's American passport. He smiles when he finds what he was looking for: an Algerian visa.

FIGURE 26. Gendarmerie Surveillance and Intervention Platoons, place de la République, March 2020. Photo by K. H.

"Ah, *voilà!*" He laughs and shows the visa to the other officers. "Listen, we have enough thugs [*racaille*] here, we don't need to handle other countries' scum. So, do us a favor, will you, and go back to your country!"

They hand us our papers and, with a short wave of the hand, signal for us to leave.

"And don't let us catch you fooling around like this again," one of them yells in our direction. We walk away, exhausted by the interaction.

April 2016. Dawn. I am walking home with friends. Boulevard de la République. We've just spent the day protesting against the 2016 labor reform (La loi travail). The day ended with an assembly on the place de la République. Antiriot police used gas canisters to quickly empty the plaza of protesters. Small groups of gendarmerie and CRS run in formation through the place de la République, shooting tear-gas canisters, rubber bullets, and stun grenades. They grab protesters as they advance through the plaza, dragging them to the center of their formation and behind the police lines.

Boulevard de la République. The sound of explosions grows faint, distant. Other groups of protesters are walking in the same direction. Gendarmerie and CRS vans in the alleys. Blue lights far behind us: blue lights that seem to get closer. Faster pace, don't run. No need to run. Burning garbage bins. We pass by the Bataclan concert hall. City officials have put away the memorials, though a few bouquets still hang from the fence of the park. I feel like I have a ball in my throat. But the street seems calm, quiet.

Everything happens too quickly. Dozens of vans and cars erupt from the surrounding streets onto the intersection in front of the Bataclan. Squads of officers in formation run forward, swinging their sticks. Run! My friends are running fast. They're not looking back. I look around to see if anyone has slowed down. Yasmine is right in front me. Run. A squad appears in front of us. Our friends made it out. We turn around. Cops. A terrace. Cops. A wall.

"On the ground! On the ground!"

I can't understand what he's saying. Sounds. I hear the sirens and the boots. I raise my hands, drop my bag.

"On the ground!"

"I'm not armed. I don't have anything on me. I have my hands up."

"On the ground, you dirty Arab!" he yells one last time, close enough for me to finally make out his words.

The first strike of the baton lands on my right jaw. I am surprised I am still standing. I stay upright. Another one. I lock my elbows around my face. A second one in the ribs. I bend over. In the shoulder. Again. I fall on the ground. I hear screaming. Yasmine's voice. Another woman's voice; she sounds like a resident pulled out of bed by the commotion. A man's voice; maybe a journalist. The officer keeps screaming for me to get down.

His superior officer pulls him from over me.

"There are cameras, calm down. Shit."

I am lying on my stomach. Hands held together by the officer kneeling on my back. Another one has his boot on my neck. I hear him yell to a colleague, *"Chope-moi le negro la-bas!"* Grab that Black man over there.

Yasmine, a teenage girl, two other men, and I are lying on the ground, hands on our heads. They pull us upright and line us up against the wall. Pat down. More invasive than usual. An officer grabs my face and looks at my injuries.

"Take him in," he says. "We've got resisting arrest [*rebellion*] and assaulting an officer [*violence contre agent*] charges here."

Handcuffed in the van, a police officer by my side.

"You can't take him," I hear Yasmine talking outside. "Take me too, then. He's not going in alone."

A superior officer tells her something I can't hear. She continues to talk to him. She's extremely calm. Yasmine's voice and the officer's get closer. I feel her hand on my shoulder. An officer grabs me by the elbow and pulls me out of the van. I stumble as he quickly slices the plastic handcuffs with a knife.

"Get the fuck out of here before I change my mind."

As we walk away, a squad arrives with more arrestees. We recognize a boy from earlier that night, at the plaza. He lives in a social housing block between the place de la République and the Canal Saint-Martin. Curious about the noise, he snuck out of the family home. They throw him on the ground, in front of the van's sliding door.

"You liked it, huh? You liked fucking with us over there, didn't you?" The officers recognize him too. "Well, we're gonna do you like we did Salah Abdesslam [one of the attackers on the Bataclan, later incarcerated]."

One officer lifts him by the arms and drags him on the seat.

I want to say something, to stop them and pull him out of the van too. My face keeps swelling and no sound comes out of my mouth.

"Let's go," Yasmine says as she pulls out her phone and calls a cab.

I try to say thank you.


July 2017. Five o'clock. I spent the day introducing myself to groups of young men and boys who spend part of their days outside, in public places such as parks, plazas, restaurants, barbershops, and local grocery stores. I sit on a Ping-Pong table with Oumar and Adama, two fourteen-year-old boys who've agreed to speak with me.

"Here, the police stop-and-frisk all the time," Oumar explains. "They stop, search, and pat us down. You never see them pat down white people. It's always Arabs [*rebeu*] and Black people [*renoi*] that get pat down like that, huh?"

Oumar looks me straight in the eyes, and when he does not he gazes into space thoughtfully touching small scars on his neck and shoulder. He continues, "Never. I've never seen them do that to white people. Maybe they stop them, check their ID. But they'll never do what they do to us, where they *touch* you and stuff."

Adama lets a silence settle and adds, "What they do is that they *haggar* us. It's the *hoggra*, here. You understand? It's for the humiliation that they do this."

The word *hoggra* comes from Algerian Darija. At one time used to describe the practice of power by French colonial officials and settlers, the word is now part of French slang. *Hoggra* denotes a form of humiliation inflected by the perpetrator's intention to dominate another. To *haggar* someone is then to make them a *mahgour*, a humiliated person, and produce a situation of *hoggra*.

Adama looks at me, and raises his eyebrows to make sure I've understood. I nod.

"In fact," Oumar continues, "with the police, it's simple: they're corrupt. They don't come here to protect us. They come to stir shit up, so that we can't live [in peace]." I ask him if, with time and repetition, he's gotten to know the officers personally. Oumar laughs cynically.

"Yeah, we know them. And they know us too, you see. They know our names, nicknames, where we live and stuff. You see they know who we are but it's to *haggar* us, actually. Sometimes they're justified in what they doing, though . . . "

He sips on a juice box and crunches it in his fist.

"But yeah," he goes on, "we know them well. We even know their nicknames. Some of the nicknames they use, we came up with. There's Grey Beard, there's the other bearded . . . "

"There's Grey Beard, and Blacky," Adama completes Oumar's list. "And there's Bylka, Karim the Kabyle, the *bacqueux* [member of the BAC]."[18]


Later, the same day, after speaking with other boys and men, I reconvene with Oumar.

"I was thinking," he says when I greet him, "and the cops, you see, they come and every time they tell us to move. They never let us stay where we want. You see, we're hanging out with our camping chairs or on some abandoned couch—or just on a bench in the park! But it's no use, I mean, the park is for everyone, nah? The street is public. It's not their mother's street. And so we move to another spot, and again 'Get out!' Sometimes they come and they tell us to move, and if we talk back they gas us [with pepper spray]. But just like that, you see. They get here with the canister in hand, ready."

Oumar stops for a second.

"There's plenty of examples. The other day, they arrested a guy, there." He points to the bench across from us. "All right, I'm not gonna lie, they were doing their patrol and we got a little rowdy, you see? But I mean, we make some noise and the police come and hit us like we're criminals? I think we're children and like all children, we're noisy. . . . And so this guy, they kicked him in the head even though he was handcuffed, lying on his stomach."

"It's not only that," Oumar continues. "In the winter, during ID checks, when they search us they tell us to take off our coats, you see, to frisk us. But they make us wait like for thirty minutes at a time. And then they leave without saying anything. Sometimes they cut our laces. You know how they have these knives, they use them to break the [contraband] cigarettes. Yeah, well sometimes they'll cut our laces with those. Sometimes it's our papers or telephone that they take, as if we'd stolen them, and then they throw them on the ground and say 'go fetch' as if we were dogs. They do this to humiliate us."

Oumar and I continue to speak. He asks me more questions about the research, the police documents I've read, the histories I've looked at in order to understand why all of this is happening here. *Why?* is a question that comes up repeatedly. We talk about school. About continuing studies. The streets start to smell of spices, wheat, and fish. I urge him to go home to his mother and eat.

July 2017. Late evening. I'm sitting with Yacouba, an eighteen-year-old man, who has agreed to talk with me about the police presence in the neighborhood. "It's important," he said when I introduced the topic of police checks and abuses earlier that day. He starts by describing the neighborhood, the difficulty of finding dignified labor, and the ease with which selling weed presents itself.

"That's it, we're locked in. Somewhere within all this we're locked in, without money, with police violence that comes over it all."

I ask him about his first interaction with the police.

"Here, you're young when it starts." He pauses. "You see, it starts when you're a child. You see, a control, with the search and pat down and everything, it's not for security purposes or to know who you are. When they touch you like that." He pauses again. "When they touch you on the—it's not for . . . "

Yacouba stops and shakes his head, looking at me knowingly but refusing to explicitly voice the pat-downs and the experience of sexual humiliation they invoke.

Then, more confidently, he continues, "You see the kids over there, they get stopped and searched. The thing here is, it's not quite like other neighborhoods. Here the police station is in the heart of the neighborhood, you see what I'm saying? In other words, the cops are always two steps away from where we are, wherever we may be. You see what I'm saying? We grew up with the police, we grow up with the police. We know them, they know us. I'm not gonna give you names—none of that—but you would know them too if you've lived here for a bit, you got stopped by the cops. But yeah, that's it, the thing is that the cops *they see us,* they see us grow up. And that's the case for us who are getting older now, but it's true for our little ones too."

He continues; we talk about violence—the kind we inflict on one another.

"You see, the problem here is that it's true, there is violence. But us, now, we try to be careful. You see, as you grow up you realize it's no use assaulting people, stealing from your neighbor, you see what I mean? If you steal here, you steal from your neighbor. You're stealing from someone who's in need just as much as you are, you see. So we've stopped stealing, assaulting people, it's not something we want to be doing, you see? It hasn't always been like that. There was a time when we'd put ourselves through endless neighbor-hood wars. For instance, I'll give you an example. So, we were playing a soccer game with some guys from Plaisance [a neighborhood in the 14th arrondis-sement]. No hassle, easy going. And then we lose. So, then people start yell-ing, 'Foul!' You know how it is, we start beating each other up. One of their boys gets roughed up, and ends up in the hospital, you see. So, later, they came here in the neighborhood and roughed people up here too. It calmed down after that."

We both let a silence settle. Yacouba scratches his scalp and lights a ciga-rette. I mirror him; we sit still, pensive, exhaling the smoke. Our conversation picks up again, more tentatively this time. We talk about overcoming such violence. That rupture often relies on a return to the homeland, a form of displacement that allows one to move away from the ambient heaviness of the neighborhood. That movement away from the neighborhood can be physical, but it is more often metaphorical. Returning to the *bled* (village back home), in the sense of an often unfulfilled intention or obligation, becomes a means to find ethical ground distinct from the individualistic mentality of the neo-liberal city in which we live.

"But it's mostly as you grow up, you ask yourself some real questions about all of this. You don't know who's in front of you. It's quite possible you end up stabbing a cousin of yours and you'll only find out when you get news from the village back home [*bled*] that someone's died, you see what I mean? It's not possible to play around with things like that. So yeah, theft is another thing we don't do. But the issue is that there's no solidarity between people here. It's 'every man for himself' here. That's why we gotta get by and find some money to help out at home, because it's 'every man for himself' here. . . . You know,

FIGURE 27. Minors handcuffed and lined up during an arrest, based on images of the mass arrest of 6 December 2018 that took place in Mantes-la-Jolie, December 2020. Sketch by K.H.

at the end of it all, my question is this: who starts the violence? You got me? [*Tu m'as compris?*] Because we're not mean, not more than other people, you see. We all have our own stories and stuff, you got me. But then the question is: who, what, where? When does the violence begin? You got me?"

He looks me in the eyes and waits for a response.

"Do you mean that the police plays a role in this?" I ask.

"We're not mean," he continues. "People say we're violent, but we just had to learn to defend ourselves."

I pause for a few seconds, quickly writing his words on a notepad, and ask, "Is it the police that forced you to know how to defend yourself?"

Yacouba nods. "You got me [*Tu m'as compris*]."

Historian Emmanuel Blanchard has described ID checks in France as "degradation ceremonies." He locates the degradation in the act of stopping. Like Ahmed, Blanchard finds the suspicion, the public nature of the control, and the sociopolitical implications of stopping citizens because of their appearance as central elements of *symbolic* degradation.[19] But there is something more to be said, something more than symbolic degradation at play here. Sexual violence during ID checks is what comes out as the most significant and yet unaddressed aspect of police officers' contact with young men and boys in the neighborhood. Children as young as ten interact with police officers, on their way home from school or in parks, and experience situations of assault during which a refusal to consent could land them with "refusal to comply" charges (*refus d'obtempérer*). They learn to control their bodies, as well as their emotional reactions. They learn to refrain from speaking out about the violence they have experienced. They learn that, even when they are believed, little can and will be done to defend them from more harm.

Learning to interact with police officers is an education in how to manage violence. Experiencing violence at the hands of the police and struggling with the subjective impressions left by events that I preferred to forget forced me to engage in a work on the self. I had to learn to speak about the sensations that ID checks left in me, about how I processed sexual violence and brutality. I noticed myself falling into a nervous masculinity. I expressed myself through silence. I censored part of myself in order to appear as strong as I wanted to feel. I withheld information and hid how poorly I felt. I got angry with myself. Within the walls of my home. In the streets. I was depressed. The lump in my throat, the bitterness in my mouth. I am not sure of the extent to which these changes were perceived or if I was indeed expressing as much aggression to others as I felt toward myself and the people who had stopped and assaulted me. What I am certain of, however, is that I internalized police brutality and it considerably inflected my gender expression. I came to rely on Republican perceptions of my body as that of a virile young Arab man. Internalizing sexual violence meant that I progressively appropriated and rearticulated the forms of masculinity that the officers has assigned me to. I erased the plurality of my own gender in the same movement that we, as a collectivity of aphasiac young men, abstracted women and feminine persons from the community of experience we shared.

Thinking of police brutality and violence in abstraction of women and femininity contrasts with the central place women take up in the neighborhood and in other *quartiers populaires* in France. Older and younger women interrupt violence, mediate tensions between men, boys, and police officers. What Yasmine repeatedly did for me—in keeping me safe from the police, and away from holding cells in police precincts—illustrates a position that women inhabit and practice when their loved ones are caught by policing and incarceration. Women continue to maintain contact with incarcerated families or community, taking on legal fees and commissary. Some, acting as wives, sisters, or mothers, even take on legal battles against police officers who have killed or maimed: eventually becoming public figures like Amal Bentounsi, Ramata Dieng, Assa Traoré, and Aurélie Garand.[20]

This contrasts, again, with the actual policing of women in the ZSP. While one can easily argue that women negotiate situations of mediation, it is impossible to reduce Black and other women's relationship to the police in the ZSP to these situations only. Indeed, while the ZSP is oriented toward young men, boys along the lines of immigration and drug legislation, it is also oriented toward specifically feminine targets. These targets are categorized in terms of economic activity, such as sex work, theft, contraband, and so on, and in terms of ethnic or national origin, such as Roma, Chinese, Nigerian, Congolese.[21] As a consequence, women that fit the officers' typology risk getting stopped and frisked. They, too, risk a beating and arrest if they do not signal complete compliance with the police check.[22] The multiple ways that feminine persons are made both central and peripheral in collective experiences of police contact attests to the multiple normative imperatives that are applied within the neighborhood, as feminine persons negotiate the norms of the police-penal pathways of the ZSP in addition to the cultural and commercial norms that emerge from the neighborhood's particular spatialities of exile and commercial centrality.[23]


## THE ARCHIVES WE CARRY

In a context where state sovereignty is played out not only on territory as such but also on and through bodies, taking tentative steps to reclaiming a certain control over one's body is a way of working toward personal and collective autonomy.[24] As Rashad Shabazz explains in his work, the spatialization of race is also a process of gendering: it produces particular expressions of gender as consequences of spatial containment. Reclaiming space, in producing urban rhythms distinct from carceral urbanization, must then also be a work of reclaiming masculinities. It becomes a praxis and a poiesis of masculinity that rips it from its forced proximity to carceral institutions.

In the specific context of the Goutte d'Or, inscribing oneself in rhythms that put the police and the prison at bay—to the extent that it is practically feasible to do so—can help navigate the neuralgia of the city without inscribing oneself fully within it. Prayer and meditation, as practices of reflection, of submitting the body to distinct daily and spiritual rhythms, help some find peace. For others, music or sports help foster self-awareness. Whatever the means, there exist ways to extricate the body out of what appears—and only is in appearance—predetermined and inescapable. Habitus and hexis are thus shaped by the social, by practices, by one's relationship to institutions, spaces, and other bodies. But the social is neither fixed nor predetermined; praxis and poiesis, as a deliberate work applied on the body-subjectivity, become methods for making habitus and hexis anew.

There remains the absent presence of colonialism and enslavement. For what lingers are wounds that are often untold and leave no trace but a blank or a gap. Negotiating one's place beyond these histories and the categories they have produced does not undo the fact that bodies act as conduits of history and that the blanks are passed down. We carry histories. We carry biographies and memories, like an ID check repeated every day for years or a calculated pace in a prison cell. We carry strange archives of things at once present and absent; we carry bodies in spaces that welcome us yet do not extend our shape. The materiality of the streets has a way of catching up with us, still.

*K. H.*

## INTERRUPTION: GIVE ME YOUR FAMAS

*Monday, 18 December 2017*

The weapon each Opération Sentinelle soldier carries looks flat and wiry, as if the dark innards of a brooding machine lay exposed. The soldiers' weapons are generative products, as are their trained, clipped bodies. Each rifle sculpts and scopes the imaginative, physical, and technological ground of a body, weaponized bodies, vigilant bodies, even when a body tries like a fugitive to escape violence and its violent deterrence. When the soldiers patrol the streets of Paris, spatializing violence and vigilance, they hold the rifles close to their bodies as they navigate the perceived dangers of the social world. The weapons are pointed toward each social field encountered. The soldiers' bodies and the guns they carry generate images, traces, and potentialities that unsettle.

In observing the soldiers, my eyes grew curious about the design and history of the rifle's ballistic potential. Within a few swift hours I find myself strolling through words and images found online and listening to bits of speech passed amongst residents of the city. FAMAS (Fusil d'assault de la manufacture d'armes de Saint-Étienne) is the name of the assault rifle that each soldier carries. Conceived and produced in the early 1970s, the ergonomic design of the FAMAS responded to the military's desire for a powerful tactical weapon that had reduced weight and was easy to use and maintain. The rifle is a bullpup configuration, with the "action" behind its trigger group, bringing the advantage of a larger barrel and increased muzzle velocity and accuracy—while the heat and rapid force of the firing action is close to the face, eyes, and cheek of anyone firing the weapon. The receiver housing is made of a special steel alloy. Fire mode is controlled by a selector within the trigger guard, with three settings: safe, single shot, and automatic fire. Automatic fire can be in three single-shot bursts, *rafale,* or fully automatic, capable of 1,100 rounds per minute. Feed system of the FAMAS-G2: thirty-round detachable box STANAG magazine. Effective firing range: three to four hundred meters. Weight: 3.8 kilograms. Cost per unit: around three thousand euros. Designer: Paul Tellie. The standard NATO Accessory Rail affixed to the FAMAS-G2 allows a variety of sights to be mounted, including red dot signals and night vision units. Also standard is a grenade launcher sight, grenade support, and 22mm rifle grenade launcher. The rifle functions best with French-specified steel-casing 5.56x45mm ammunition; using standard brass-casing NATO ammunition of the same dimensions can create overpressure and case ruptures in the FAMAS, which can lead to severe malfunctions; minor injuries have resulted from the use of improper casings. This irregularly shaped rifle is said to be affectionately known by French-speaking troops as *le Clarion* (the Bugle)—the narrow muzzle resembles the mouthpiece of a horn as it gradually expands into sound and air. I wonder if any soldiers have ever placed their lips sweetly against the muzzle and blown faintly into the stem or daringly slipped a silent potent mouthpiece into an enemy combatant's mouth.

The FAMAS was first used in Chad during Operation Manta (1983–84), followed by Operation Desert Storm. French soldiers have also carried it in various peacekeeping missions. The rifle has also been employed in the Gulf War, the Bosnian War, the Syrian Civil War, and, since 2001, the war in Afghanistan. Along with French Armed Forces, the FAMAS has been used by military forces in Lebanon, Papua New Guinea, Gabon, Serbia, United Arab Emirates, and Venezuela; the weapon has traveled from the Republic of France to former French colonies to select nation-states. The apparitional force of the assault rifle and its violent imagining has also made its way into video games, including the series *Call of Duty, Army of Two, Battlefield, Tom Clancy,* and *Phantom Forces.* By now I have watched several videos of the games that show the rifle, including one that shows the FAMAS as it appears in thirty different video games. The simulated gun is held with simulated human hands, gloved or ungloved; one sees its fierce power through the POV sight, the cartridge firing rapid bursts of ammo into shooting ranges, desert terrain, warehouse battlefields, woodland fauna, African savannas, and open, cumulus sky; rapid bursts, cartridge released, reloaded; within seconds there is a monotony to the action, repetitive fire samples; no one is shot, nobody seen.

"There's no question about it," says the commentator in another video, as if evaluating the merits of a new cyber-technology. "The FAMAS assault rifle deals massive, massive damage in close-quarter combat and can drop people faster than any other assault rifle in the game." A potent beauty. On the YouTube channel VICKERS TACTICAL, Larry Vickers explains the rifle's features and demos its firing capacities. The video shifts from real-time firing to extreme slow motion, when the gun fires and the bullet casing releases from the chamber, the sleek sexed sound of metal sliding against metal; another bullet takes its place, fired again, smoke seeps from the nuzzle in a potent scene of erotic steel. In the comments posted below the video, a French military officer and shooting instructor notes that the FAMAS "has been a great rifle for many years and has been successful in many operations. . . . The bullpup design helps us greatly in urban combat and it is a pretty reliable gun if you use the correct mags."

"I slept with my FAMAS," said one man of his military training in the remote wilds of southwestern France. "I didn't like that so much. The rifle is heavy, and bulky, and cold, and I had to sleep cramped next to it in the small sleeping bag that the army provides."

In awkward sleep this man's body was viscerally adapting to the contours of the weapon. Like a student learning a lesson and putting it into practice, he was also acquiring the capacities of a body that could become a weapon of the French Republic. In the socialization process of military training, through which a soldier's corporeal *habitus-hexi* are acquired, techniques of the body and techniques of violence are sculpted together in forming a potential kill unit, which then might lie dormant. Long finished with his military service, the man quoted now manages a bistro in the 12th arrondissement; on days off he enjoys picnics with his wife and children on the grassy hills of Parc des Buttes-Chaumont. If the government instituted a new law of conscription in times of war, he could be called up to fight for the Republic, a state summons that would mobilize his body's simulant training into real-world combat.

Someone tells the story of how, in the streets outside the Bataclan the night of 13 November 2015, a police officer asked an Opération Sentinelle soldier stationed outside the Bataclan if he was going to intervene in the ongoing attack. The soldier replied that he did not have orders to move. "Then give me your FAMAS," said the policeman. Pass it to my trained body, and I will take the shot. The soldier refused to hand his assigned rifle to the policeman.[25] He had different orders.

Currently, the potentially deadly weapon moves within the streets of Paris, held in the arms of young men and women who years or months before (or that very morning) might have been shooting simulated versions of the rifles in video games played in bedrooms back home while destroying phantom jihadists, guerrilla fighters, or Russian spies. And now as I too move about the *névralgique* streets of Paris, physically, imaginatively, nervously, a ghost sentinel following in the wake of militarized sentinels, I try to track the rifle's material and apparitional configurations. I find, after days of watching and writing, drifting through the film of different media and perceptions, that there's no great divide between the sight of the assault rifles on the streets of Paris and the emanation of them in video games, news feeds, video documents, or fanciful imaginings. The workings of body, perception, metal, image, and the phantom image of metal are rolled into one fraught vehicle of force and consequence, the explosive horror and beauty of violent things. Rhythms of bodies seen, captured, wounded. *Give me your FAMAS*. Despite the dread a body senses in the rifle's assault, I find myself wanting to reach out and touch the stem of the bugle muzzle and feel the heat of its automated firing.

"The weapons vanished in the abyss like fleeting images, like pictures one throws into the fire. New ones were produced in protean succession."[26]

In 2017 the French armed forces began the retirement of the FAMAS in favor of the German-made Heckler and Koch HK 416 assault rifle, "the next generation of standard assault rifles for the French army."

R. D.

# FIVE

# *Archive sorrow*

The archives belong to the government, it is for this that they exist.

LÉON DE LABORDE,
Director General of the Imperial Archives of France (1857–1868)

It is not you who will speak; let the disaster speak in you, even if it be by your forgetfulness or silence.

MAURICE BLANCHOT,
*The Writing of the Disaster*

## THE DISASTER RETURNS

*Thursday, 16 March 2017*

The disaster returns.

The disaster fades, slackens, disestablishes itself.

The word *disaster* carries the vague, fragmentary sense not so much of a single term or distinct name but rather an interminable sentence, a history of language and sensation unclosed, unfinished, incessantly sliding toward a "rip forever ripping apart."[1] And so one searches for the long, interminable sentence of the disaster by writing about its verbs and nouns, its subjects and actions, tracing the turns of its language as it moves from a sense of cosmic collapse to the "tormenting vicissitudes of the near at hand (the neighboring)."[2] Words fall outside of language, tensions never resolve; a system of meaning is never complete. The disaster cannot be known in any direct or clear way. Any knowledge of it entails a disastrous, fragmentary knowledge.

The disaster recurs. I returned to Paris in January 2017 in order to further trace marks of the violence of that night—and, now, other nights. I landed in Paris while the city was in a cold spell. In pallid daylight people walked frigid streets bundled in coats and scarves, their breath steaming in the air. Canal Saint-Martin had frozen over. Torn cardboard boxes lay strewn on the ice surface close to discarded wine bottles and empty beer cans.

The waters soon warmed. I took up residence in a sublet apartment a few streets from the canal, a five-minute walk from Le Carillon. When I approached the intersection the day I arrived it was as if I was returning to a research field site (*terrain*) after being away for months. This was fieldwork in disaster, within the disaster of fieldwork. I visited the bar several times in those winter months. Most often I went there in the morning, to read and write. I liked the rhythms there. It's a charmed place, with a tragic history.

Whenever there I felt voyeuristic. Even if I was intent on reading a book, or writing out unrelated thoughts, I always seemed to have an eye out for marks in the wake of violence. Recently I came upon a few notes typed up in February.

> The mood at Le Carillon: lighter, postgrieving. A., shouting, with energy, enthusiasm, when he returned, after being out for a while.
>
> In the mornings I hear A. speaking what I presume to be Kabyle.
>
> He barely remembers me, if at all. I am a fleeting impression to him; a face he once saw. One of many in a passing crowd of patrons and phantoms. He has started to recognize me again. I am a new form, a personage.

A. is the owner of the bar who was there that night and despaired of not being able to save anyone. His body is thin and wiry, compact of restless energy. I feel great sympathy for him. To have been devastated by the events of that night, watching the eyes that continued to look at him, fixed by memories, and to return to Le Carillon each day, opening it up in the morning, staying until late, talking with neighbors; in this I find a way of living on, past the disaster, persevering in troubled life. He does not know I write about him, that I quietly care for and support him. I see him smile and feel relieved. Despite the differences in our lives I trace a secret intimacy. He does not know who I am. To me he is an apparition, a figure within sequela of violence. He is shifting phantasms. Does he inhabit a double temporality himself? I have tried to establish a gentle, quiet mark of copresence in his company. Of this he knows nothing.

He began to recognize me when I walked into the place. I did not follow his eyes. I dwell on the margins of his history. I am a lichen of sorts, growing on damp alga surfaces. Life's notetaker, annalist of death, I scratch graffiti on the margins of the event, these words a semilegible "tag" etched onto a side wall.

I thought of writing an open letter to A., for the indirect purposes of these pages. I was going to title the letter *Salut,* as a gesture of salutation and respect, a wish for well-being; to word him away from harm, danger and death. *Salut, A.* Through words I wanted to mark a silent link between us. I imagined writing my concern for his life while seated at one of the wood tables inside. I would draft the letter quietly, intensively, as he worked the bar. He would not know what I was writing. I have since lost the spirit of those words. That fantastical memory is in ruins. What remains is the word *salut.*

*Salut à toi. I wish you well. May you not be harmed. May you survive the pain of that night. Salut to silent affinity, to connection from afar. Salut to obscurity in knowing. Salut to friendship and the strangeness of others. Salut to writing on life in all its haunting complications.*

Why is it that I cannot say as much to A. when I visit his place? I do not want to be a stain on his consciousness. I do not want to mark him or cut him with words. He has enough ghosts as it is. (But if, at a later date, he reads these words? Writing is stain abrasion. Writing can wound.)

I stopped going to Le Carillon—not because I found the place haunting but because I was haunting the place. The anthropologist is a guest, ghost, *geist,* spectral visitation troubling a place and time.

Violence marks damage within the phantasms of the Parisian quotidian. A few days after I arrived in January I sat and sipped an espresso at a neighborhood café near the metro station Jacques Bonsergent. A group of family and friends had gathered there for, it seemed, the start of a Sunday together, a day-off ambiance of carefree fun and pleasurable foods and drink. A boy entered the café and playfully snuck up on a man (his father? an uncle?) and leapt on his back with a shout. The man showed alarmed surprise. *"Je suis terroriste!"* said the boy, with a smile. *"Je suis terroriste des bobos du dixième!"* The man scooped up the boy and hugged him in feigned horror and delight. The child was playing at terrorist of the bourgeois bohemians of the 10th arrondissement. Imageries and ghostings of violence are seeded within forms of play and imagining, fantasies of fear and the pantomime of assault and rescue.

As the winter wore on I found the mood in Paris had altered from the previous summer. The atmosphere was less tense than in those heated months. The city appeared less wounded. Life was not as pained or mournful, as if a *cicatrice* scar was forming over a tender wound. Calm ran through most days—until the *névralgique* flared up, as in early February, when the city was alerted that soldiers at Le Louvre shot a man wielding a machete.

In the air was knowledge of the brutal assault and rape in early February 2017, of a young black man, known as Théo, allegedly by police officers during an identity check in a *cité* of Aulnay-sous-Bois, a poor neighborhood northeast of Paris. The phrase *Justice pour Théo* became a rallying cry. There were protests in Paris and in the *banlieues*. On Saturday afternoons police helicopters lurked and threatened like scavenger hawks above place de la République.

The letters *ACAB* are painted onto street signs and lampposts. *All Cops Are Bastards.*

It's a matter of oscillations—shifts in perception, consciousness, memory, states of concern and vigilance. Forms of awareness and remembrance vary from moment to moment, day to day. One moment you're sitting on a pleasant terrace. The next you find yourself in a perilous threshold, exposed to attacks.

"While walking here I started to think there might be a bomb in each trash can," said an American in Paris one afternoon. "On other days it's not like this. Everything oscillates."

Some live within a constancy of fear and anxiety. "Usually I'm concerned about the state of exception, and states of emergency. But I live in fear," said a woman from Strasbourg who often visits Paris. "I'm afraid most of the time. I avoid any places where a lot of people gather. I'm afraid whenever I go into the metro or take a TGV train. I worry that there will be an explosion."

For some, the fear of terror is seeded into the thoughts and expectations as they move through everyday intensities of space and time. Etched into perceptions is a plaguing concern for the combustive dangers of life in France; terrorgraphies of body, mind, emotion.

I DON'T LIKE TO REED THE NEWS. IT'S SO HARD TO SLEEP AT NIGHT.

These words are painted onto the side of a building near Canal Saint-Martin, amidst a tableau of spectral figures.

In listening to people speak of the night of the attacks, their memories of the deaths and wounding, I sense the tension in their bodies. The muscles of the back become tighter, shoulders are drawn in, as if to protect the body from possible pain felt, recalled or imagined.

"It gives me the shivers," said one woman in reflecting on the attacks.

"Look, my hands are shaking, just from talking about it," said another in relating what she and her husband went through that night, worried for the safety of their young children, asleep at home. "My hands were shaking that night, as well."

The memories are there, still fresh, raw in bodies nervous from fear and assault. The disaster returns in bodies, in dispersed ways.

Others have left Paris altogether and gone to live elsewhere. For them, the attacks on the city's streets and structures held far too many reminders of terror death and lost friends and family. They sought for good reason to flee the tangible spaces of disaster, though the disaster follows them still.

If you walk in Paris long enough and have an eye out for certain marks you can begin to trace the scars of past wounds, deaths, and terror. One man tells me that on weekday mornings he walks from his home near place Saint-Marthe to place de la République, where he takes the metro to his work place. Each time he takes one of two routes. The first crosses the site of a barricade built along rue du Faubourg du Temple during the Paris Commune, where national guard soldiers were overrun by the French army during *La semaine sanglante* in May 1871. The second passes by the intersection at Le Carillon and Le Petit Cambodge. "Each morning," he says, "it's like I decide which ghosts I'm going to see."

## MONUMENTS TO THE DEAD

There is a politics to traces, a struggle and play of forces that effect which marks are effaced, canceled out, demolished, which traces remain and recur, and which signs are given the authority to stay fixed to a wall and designate the collective memory of a nation.

In returning this winter to the streets by Le Carillon I found that the marks and images once graffed upon a wall standing across the way from the bar and Le Petite Cambodge were gone. The only piece of writing currently affixed to the wall is a plaque made of fine marble, bolted into the coarse material of the upper portion of the wall, some three meters above the ground. This *plaque commémorative* bears the inscription:

> *EN MEMOIRE DES VICTIMES BLESSÉES*
> *ET ASSASSINÉES DES ATTENTATS DU*
> *13 NOVEMBRE 2015*
> *AUX 13 VIES FAUCHÉES EN CES LIEUX*
>
> In memory of the victims wounded
> and assassinated in the attacks of
> 13 November 2015.
> To the 13 lives cut down in these places.

FIGURE 28. Commemorative plaque, rue Alibert, March 2017. Photo by R. D.

The word *fauchées* carries connotations of "mowed, reaped, flattened," an action that can refer to cereals or stalks of wheat severed from the earth with the use of a scythe (*faux*) or with a machine. The language is militaristic in imagery, as with young men cut down in battle on the plains of France. The word is linked to the scythe that the Grim Reaper carries in his hand in approaching those who are to die.

After this inscription runs a list of the names of the thirteen persons who died that night. There is a sensible reason for the plaque to be set upon this wall, as it's the clearest and most expansive vertical surface in the vicinity of the attacks. The curving wall of the hospital's exterior faces the intersection of streets in a direct and open way.

The plaque stands at a distance, in visual communication with the bar and restaurant. It can be seen through the windows of Le Carillon. The marble inscription looks upon the scene from a position of authority and perspective within a geometry of measured observation and statement. While seated at Le Carillon I've noticed people walk toward the plaque and read its inscription, look around, look toward the bar and restaurant, talk among themselves, walk on.

The memorial plaque was installed the morning of 13 November 2016, one year to the date of the attacks. A ceremony took place at the intersection, as well as at other locations in Paris where the attacks happened that same evening. The route echoed the pathways of the attacks. Those attending the ceremony included François Hollande, president of France, and Anne Hidalgo, the mayor of Paris. One newspaper article on the ceremony of observance near Le Carillon includes a photograph of these government officials standing closest to the plaque, looking up toward it, in a moment of silence.[3] No speeches were given. Beyond the two dignitaries are rows of other participants in the ceremony, presumably the most elevated and politically important standing closest to the shrine; or they are mourners, family and friends of the persons named in the plaque, and then on to mourners and spectators of possibly diminishing relation to those who died in the attacks—a political hierarchy of mourning and remembrance. Beyond the group assembled stands Le Carillon, its maroon awning apparent on an overcast day.

Those visible in the photograph are looking toward the plaque, away from where the shootings occurred. The eyes of most there are set on the space of commemoration, at the materiality and aura of that collective remembrance, rather than toward where the women and men were killed. A few are looking toward the ground. One man is looking up, as if toward the sky or the heavens. No one is looking toward Le Carillon or Le Petit Cambodge. They are regarding a site of memory that is becoming standardized and nationalized. The focus of regard toward the memorial plaque rather than the sites of the deaths implies a shift in perception, a movement away from the actuality of the violence toward a structured emblem of violent history.

What would the designated mourners and any other participants or observers have thought of this ceremony? Would they have found it comforting and reassuring, this political support and acknowledgment of loss and mourning at the highest levels? Or would they find something absent in this, something lacking, or exposed, in the formal enactment of civic mourning?

The plaque set across the way from Le Carillon and Le Petit Cambodge is much like other memorial plaques in Paris, as well as in France more generally, where *les monuments aux morts* can be found in most towns and villages, usually near the town halls, within the space of a public sphere. Inscribed in these plaques, made of metal or marble, bolted into the sides of buildings or set in stone, are the names of locals who died in wars, including the First and Second World Wars—*morts pour la patrie.* Meanwhile, set alongside the highways of France are neat and uniform panels that speak of cultural historical sites—the amphitheater of Nîmes, the vineyards of Burgundy—"in ways that reinforce a certain understanding of the country," to quote historian

Tony Judt, who writes of encountering such panels while driving through the *autoroutes* of France. "And as we reflect upon the variety and the wealth of the country, the ancient roots and modern traumas of the nation, we share with others a certain memory of France. We are being led at seventy miles an hour through the Museum of France that is France itself."[4] With this landscape of official memory, one might find a lot of contemporary anxieties about past glory being, indeed, past and perhaps not so glorious after all.[5]

Similar kinds of historical monuments and landmarks are found in other countries of Western Europe, from Sweden to Belgium, and, notably, Germany, where postwar monuments work to honor and memorialize the victims of Nazism. Within the current "era of commemoration," as Judt remarks, "The western solution to the problem of Europe's troublesome memories has been to fix them, quite literally, in stone."[6] Constructing monuments and museums and the state-supported culturation of sites of memory has tended to be a Franco-German solution to difficult historical memories. In Eastern Europe and Russia, in contrast, structures of cultural memory "are temporal rather than spatial. Its units are memory events rather than sites of memory," or so historian Alexander Etkind finds. "In Russia and eastern Europe, novels, films, and debates about the past vastly outpace and overshadow monuments, memorials, and museums. . . . Cultural memory is hot and liquid rather than cool and crystallized."[7]

The crystal-cold commemorative plaque affixed to a wall near Le Carillon is a monument to the dead. It's a war memorial of sorts, shaped to landmark a state-sanctioned site of memory within the archival terrain of Paris and thus contribute to the collective memory of the nation, one that tends to conceive of history as conflict and conflict as history.[8] Through the state-centric uniformity of its design, and its minimalist death statement, the plaque signifies a historical event of national importance while masking the complexities of the political histories surrounding that event. It signposts a scarred hurt, lasting puncture to the Republic. In years to come, this plaque will probably exist like so many of those placed around the city, which speak in abstract ways of people cut down during uprisings or by invading forces, or children taken away by the Nazis, through lasting inscriptions in which the names no longer signify much at all in terms of their specifics, except within the memories and inheritances of a few descendants. The statement will stand as a general collective memorial to lives lost at this site, or stolen away—the Republic under attack. The names erode in time, lose their intensity.

FIGURE 29. Memorial in park across the street from the Bataclan, boulevard Voltaire, December 2017. Photo by R. D.

The site of the attacks has become a site of history, marking an event in historical time. The intersection is getting covered over by layers of memory and perception. The disaster is disestablishing itself. It's changing, getting forgotten some. The plaque on the wall is like a cicatrix formed over the site of a wound.

"This is death," said a resident of Paris in viewing a photograph of the memorial plaque, along with photos of the poem and images once set upon that wall. "There was life there before. Now there's death."

To draw on Blanchot's terms, death (*la mort*), as a clear formation, as an illusory refuge, replaced the dying (*le mourir*) in the disaster.

In a small rectangular park across the way from the Bataclan stands a squat heavy stone with a flat marble façade bolted onto its surface. This monument lists the names of ninety people who were killed at the Bataclan the night of 13 November 2015.

At the Bataclan itself a commemorative plaque is set on a wall close to the entrance to the music hall. The script reads:

*EN MÉMOIRE DES VICTIMES ASSASSINÉES*
*ET BLESSÉES EN CES LIEUX LE*
*13 NOVEMBRE 2015*

Along that wall there is writing close to the plaque, words in French, Spanish, English, apparently left by people who visited the Bataclan since the time of the attacks.

*Siempre.*
*On ne vous oublie pas.*


## THE DIGITAL ARCHIVE

Still apparent on the wall near Le Carillon are the words *NE PAS ARCHIVER*. Of the hand-marked inscriptions around Le Carillon, this negative statement, fixed in strong black ink, might last the longest.

I gained a sense of the potent work of archivization one day in February when I visited the Archives de Paris, set in a modern building a short walk from the constant traffic of boulevard Sérurier in the 19th arrondissement, close to the Périphérique. For several months an exhibit stood along a wall just past the entrance to the archives. The exhibit went by the name *De la rue aux Archives: Le cas des hommages aux victimes des attentats du vendredi 13 novembre 2015 collectés en janvier 2016.*[9] A span of cabinets with protective glass planes contained displays of materials left at different sites of attack, arranged according to location. I was struck by the papercentric quality of the exhibit: the archives shown consisted entirely of writing on sheets of paper in various formations—letters, handmade cards, poems, drawings, paintings, and a few books, like Paul Éluard's *Capital de la douleur* and Hemingway's *Paris est une fête.* Each item carried a shadow history of connection and wreckage, the tacit residue of something felt. With these documents set behind glass, like a museum exhibit, there were ghosts nearby; the graft voices of authors and those written about; specters, all. Writing is a spectral affair.

On display were words of defiance, anger (*VOUS ÊTES MÉCHANTS LES TERRORISTES!!!*; solidarity (*"Le Maroc Avec Le France Je suis Marocain et j'aime La France"*), and discourses of healing (*PANSER, PENSER*). A passage from a letter left near Le Bataclan, signed by *Michel* on 27 November 2015, brought to mind aporias encountered months before.

> I do not hate those who committed this inhuman act. How to explain that human beings, raised in the love of a father, a mother, brothers and sisters, can one day want to kill humanity?
> I do not know.

I do not understand . . .
But what I do know is why I came here today: it's to tell you that
I LOVE YOU.

It's unclear if the author of this letter, addressed to *"Chers enfants,"* was aware that his writing was appropriated by the Archives of Paris and eventually put on display. This piece of paper, like other documents on exhibit, inhabited an uncommon liminal space between the private and the public, the personal and the collective. Such is the social life of the archival: a handwritten, singularly authored letter, addressed to the "children" of the attacks, placed at a site of collective mourning and memory, is taken by agents of the archive, cleansed, dried, preserved, digitalized, and exhibited behind glass in the lobby of the Archives of Paris, to be read and stared at by visitors walking past the displays; and then photographed by an itinerant anthropologist who writes about that November letter in these remnant pages, as if the letter held a trace of mourning and aporetic incomprehension; the letter is then destined to be kept in a black box for years on end, where no light enters, where it will go untouched by any human hands, while a digitalized copy can be found online, subject to generations of historians who might look back on that critical event in the history of Europe and the world at large. Such a curious destination for a handwritten note left at the side of a building.

The exhibit comprised a small selection of the 7,689 documents collected by archivists from the sites of the 13 November attacks. Included in the display were photographs of several "agents des Archives de Paris" sifting through piles of flowers to retrieve desired objects and then placing the gathered materials in boxes to be taken away in trucks. The materials were separated from other materialia deemed to be refuse, elements refused by the archival process, and then the archivable content remained. Once at the Archives of Paris, set within its architecture of power and survival, the documents were sorted, disinfected, dried, classified, scanned, and digitalized. They were carefully enclosed in black boxes, lined up on of shelves. "From now on the originals are untouchable, even by the researchers and experts."[10]

The documents are now kept within a space of domiciliation, "this house arrest," where they are kept, monitored, and controlled by civil state archivists, who by governmental decree have the power to possess, guard, and permit or deny access to the archive's holdings.[11] The state and its civil servants largely manage and control the holdings of the national and city archives. It's not the objects themselves that circulate but rather their simulated images, their codified simulacrum. The originals are preserved onto an infinite future, never touched or handled, rarely seen or shown, as if they were sacred texts kept in a reliquary of a church, not to be touched by unsanctified hands.

"The archivization produces as much as it records the event," Derrida observes.[12] This was the case with the archiving of materials from the memorials that emerged in the wake of the 13 November 2015 attacks, for the archive came to encode and advance a reinscription of those events and their aftermaths. A certain (post)writing of the histories involved is in effect. This historiography is in line with the interests and political narratives of the state—a tragic event in which innocent people died; trace remnants of shock, sorrow, and nationwide mourning; the pressing need for a state of emergency. Other possible archives and forms of memory and memorializations are regulated to the margins, or they do not appear at all. With the archives of the November 2015 memorials aspects of the violent events are kept visible, preserved in a visible virtual light, while events surrounding the event remain obscure and unseen. There is no archival mention of the violence enacted on residents and "noncombatants" of Iraq and Syria by French military forces and recent bombing campaigns against ISIL, or of the damage inflicted upon persons and families in France through the harassment, arrest, and house and bodily searches authorized through the powers of the state of emergency; there are few archival traces of other forms of violence that sear through everyday life and death in Paris. As far as the state and its archives are concerned, such events and their histories have been withdrawn into invisibility; they have been elided and exscribed in contemporary historical conditions.[13] The state's archive conjures a magic trick, with document misdirection, *read this, not that.* While other disasters go unarchived by the state.

One reason that the archivists put so much care into preserving materials left at the site of the November 2015 attacks is that little of the sort had been done with the memorials that emerged after the *Charlie Hebdo* attacks in January 2015. Nothing had been archived by the city.[14] "We regretted that," said a *premier adjoint* of La Mairie de Paris. "The first time, we didn't know how to do it."[15] Archive regret, archive longing, archive envy, command and control—the governmental psychodynamics of the state's urge to archive. With the next attacks the city was prepared to preserve and record. A concerted archival desire emerged in part from a sense of failure, responsibility, and civic duty. In the compulsion to repeat one tries to do better the next time, record better, preserve better. Implicit was the concern that much would be lost and forgotten, that the materials left in the wake of the attacks would be effaced and erode into a vague oblivion. The managers of the city and its archivists felt compelled to retrace the event and its aftermath.

The compulsive drive toward an archive was spawned by a fever (*mal de*) of absence, lack, regret. The archivists wanted to prevent the death of a certain kind of memory and the absence of a certain kind of memorialization. The state wanted to control and manage any archival holdings of the disaster. Archive fever is to burn with a passion for preservation. It is never to rest, interminably, from searching for the archive right where it once slipped away.[16]

What came of this archival desire was the perceived civic duty to preserve and record. Within days of the attacks an archive was deemed necessary and its machinery kicked into gear. As the director of the Archives de Paris related in 2016: "As of 17 November 2015, the office of Bruno Julliard [first deputy to the mayor of Paris] began to reflect on the preservation of all these tributes. Here we archive the documents of the history of Paris from the Middle Ages to the present day. Naturally, we have worked on it. The preservation of the original documents was for us a crucial question. . . . We make no selection. We kept all the documents in good condition."[17]

Traces of an event can easily perish, and so with pressing urgency a team of archivists collected "documents" within weeks of the attacks, in ways attentive to varied interests and concerns. "We had to help the affected institutions to reopen," said the director. "At the same time, we had to allow

Parisians to pay a long-enough tribute to the victims in respecting a period of mourning. But we also had to allow the inhabitants to find a less oppressive living environment."[18]

From the start, the materials collected were destined for the future. In speaking of the work of preservation, one archivist told a journalist that he had the impression "of creating material that will tell the story in a hundred years."[19] An archive's prime responsibility is to the future. An archive is for future readers, publics, future histories and historians. As Derrida writes, "The question of the archive is not, we repeat, a question of the past. . . . It is a question of the future, the question of the future itself, the question of a response, of a promise and of a responsibility for tomorrow."[20] The archive of the memorials of the 13 November attacks is designed for a future readership, to maintain a link between the past and the present of any future time. The archive entails a promise, a pledge, in which artifacts of a critical event in French history are kept for a potentially infinite number of years. "The archive has always been a *pledge,* and like every pledge [*gage*], a token of the future."[21] To think the archive is to imagine a future, the future as specter—what Derrida called "*l'avenir comme spectre.*"[22] The future of the archive appears spectrally, as vague potentiality, an abstract time and materiality and readership imagined. The archive of the future will probably tell one kind of story, while neglecting others.

The first future for the archive arrived in February 2017, when 7,348 documents appeared on the website of the Archives de Paris, under the rubric *Hommages aux victimes des attentats de 2015.*[23] Within a sleek, efficient design the documentary corpus of *hommages numérisés* (digitalized homages), has been organized according to the sites where particular documents were retrieved and the dates of collection—5,305 images for the Bataclan alone. The program design is the work and product of a business called *Arkothèque.*[24] The program itself carries the name *Visionneuse*—"Place your images in an ergonomic, intuitive, and seductive space!"[25] The seductions of the archive: search filters enable researchers to identify particular places and times and then work through the results of that search. Each image file can be brought to full screen mode and scrutinized in detail; one can zoom in on specific features of an image and consider closely its composition and textures; each image file can be printed, even in close-up; you can look as long as you want, and study the grain of emotion kept on paper, and then move on, whenever you desire; eroticarchivally seduce, and be seduced.

The database of digitalized homages hosts a "consignation," a gathering together of signs.[26] As Derrida notes, "there is no archive without consignation in an *external place* which assures the possibility of memorialization, or repetition, of reproduction, or of reimpression."[27] The signs of "witnessing and homage" are gathered within spaces at once actual and virtual—the holdings of the archive, the data cloud of the Internet, or on a laptop. Worth noting is the stratum of the digital archive: its holdings and potential uses rely on technologies of digital mimesis and documentation, systems of coding, virtual dissemination, and remote duplication. These technologies shape the forms and contents of *l'archive des hommages*. Other forms of inscription, other techniques of recording and display, would bring other archives.

As of this writing, the data set for Le Carillon holds 446 image files, with 436 of those related to materials collected at the site on 14 December 2015. (The other "date of collection" for Le Carillon was 19 January 2016). Each image has been assigned an identity code. For instance, "Le Carillon 3910W 1(9), 14/12/2015" denotes an image of writing traced in blue ink on lined paper, *Seb, tu resteras pour toujours dans nos coeurs, pour toujours.*

Scrolling though the many files brought images of poems, statements, declarations, laments, and messages to the dead written on papers of various sorts, since smoothed out, flattened, and digitally photographed. I felt uncomfortable reading the more personal statements, addressed to those who had died. Such examinations felt voyeuristic—as if I was opening and reading an intimate letter addressed to someone else, messages cast toward a spectral readership. I zoomed in on several of images. I could see the grain of ink where a pen marked the surface of paper. Some of the papers imaged show signs of having been affected by water or contact with the biology of flowers.

I found the collection sterile. It was as though the damp dying spoor life of the messages had been dried out of them. The wounds of mourning, of loss, shock, defiance, love, of violence and hatred, all this had been flattened out, and a reader was left with scant traces of an earlier time. Still, the voices were there, diffuse and masked, in murmurous script, like the chorus of an ancient drama commenting on a tragedy.

The archive has been digitalized. With the preservation and digitalization of the archived materials come a series of transformations: the materials change from wet to dry; from degrading matter to preserved form; from ephemerality to permanence; from bunches of aggregate objects to a corpus of separate, individuated legible documents; from an absence of codes to systematic coding; from semi-private authorship to direct public display; from myriad materialities of numerous forms and dimensions to distinct *fichiers images* (image files) resembling flat surfaces. The various materials and inscriptions of any number of communicative gestures are converted into documents of "*témoignage et homage.*" As the materials move from the street to the archive the process of archivization changes the objects collected in lasting and irrevocable ways.

Perhaps it's the prospect of such transformations that the statement *NE PAS ARCHIVER* works against. That negative command could have been marked on stone during those days in December 2015 when agents of the archive were coming to the sites of the attacks to collect materials for the archive. They took away elements integral to a memorial and, through the work of archiving, permanently changed them.

The words *do not archive* anticipate the potential threat of archival violence. This is a gentle, seemingly benevolent violence, as is often the case with the work of a government or bureaucratic system. Through such work the substance of lives and deaths is shaped and transformed. The work of the archive at once indicates and asserts the power of the state, particularly in terms of the power to set the terms for a particular kind of national history and to establish certain traces of violence.

The transformations were perhaps destined to occur. The bodies of the dead were recast and the deaths transformed. The process of archiving the materials of the memorials recalls the response to death in many societies, in which the process of dying and death is not complete until a body changes form in a lasting way. For some peoples, the corpse is first buried in a temporary grave and then, after some time, often several years, the skeletal remains are removed. The bones are cleansed, dried, and kept together in a location separate from everyday life, such as an ossuary or a container kept in the home of family members. These physical transformations parallel the transformations that the soul or life force of the deceased is itself undergoing, which itself parallels transformations undertaken by mourners.

Symbolically, phantasmally, the archive is an ossuary in which the bones of the dead—letters, cards, and drawings left at the site of the dead—have been taken from a temporary grave—the streetside memorials—and cleansed, dried, ordered, and collectively preserved in a rarified domain apart from everyday life. Paper, then, as bone, and relics of dried ink. The work of archiving implies a work of mourning, a means to transform the relations of the living to the dead. The appearance online of the digital archives, some fifteen months after the attacks, could be seen as coinciding with the end of the mourning process proper; matter, souls, and mourners transformed. By then, life in Paris had returned to a semblance of normality, though the trace-pain of the attacks lingered.

Research on the archive can entail a work of mourning, a way to come to terms with violence, death, and traumatic shock. The archive promises knowledge of the wound, or at least its history. Studying the archive can hold the possibility of reducing anxiety and uncertainty amongst lives jolted and disarranged. In writing on the archive I intuit the desire to archive the archive. With such meta-archive fever comes the desire to study the archive, retrace its traces, research its assemblage of language and matter; document and number the bones in the ossuary. The materials, neatly arranged, are virtually apparent, viewable. They are ripe for semiotic analysis. It's an easy thing to fetishize the relics stored there. One can be seduced by the archive, or one can try to resist those seductions.

## SHADOW ARCHIVE

Khalil Habrih's writings in these pages can be read as a shadow archive, an *anarchive* that runs counter to other archives, founded and controlled by the French state, as well as certain media, journalistic, artistic, and scholarly portraits of life in Paris.[28] This counterarchive works against the state's archivization of the bodies, spaces, discourses, and materialities of north Paris; as though the creative work here is to say *do not archive us,* do not let the state's mandates and phantasms be the only archivic mythology of our lives, do not fix us in damaging words and images; do not name us; we have our own words and images, which we find to be altogether vital, concerned, contestive, engaged, poetic, spirited, and joyful; this can be shared with others. This archival art, unsealed, plural, co-consigned, dispersed and dispersive, syncopated and counter-rhythmed, counterinscriptive, at once actual and virtual, without fixed domicile, stands in the shadows of the archives and language and political culture of the state. Such efforts imply an "alter-politics," a search for alternatives in the construction of society, political economies, perception, and social life.[29] Agents of the French state might well deem many of elements of this living archive as being marginal, irrelevant, interruptive, unregulated, disordered, of errant disarray—or dangerous and illegal, even, *hors la loi*—at least when it comes to the interests, procedures, legal codes, and capital investments of that state. But still these elements live on, in vital and significant ways. This is not Khalil's archive alone so much as it belongs to the peoples he has worked with and lived among; it's also the living, embodied trace-archive of his family and relatives and that of other families and generations who have moved from the Maghreb to France and live with the effects of colonial drag and political histories. Likewise, it's the visceral, sentient chronicle of his own body, alongside others; "the archives we carry." The archives—which are variably gendered, no doubt, and variably positioned in people's lives—encode and annotate the trace-inscriptions of state, colonial, and police forces on people's lives, bodies, homes, speech, remembrance, and forgetting. These archive-bodies and archive-voices hold memories and erasures, inscriptions, statements and silences; they carry great potential.

Khalil Habrih writes in part to archive otherwise.[30] If there is any archive fever stirring here, in Khalil's thought and writings, then this feverish need to write, trace, and document interruptively—"a *mal d'archive,* a feverish, almost nervous urge"—comes, I take it, from a desire to speak and write about the lives and concerns of those who live in north Paris, lives that tend not to be represented by others in accurate terms and nonviolent, undamaging ways; or they are not represented at all. This *mal d'archive* is to burn with a passion against injustice, oppression, and state violence. It's to burn with a passion against forgetting. This is a striving toward memory, "to graph onto paper" one's collective memory. The holdings in this counterarchive make other actualities and potentialities visible, the voices and histories of various peoples, as well as dispositions and memories that women and men carry in their bodies, including the tracework of colonialism, racism, and marginalization, *the strange archives of things at once present and absent.* They source a creative rewriting of identity, thought, and political action. In entering into the spaces of this shadow archive we are asked to read and listen otherwise.

*R. D.*

## INTERRUPTION: LISTEN TO THE PASSING OF TIME

*Friday, 19 August 2018*

I met Samir on the day I visited the shop of hip-hop group Scred Connexion, at 80 rue Marcadet.

I introduced myself and we shook hands. I quickly explained my research project, mentioning that I appreciated the texts and sampling that the Scred

Connexion had and still continued to produce. He smiled and thanked me. I looked at his hands—although the vinyl had stopped turning, his index still hovered toward the edge of his turntables.

"Are you *the* DJ?" I asked.

He smiled and nodded. Samir, also known as DJ Diemone, managed the hip-hop collective's online shop and storefront. When we met, Samir also performed live with the rappers of the Scred Connexion: Koma, Mokless, Mourad, and Haroun. In line with the hip-hop collective's mentality, Samir greeted me with respect and humility; with discretion.

"So, tell me, what can I do for you and your research?"

Throughout the summer of 2017 I met with Samir a few times a week. I took the habit of bringing him a can of Coke or a cup of coffee. We'd sit in front of the shop. I often brought up interviews, conversations, or scenes that I'd seen. He reacted, willingly partaking in the analysis of my "data" with me. I asked him questions about himself, too, as he brought in his generation's historically situated perspective on police presence and proximity. Samir and I got to know one another better. He had grown up in the housing projects of the Baconnets in Antony (Hauts-de-Seine, 92). When we met, Samir was living in the private housing project Les Roses Rouges (The Red Roses) in Villejuif, where I had spent my childhood.

"I think there used to be a construction site right beside the building I lived in with my family. That's where the elders prayed in the sand … " I recalled one day as we sat on the curb. "But I don't know, man, my memory's fuzzy. Most distinct thing I remember is the sound the fence made when I hit it with branches."

"You remember well," he said with a laugh. "It's an actual mosque now, with green tiles and everything. *Shouya bi shouya* [bit by bit] we settled in."

*Samir:* There's something fundamental. Write that one down. It's a question of age. I'm older now and I don't experience things how I used to. I see things with a little bit of distance. And my vision, then, is a little bit more overhanging, you see. The kids in the square Léon, they're steeped in it. … They have their whole head in there and, *voilà,* it's a different experience from the one I had. Things change as time passes, and between generations today experiences are different too. These kids won't necessarily tell you the same things I tell you. Us, with hindsight and with the situation we've made for ourselves here, we see things differently.

*Samir:* Our parents too, they were traumatized by the things that happened to them. We all grew up with those "Don't forget your papers." For sure, they went through crazy things, back then when you had the first undocumented people [in the 1970s] and the beginnings of immigration [in the 1950s]. Nah, that's it, they passed that on too. I remember, my mother, she'd stick her head out the window and yell, "Identity card!" Loud, like that, in the street. But we didn't give a fuck. In any case, it's an experience I share with you: parents who worry and always remind us to have your ID with you. And back then [in the 1980s] it wasn't the same. If you didn't have your card, straight to the police station. Not like today, with everything digital. You'd end up in the precinct for two, three, four hours eating shit. I took a lot of phonebooks in the face [during interrogations].

And, you see, it's not for nothing that I got this tattooed [on his arm, I read the words *Music is my therapy*]. After some time, cops see you with your bag full of vinyls and they don't stop you anymore. They see what your job is, my drug was music. You see what I'm saying? That was after going to the pen. I fell. I was accountable. I did my three months in prison. Jail wasn't for me. And that's when I really started scratching [vinyl records]. I was lucky enough to have a neighbor DJ who introduced me to it.[31] After, at some point, I didn't even worry about the neighborhood, I went home and I'd prepare my playlists with all my vinyl records, you see what I'm saying? I went to my concerts, I worked on my sound, and I traveled too. Music really saved me in a way, it opened doors for me, intellectual doors, you see? In the hood, you got positive and negative at the same time: but it's always the extremes. You see, I knew Drogba when he lived in the same neighborhood as me, and his escape was football.[32] So you see, it can be total negativity, but it can also create really positive things. So, you had people who dealt. There, drug dealing was all there was, everywhere, everywhere, everywhere. And you had music or sports to avoid it: that's when the people you meet are fundamental to changing your trajectory in life.

*Samir:* For sure there will always be a continuity between the elders that were tortured by the police, my generation, and the young ones, like the ones that get beat up by cops in the square Léon. As long as there are racist cops, as long as there are fascists in the police, that experience will be shared, that's inevitable.

Here, listen, I don't know if I told this story. It was a few years ago. I was with my mother and two little cousins. It was on the day of Eid [*Eid al-Fitr,* the religious holiday that marks the end of the month-long fasting of Ramadan] and we were going to the mosque for the great prayer. You know, for Eid you have to get there super early because it's a long prayer. We were all dressed super well for the mosque, my cousins were in the back, I was on the passenger seat, and my mother was driving. We were going to Créteil if I remember correctly; they had just inaugurated a Great Mosque, and we were all happy to go there for Eid.

So, my mother was driving, we're on our way and everything, and there I see a police car go by in the opposite direction. I tell myself it's not for us, we don't look suspicious, there's my mother, the little ones in the back. But, you know how it is, always keep an eye open because you never know, and there from the corner of my eye I see the cops do a U-turn. I tell myself, nah, it can't be for us, they're making a mistake. They pass us, block us, and get out of their car like cowboys. Car registration, ID card, driver's license, and so on. And I tell myself, all right, someone must have messed around with a car that looks like ours, or a similar car was stolen. I don't know, but I tell myself they're in the wrong and that, in any case, our paperwork is all good. But, you see, we were dressed to go to the mosque, and they looked at us sideways, straight away. So, they ask for the papers and so on, and I start to speak to him [the police officer].

And he tells me: "I didn't talk to you, I'm talking to the lady."

Straight away, you feel they're only looking to stir shit up, actually. After they searched the car, you know how they do, open the trunk and everything. They start asking questions like, "Since when do you have this car?" "What are you doing here?" An interrogation, really. And there, I felt my nerves rising, you see? But really, my nerves were rising [he grabs his throat with his hand]. I really wanted to fuck them up. And they keep talking bad, looking bad. And there I must've said something like, "All right, you did your search, now let us go. Listen we're just going to the mosque. Huh, you don't have anything better to do?" My mother, *meskina* [poor thing], you know how they are, she can sense that I'm all tense, and she wants to calm it down. The cop, though, goes around and makes me get out of the car. And they start to circle me and to push me against the car, you see what the scene looked like. I tell them, "Look, there's kids here," and he answers: "We don't give a shit." You see how they talk shit. And for me, that's it. I do him like that, "I already fell and did my time in jail and you weren't even born you dirty bastard, I'll fuck you and I'll go back." Because they're not even in their twenties yet, these cops. That too makes you furious. And then, the fight starts. And by then my mother, *meskina,* she had gotten out of the car, on the other side, and she was screaming, she was screaming, you know how they are. And, you see, I was wearing my tunic, my *gandoura*. You can imagine the scene.

And there, you got another patrol car that arrives. And an Arab [*rebeu*] cop gets out of the car. He grabs the cop that was hitting me and he starts yelling at him, you see. And during that whole time, that Arab cop wasn't looking at me or my mother, he was looking at the kids in the back. He was looking at my cousins. And you could feel that it was doing something to him. And the little ones didn't understand at all what was happening. They were there in the back, you know, dressed in their *gandoura,* and they didn't understand the scene. And then the Arab cop gives us our papers back and we leave for the Great Mosque for prayer. But, you see in all this, we weren't at fault, we weren't in the wrong. It didn't have anything to do with us, it's those fascist cops that had a problem. Because if we had been on our way to church nothing would have happened. It's only because we were going to the mosque, these fascists couldn't stop themselves. And the other one, the Arab, was yelling and trashing them.

That's also to say that there's something under the uniform, be it a fascist or a good guy. For instance, I felt, when I told him that I had already gone to prison and that I wasn't scared to go back, I felt that he took a couple seconds to think. He stepped back a bit, you see what I'm saying? They're human beings. So, about what we were saying, you know, these people aren't completely exterior to the hood, they live with us, that's for sure. At the same time, it's not a coincidence they send us cops from the south of France. Of course, if you send some guy who grew up in Orange [a town in Provence where the fascist National Front political party is deeply embedded] to patrol Barbès, that's not going to keep the order. But these cops, once they're here, they're here too. I would meet some that swung by our parties when I threw down my playlists. Only mountains never meet.

Zohra is an Algerian elder, a *chibanyia*. She left Algiers as a young woman, shortly after the end of the war of independence. She lives in a municipality immediately outside of Paris and commutes several times a week to Château Rouge, where she meets with friends in a local café. We met in February 2017. On a hot summer afternoon, as we sat at a café near the metro station, I began by trying to explain the difficulty I found in making sense of the intergenerational transmission of memory when history as such is rarely mentioned within families. Often, when history was involved, Zohra brought the stakes back to the present.

> *Zohra:* "What is the place of parents within this *histoire* [history and story]?" I ask myself. Even when some parents don't raise their children with guidance and care, either by inability to do so or negligence, the question should be asked. And for parents who succeed in properly educating their children, how can they guarantee their good development in these conditions?

The question of intergenerational transmission—of collective memory, of crafts and techniques—seemed to always bring us to a cul-de-sac; it seemed to me that such questions were simultaneously urgent and ultimately made irrelevant by our contemporary context. *In these conditions?* I remembered Zohra had used the metaphor of dreams to illustrate the passing of time since the war of independence; I thought I saw a small breach out of what felt like a dead end.

> *Khalil:* You often spoke of dreams . . .
>
> *Zohra:* It's funny you remember this, that I often speak about dreams. I was telling you, we all dreamed, we all had dreams. Us, the generation that fought

[in the Algerian war of independence]. But your parents' generation only had nightmares [and the Algerian civil war]. And for yours, for your generation, I do not foretell anything good. There are no dreams, there are no nightmares. Maybe just fog.

In any case, I do not dream anymore. And I don't speak here of aspirations or dreams I would have for a brighter future—I've stopped dreaming like that long ago—I mean the dreams that we dream at night: I do not dream anymore. And then, let me still say, not all is dark: some still manage to get through the net and make it. But this surely means that there is a net through which one must know how to pass.

In an avalanche of bitter rhymes, in a track called "Bouteille de gaz" and signed by the Scred Connexion, Haroun raps: *I don't want my son to grow up here, I don't want him to live this life / I don't want him to ask himself, not even once, "Why am I here?"* Words that stick and settle in my mind. Is this what Samir's generation had to grapple with? Is this what Zohra refers to in terms of dreams, nightmares, and fog? In the same track, Mokless goes on: *We'd do well without this label that sticks to the skin / The fear of pickpockets when we get on the subway / People's vigilance, you think I don't see it every day / All it does is amplify my hatred, brings it to me for a long stay.*

*Zohra:* These are difficult themes that you are thinking about. Complex themes. Difficult too because they are humanely painful. But if you want to know what I think of it, I would define the ghetto as a return of colonialism and at the same time as a residue, a waste, of decolonization. The ghetto is this homogenization of practices and behaviors that we can witness here. It is also a product of exile, of this longing for the homeland, a land to which we will never return. The wound of separation is much too painful. As it is a longing, a quest, it is also a refuge, if I may call it that, a shelter away from the gaze of mistrust and suspicion that we receive in the rest of the city. The ghetto is also us, isn't it? We are its products, as we are the waste of decolonization. But we are also its producers. That is, in a certain way, what links us to one another. You and I, but also all the people in this café, be they Black or white, Muslim or Jewish.

July 2017. 10pm at square Léon. I'm sitting on a bench, looking at the checkers and chess tables. Around each table, small groups of men stand in circles, commenting the games and moves. Most of the men are older, dressed in modest traditional clothes. Most of them are from West Africa. Younger men and boys, like myself, come and look on as well. We sit or stand silently and listen to the elders debate.

An older Senegalese man grabs my attention as he begins to raise his voice. He is standing across from a man in his thirties, a checkers table separating them. They talk politics and punctuate their discussion with comments about the game they're looking at. They speak of exile, of the paradox of persisting exile for people born as French citizens. The younger man mentions racism and war.

Someone in the circle interjects: "It's the ghetto here, anyway."

"No," someone else replies. "There are no ghettos in France! These victim stories need to stop!"

The older man, who had caught my attention initially, wants to settle the debate.

"Look and listen," he says with the tone of a pedagogue, "for these are matters that you know intimately."

He points to different parts of the city, east, south, and north of where we stand.

"Over there, there are the Jews. Over there, the Arabs. Then the Hindus, and so on. Is it not? Am I wrong? And then, over there"—he points to the north end of the Goutte d'Or—"it is Black." He pauses and wipes his hands on the back of his hips.

"We tell ourselves that France-this or France-that," he continues, "yet here too the ghetto exists. That is to say that *race* can be inscribed into walls! Isn't it? Am I wrong?" He pauses again, longer this time. "And then, of course, it can be beneficial, can't it? And beauty can come out of it. But the ghetto, the ghetto can also be the ghetto as the *Germans* did it. And that is *total* destruction, isn't it?"

The younger man, with whom the discussion started, waits for him to pause again, and then says: "Look at the place that is granted for us here: undocumented status [*clandestinité*], moonshining, unsanitary housing."

The elder nods. "Yes, and then there are those who are stronger and steady, and those who are weaker. Some cannot take it anymore and, diminished by the experience, they go back to the homeland. Their home neither here, nor there, you see?"

A teenage boy comes walking quickly toward their table. He candidly asks if he can play a game. The older Senegalese man, more visibly tired than he looked a moment ago snaps at the boy.

"Oi, boy! There are rules here that one must respect when one wants to play. One does not interrupt a game like you just did!"


August 2017. Scred Connexion shop on rue Marcadet. Samir is getting ready to close the shop. A group of little boys come running. They stop at the entrance, out of breath. They don't look any older than ten or eleven. They straighten their shirts and flatten their hair before walking in. Each one of them greets us and shakes our hands. They all go downstairs and explore the shop, before walking back up. They look intrigued. One of them asks:

"Are you the big boys of the neighborhood [*les grands du quartiers*]?"

Samir laughs and replies, "No, no. I'm a little one [*un petit*]."

The child shakes his head and continues, frowning seriously. "No, but are you the big ones, the elders of the neighborhood? Because we're your little ones [*vos petits*], we're *your* neighborhood kids."


Samir Khirat passed away on Sunday, 24 May 2020. He was forty-three years old. Samir was loved and appreciated by his family, friends, and colleagues. He died in his parents' apartment in Villejuif (Val-de-Marne, 94). I will forever remember the humility, respect, and kindness that he afforded me.

*Allah yrhamhu.*

*K. H.*

S I X

———

## *A trace is the mark of something not there*

Writing is not destined to leave traces, but to erase, by traces, all
traces, to disappear in the fragmentary space of writing, more
definitely than one disappears in the tomb, or again, to destroy,
to destroy invisibly, without the uproar of destruction.

MAURICE BLANCHOT,
*The Step Not Beyond*

*Tuesday, 24 May 2017*

I returned to Le Carillon this past Sunday after walking for hours in search of images. In making my way home I approached the red awning and decided to stop for a drink. I walked to the entrance, stepped inside, and took a seat at a table bordering the windows facing rue Bichat. The light from the sun was of a similar angle as before, nearly a year since I sat on the terrace and wrote of the everyday and the impossible real. Friends and couples sat at the tables lining the sidewalk, sipping on iced drinks and pints of blonde beer. From my backpack I took out a worn copy of *L'écriture du désastre*. Some time had passed since I had last read the text and I wanted to return to Blanchot's writings on the disaster. What caught my eye were passages on the force and forcelessness of the disaster in time, its duration and recurrence, its dissimulation and dissipation.

The disaster disestablishes itself, loosens, slackens, writes Blanchot. "The disaster, that which disestablishes itself—disestablishment without destruction's penalty. The disaster comes back; it would always be the disaster after the disaster—a silent, harmless return whereby it dissimulates itself. Dissimulation, effect of disaster."[1]

The disaster returns, incessantly, sporadically. This brings the disaster after the disaster, a silent return, harmless or harmful, which fades in time. In Paris, time and memory have come to rest on the disaster like particles of dust.

Music from Algeria flowed from the speakers inside the bar. Someone turned up the music and the men danced to the songs, their arms raised in the air, bodies turning about, singing, smiling, the joy of dance and music filling the place. I tried not to watch or listen too closely. I did not want to be an ethnologist mapping the structures of a Kabyle bar.

In one of the restrooms a sticker had been affixed to the metal top of the toilet paper dispenser. It showed a woman pointing a finger at another woman. "Relax!" On the tiled wall above this someone had written in French, in black marker ink: *Those who are dead should not be forgotten.* When I returned weeks later those words were no longer there.

I looked past the window at the people walking along rue Alibert. I could see the bullet hole in the polished wood at the base of the bar. Just below this dark gap in the wood, glued to the surface, was a small plastic sticker with precise lines, like the centimeter markings on a ruler. It's likely the police used this device to measure and record the force and extent of the bullet's impact. The owners of the bar must have decided not to remove this piece of evidence. It's one of the few remaining material traces of the violence that night.

And yet that seemingly self-evident trace is constructed in dense and over-lapping ways. The gap in the wood has been mapped and measured; police officers recorded the evidence; the owners have sustained and preserved that mark; tourists take snapshots of the damage; in writing I retrace the marks of such tracings.

What is a trace? And how might one write of traces and tracings and so trace out their contours?

A year ago I came to Le Carillon in search of traces of violence that hit that November night in 2015. Now, in returning to this unnamed neighbor-hood, I find that I am not sure, any longer, what a trace is. My earlier pre-sumptions about the fact and existence of traces has come into question. This questioning stems from issues and phrasings invoked myself—the language and phantasms embedded in the thought of the trace.

Things have gotten rather entangled. It's difficult to say what might be a direct trace of violence and what is not. Are the memorials that emerged at the sites of the attack a trace of the violence—or of the mourning afterward? What about the inscriptions and images etched on walls near Le Carillon? Is a nightmare memory a trace of the event?

What counts as a trace and what does not? What economies of time, sig-nificance, marking, erasure, power, potential, and interpretation come into play here? And what about the scene from Eric and Ramzy's film *Seul Two,* made ten years before the attacks occurred but since posted on the Internet in homage to Le Carillon and the lives involved—has that now uncanny scene become a trace of a later wounding?

It depends. The perception and encoding of a trace depend on a perceiver's positioning and what one traces of matter in the world. Every trace requires acts of tracing, of tracing out connections, of marking events and their aftermaths. It's a matter of drawing, plotting, tracking, keeping track, drawing a line, following a course, of deciphering, discerning, searching out, marking. A trace emerges from a work of tracing. Vast economies of time, perception, meaning, and interpretation inform such acts.

The semiotics and temporalities of tracing are altogether complex. At first glance, it might not appear to be so, given commonplace notions of what a trace is. Quite often the concept of a trace bears a certain metaphysics and a direct temporality; namely, that a trace carries an indication of—an indexical link to—a past presence, however direct, fleeting, or tenuous that indication might be. A track on a muddy trail shows the movement of an animal that passed through the brush; a mark is left by the action or passage of someone; a photograph holds a graphic trace of light in a moment in time. But each of these possible traces requires complicated assessments and interpretations within complex matrices of time. Any such traces result from a work of active and selective interpretation, of "reading" an environment or an object, of giving sense to it, tracing things out in one way or another.

There is a danger of naturalizing traces, of taking them as naturally occurring phenomena, unmediated by political and sociocultural processes—the tracework that enables and sustains and complicates the idea and political force of traces. (*Tracework:* the work of traces, and tracings; work on and with traces; the ways in which traces work in the world.) There is also the risk of romanticizing traces—cloaking them in an aura of ghostly residues and past heritages, untethered to pressing political concerns and fault lines, including ongoing acts of physical, structural, and ideological violence.[2]

No trace of a presumed former presence is ever simple and self-evident. No trace is ever natural. A trace is a construct of perception and interpretation—a tracing of some kind of mark or indication. These ways of encountering and perceiving traces are informed by innumerable political, cultural, and personal vectors of thought and life.

This appears especially so with marks of violence. Violence seizes a trace, takes hold of it, makes it its own. Acts of violence lead people to know the damage in certain ways, to trace out lines of cruelty or retribution or track a story into death and maiming. Violence constrains. A bullet hole is grasped in only so many ways. That recognition involves a certain violence of perception.

Tracings are not free. Anything one traces in Paris and elsewhere is patterned by images, sentiments, figures of thought and language, powerful histories and imaginaries. Language traces us before we trace a single word. It's as if a faint outline is already in place and I am filling in the contours, following the course of the lines, without realizing the outline already there. There is, in tracing, an unworking and effacement of the subject. In tracing one dies a little. A track carries the faint mark of a disaster, a fragment of lost time, ruptured matter or displaced being, yet also the joy of ever-altering life.

Traces do not exist on their own. It takes someone, or something—an *interpretant* of some sort, to use a semiotic term—to trace them out as such. An act of *tracing* is required for a trace to exist, to be perceived. That work of tracing holds a greater relevance than a focus on traces alone, for it situates any thought involved within domains of action and interpretation rather than sticking with the stuff of marks and tracks.

The work of tracing is variable, involving different possibilities and forces, different energies of materiality and absence, which come into play at various moments.

1. Creating traces; through art, writing, speech, action; trace as image, affect, voice, inscription, *-graphy* (photography, cinematography, autobiography . . . ) (*-graphie*); trace as art, play, *jouissance,* illusion, imagination, fabulation, allegory; trace as shadow play of presence and absence; trace as metaphor, allegory, play; transforming traces; the art and poiesis of traces.

2. Interpreting traces; tracing out their implications; decoding, deciphering, reading; deconstructing traces; trace as mark, graph, sign, index, code, clue, language, discourse; text, and life-death as fabrics of traces; ichnology, the study of traces and trace fossils (*ikhnos,* "trace, track"), paleoichnology; the semiotics of traces.

3. Finding traces in an environment, or with a body of some sort; tracking traces; tracing them out; identifying, detecting, perceiving, selecting traces; hiding traces; *traceabilité;* trace as track, trail, footprint, particle, contaminant, residue, remainder; evidence, indication; the forensics of traces.

4. Preserving traces; documenting; storing, ordering, creating assemblages of trace; archiving; trace as memory; the mnemonics and archivology of traces.

5. Working with traces; recording; interpreting; writing about them; circulating, communicating them; contesting traces; trace as action, event; the rhetorics and pragmatics of traces.

6. Relating intimately through traces; touch, caress, intimacy, breath, desire as trace; trace as fantasy, memory, longing, heartache; bite, mark, hurt; the erotics of trace.

7. Effacing traces; removing traces from a scene or situation or a life; negating them; denying them; obliteration, incineration, destruction, dissimulation; obscuring, occulting traces, to make disappear; trace as absence, disappearance; the annihilation of traces.

8. Promoting traces; showing them; contesting them; denying them, stealing them; the instituted trace; assemblages of traces; trace as power and dominance, or resistance; the politics of traces.

9. Recording traces; chronicling and interpreting them; crafting, and contesting, narratives about them; carrying trace wounds of past histories of violence; attending to the complicated flows of history; archaeology of traces and trace fossils; the history and historiography of traces.

10. Living with traces; recalling them, forgetting, denying them; trace as affect, fetish, the real; as the ground of language and subjectivity; trace as screen, erasure, forgetting, substitution; blindness, occlusion; trace as shadow, scar, symptom, affliction, effraction, neuralgia, trauma, psychic force; dream, crypt; fantasy and phantasm; the phenomenology and psychology of traces.

11. Inflicting traces; wounding, marking, damaging, "touching"; incising traces on others or onto a landscape, terrain, environment; blow, cut, *blessure,* rupture, death, trauma, and grief as trace effects; burning, searing, imprinting; trace as wound, scar; marks of torture, discipline, punishment, beatings, brutality; the violence of traces.

12. Trace as specter, ghost, haunting, revenant, repetition, uncanny return, remains; ash, corpse; trace as survival, living on, cessation; descent, inheritance, thread (*fils*); echo, continuance, reiteration; trace as seed, spoor, germ; trace in relationship to life and death; the hauntology and genealogy of traces.

These various forms of tracing have been evident in the days and months after the 13 November 2015 attacks in Paris, as with other sequela of violence. A harsh violence cuts a track into the city and intersects with other trace-histories of violence. The violence of that night inflicts haunting traces on many. In its wake, people search for traces, interpret them, create them, document. Some traces are preserved, memorialized, archived; others, effaced, discarded, denied. The living contend with traces of an event through works of wounding, memory, forgetting, haunting, writing, erasure.

Traces vary in shifting form and substance; material, immaterial, actual, spectral, echoic, oneiric, bodily. With any trace there is an intricate play of materiality and immateriality, neither sheer presence nor complete absence, phenomena at once actual and imaginal, phantasmactual. A bullet hole is neutral is fragmented matter is smooth ballistic flow is a crack in the everyday is imagined onslaught is proof of revenge is people looking at a memory fetish.

"It's only when I saw the bullet holes that it felt real to me," said a woman from California upon visiting the site of the attacks.

It's not clear that the gap in the wall is, in fact, a bullet hole.

The reasons and motives for tracing out traces are manifold and ever-shifting. There is no anthropological theory to be traced here, no true ethnography, no thick description rooting traces deep into the ground.[3] Just tracings upon traces within a delirium of traces. Still one writes and traces; marks and incisions in intensity without resolution.

A trace, any trace, anything that one might call a trace, is altogether constructed and enacted, charged with intense relations of power, involving multiple obscure networks of perception, graphings, estimation, enunciation, circulation, materialities and spectralities, as well as all the processes, forces, interests, desires, fears, and phantasies that go into the tracework of a mark. Traces stem from acts of conjuring. As such, they are spectral, phantasmal in design. A trace is just as spectral as anything else—images, nation-states, words, cities, books, bars, jihadists, archivists.

There is always a politics to tracing. This ranges from incidental encounters with perceived traces to the collective appropriation of traces. Within the course of everyday life traces are invoked, negotiated, appropriated, circulated, replicated. They are written on, and about, interpreted, analyzed. Traces are fabricated, effaced, erased, dismantled, destroyed. They are contested, fought over, controlled, sometimes worshipped or fetishized; collected, appropriated, archived, obliterated.

And so, yes, a film made ten years before the occurrence of a violent event can become a trace of that event once a certain tracing, a drawing of lines and connections, is in effect. There is no point in sticking to the idea that traces simply involve the vestige of a past passage or event. That brief scene shot at the Carillon, humorous in effect, is haunting, tinged with spectral forces. The scene is an anterior trace of a future tragedy.

Time is fraught with traces cutting here and there, splicing in and out of memory. One moment you're walking down a quiet street; another, you're reliving someone's reliving of a painful night. Traces involve complex, recursive loops of time, discontinuities in time. Traces are multitemporal. Coursing through marks are multiplicities of time suspended within interlacing dimensions of past, future, present. We might think we live in linear time, yet life is never lineal. We have never been linear.

Traces are patched together. Traces are never natural. Tracings carry a complex temporality. Tracing is political. And just about everything is composed of traces. Apparently people live—and die—in a world of traces, where everyday life is trace, where writing is tracing, speech is trace, image is trace, where violence marks, where mourning is painful trace and lost presence. To kill is to trace death into the world. All is traces upon traces, with no real presence or first or final tracing or retracings in sight.

Erasure belongs to the structure of traces. A trace carries the absence of what it indicates, points to, recalls, tracks, or retraces. A trace is not a presence but the shadowy, spectral sign of a once-there presence (which might not have been there at all, to begin with). Absence, deferral, displacement, and illusion mark the parameters of traces as much as any ideas of retention, continuity, presence, remainder, or evidence—with all such aspects included, paradoxically, within the specter of a trace.

It might be that it would be best to write about traces in such a way that the word and concept of *trace* is put *sous rature,* under erasure, inadequate but altogether necessary. One needs to write trace as ~~trace~~, as if the word had been grafted onto a Parisian wall and crossed out by the hand of another . . . and then, eventually, all such marks are effaced in time. Traces are under erasure. A trace is empty—at bottom it does not exist. A trace is a mark of something not there.

In parting there is disaster. When I left Le Carillon the other day, the sun had fallen past the horizon and a chill had settled in the air. I grew tired of reading and writing. I gathered up the books and notebook and walked toward the door. The man working the bar was engaged in conversation with two men standing near the beer taps.

*"Merci. Au revoir,"* I said, faintly.

The bartender glanced my way as he spoke with the others there. Transient, harmless, a passing specter, I caught his eye for the briefest of moments. He did not respond to my words.

The mark of something not there.

R. D.


INTERRUPTION: 3ALESH? WHY?


*Wednesday, 23 August 2017*

*Rencontre* in square Léon, July 2017. Heat wave. It's around 3pm and the sun is at its zenith, blazing over the square. The few people that are in the park are resting in the shade, sheltered by the trees. I walk through the square from rue des Gardes, heading north toward rue Myrha. My pace is slow. A man, fifty years old or so, approaches from behind. He is walking faster than I am and quickly passes me. He ignores me at first but, turning his head slightly, looks at me discreetly from the corner of his eye. He slows down, as I catch up, and we walk next to one another.

"*Ya Allah* [Oh God]" he says, "some people are at the beach, and here we are in the square Léon of Barbès. Brother . . . "

I laugh quietly and nod. He is as slim as me, but slightly smaller in height. He slides his large hands through his oiled hair and adjusts his collarless shirt, as if to punctuate his sentences. He continues. "Ah! Some are at the beach, in Barcelona, in Ibiza, in . . . in Skikda. And us? We're here in Barbès, *3alesh* [why]?"

He twirls his hand in front of him, a physical point of interrogation.

"*Eh oui,*" I answer. "We make do with what we have."

As we reach the northern entrance of the park, he turns toward me and extends his right hand. "*Moutcharif,*" pleased to meet you. We continue walking next to one another, going left, then right, walking without paying attention to where we are going. He scratches his throat and tells me, "You know, I arrived in France fourteen years ago. Fourteen years! And I haven't gone back to Algeria since. Never! But it's over now, I'll go back in August, *in cha Allah* [God willing]. I'll go back home in Algiers, *in cha Allah.* I left everything to come here, my friends, my neighborhood, my family. Ah, *in cha Allah* I will go home."

"*In cha Allah,*" I answer.

"Yes, I am done with France. It's not a country. *Blad maqaouda* [fucked up country]. It's true. You know, I got here fourteen years ago, to work, to make something of my life, you see? And after six months here, I ended up in the jail for foreigners."

"The CRA [Center of Administrative Retention]?" I ask.

He nods and continues. "Yes, exactly that, *khoya* [my brother]. Thirty days because I got stopped and checked by cops and I didn't have papers. I burned the border, that's why, you understand.[4] And there, *fil* CRA [in the CRA], I saw what they do: they deport the good people, the people who work hard, the good ones; and they let the hoodlums out! I saw it. Ah, it's not a country. Anyway . . ."

He slows down and pauses, breathes and lights a cigarette, a *mboro blad* [Marlboro from Algeria]. He drags on his cigarette and resumes. "You know, after that I wanted to fit in, to work, to contribute, to make something of my situation. I worked. But you know how they are *gaouri* [the French]: they exploit, they humiliate. Me, I've always worked because I wanted to. Always, I want to choose, you see? I'm not going to stand defenseless. So, I worked, understand me well though, I worked in the restaurant business for French *zmigris* [French people of Algerian descent, immigrants], to make money. But when you start without papers, the contracts often stay the same, even once you get a residence permit. Meaning, I've been doing undeclared work this whole time.[5] So after ten years in France, I had the residence permit and everything, I applied for nationality. To be French, to have rights, you know this. Denied. Denied?! You want to know why?"

He stops and looks at me through his Aviator sunglasses.

"Tell me," I answer.

"Denied," he resumes, "because 'no ties.' No ties?! *ʒalesh*? *ʒalesh* no ties?! Of course, I don't have official ties if I do undeclared work. I'm not going to incriminate my employers or the friends for who I work! No ties . . . *ʒalesh*? They tell me no ties, no ties, in the meantime I lost all my ties *fil blad* [in Algeria]. *Ya Allah! ʒalesh*? It's over for me now. France isn't a country. How could they say no ties? I speak the language; I know the culture. I was born French! They make me a native *fil colonie* [in the colony] and then they tell me I have no ties to France?! *ʒalesh*? *Le la* [no] that's not possible, still! I'm going far away; I'm going back to the *bled*. Nah, it's not worth it, *ʒalesh* continue like this here? Nah . . . *In cha Allah* I'll go home by the end of August. *In cha Allah*."

"*In cha Allah*," I answer.

His phone rings and he picks up.

"*Allô! He, he* [Yes, yes]. *Win enta* [where are you]? OK. OK. OK, *amam almasjid* [in front of the mosque]? OK."

He puts his phone away and extends his right hand.

"Thanks for listening to me, young man. Take care of yourself, *ya ould* [son]. *Bislama* [with peace]."

"*Bislama*," I answer, as he promptly walks away.

*K. H.*

———————

# SEVEN

# *"Where wounds are barely scarred over one is cut anew"*

But the war goes on. And for many years to come we shall be bandaging the countless and sometimes indelible wounds inflicted on our people by the colonial onslaught.

FRANTZ FANON,
*The Wretched of the Earth*

## COURSE WORK

Student: Khalil HABRIH
Teachers: Alban BENSA, Manon CAPO, and entire organizing team
Course: The Making of Political Subjects
Diploma: Social Sciences, distinction Sociology, M2
Institution: École des Hautes études en sciences sociales
Years: 2016–2017

*Traces of violence in a post–November 13 Paris:
Phenomenological anthropology and urban* dérive *in north Paris*

*Introduction*

Phenomenological anthropology is interested in lived experiences, in violence, bodies, aesthetic efforts, subjectivity, and intersubjectivity. As Robert Desjarlais recalls, the contribution of phenomenological anthropology in the last twenty-five years has made it possible to reconfigure the understanding of the human, the body, suffering, and healing. By refocusing on the body and subjectivities, while focusing on an effort of deconstruction, Desjarlais tries to make sense of the traces of violence: it is a question of finding a coherence in what seems insensible. In the social sciences, the idea is to understand the social space as it reveals itself to the observer, in its immanence.

As a social science, phenomenological anthropology is part of a *cumulative* history of the production of knowledge about the human as a social and political animal. Robert Desjarlais draws on the American pragmatism of William James and John Dewey—a pragmatism complimented by the existentialist and phenomenological approaches of Husserl, Heidegger, Sartre, Merleau-Ponty, Arendt, and Levinas. He also draws on the hermeneutic phenomenology of Dilthey, Gadamer, and Ricoeur, as well as the ethnomethodology of Garfinkel and Sacks. At the center of his research practice lies, finally, the deconstructivist phenomenology of Jacques Derrida: the subject, ultimately, of the presentation of his work.

By seizing on Derrida's concept of *trace*, Desjarlais tries to bring out the physical memory left after the attacks of 13 November 2015. Commemorative plaques, official speeches, commemorations where the popular and the state mingle. *Je suis Charlie* as an ideal posture; *Je suis en terrasse* as a commemorative hexis? Is the production of memory state-centric, or can it be honestly described as a popular, grassroots movement? Desjarlais is addressing these and many other issues by focusing on body and memories. He articulates his research through the perspective of understanding the presence of the past in subjectivities and intersubjectivities: in consciousnesses. To do so, he addresses political violence, through lived experiences and everyday life, to access the political subject. This is the perspective of the phenomenological approach, distinct from political anthropology.

Desjarlais's study focuses on what he calls "apparitions" of violence in everyday life. It is therefore a question of grasping and putting into writing the *atmospheres* involved and identifying what are indeed traces of violence left by the attacks of 13 November. On this subject, Le Carillon is indeed emblematic. It is, at once, a place of *lightness*—there is, after all, a terrace—and a place inscribed by the severity of the massacre perpetrated. He develops a writing of the everyday that tries to capture these double temporalities; these double spatialities, as well. Because space is officially invested: by the state in its production of an official memory, yet also by residents, neighbors, and patrons who frequent these public places.

This doubling, an entanglement of memories and experiences significantly different from one another but all rooted in a common experience of violence, is a matter of a certain dialectic. Alban Bensa thus speaks of the dialectic between the cult formulated by the state and the one formulated by "popular culture." The example given by Desjarlais is particularly telling:

during the official commemoration of the massacre that took place on the Carillon terrace, the members of the assembly, including President Hollande, look to the commemorative plaque that has just been unveiled. The terrace is behind them: where is the observance? Is memory the product of a shared subjectivation process or is it, roughly, a product that inscribes itself in a national story narrated by the French state?

This question . . . leads us to another one, central to Desjarlais's methods: that of the archive. Derrida indeed wrote that "there is no archive without violence." The "politics of the archive" is thus a matter of a fundamental violence: the formation of the archive is a dispossession of subjects. . . . The traces of violence left by the attacks belong to a work in dialectic between the inscription of the memory and its forgetting. . . . This is therefore akin to a destin*errance:* the commemorative photo left at the scene of the crime will end up in the archival cases in underground offices.

### *Urban* dérive *in north Paris*

Robert Desjarlais's aim, which I have quickly summarized, allows one to discuss "conflicts of memories" in France. During the seminar I put forward the question of alterity—as historical production—and its relation to the questions posed by Desjarlais on the attacks of 13 November. As interesting as his questions are, it appeared to me that elements were sorely lacking in the construction of a faithful portrait of traces of violence in Paris. I invoked the returns of colonialism in France, the traces left by state antisemitism in the arrondissements of north Paris, and the memorial legacy of immigration and exile. If some witnesses to the attacks expressed a deep distress and irresolvable incomprehension in the face of these acts of violence—"I do not understand!"—how could one access these hidden texts, which would broaden the scope of his study and refine Desjarlais's brushstroke and the portrait of Paris he was drawing? A student proposed that he go to Saint-Denis, where the RAID operation that cost the lives of several of the suspected terrorists had displaced the residents of a building on rue du Corbillon.[1] These collateral victims of the massacre—victimized not by terrorists but by the response of the state to this violence—could expand the vision that Desjarlais was developing.

Robert suggested we meet so that we could talk further. I suggested that we meet at the plaza in front of the Gare du Nord. We could then go for a walk in the 18th and 19th arrondissements. On Thursday, 20 July 2017, I met Robert Desjarlais . . . and we began our urban *dérive*. For reasons of composition, and in an effort to maintain the immediacy of our conversation, I switch here to the present tense.

I arrive at Gare du Nord a little late. . . . Robert and I greet each other warmly and exchange a few words: his travels in France, in Nice, the writing of his work. I tell him about the ethnographic study I have been working on at the same time in the Goutte d'Or. We walk through the station; I point out to him the *Eurostar* trains and the great barrier, white and barbed, which marks the Franco-British border.

"Migrants have died here trying to cross the border into England," I explain. "A young man died here in early May."

He looks through the station, and we then exit onto rue de Maubeuge, walking all the way to the boulevard de la Chapelle. Arriving at a red light, I hesitate: should we go to Barbès? Wouldn't it be better to go along the boulevard, toward place Stalingrad? To not plan one's wanderings is a distinctive feature of the urban *dérive*. I turn right and we walk to the place de la Chapelle, along the overhead bridge of line 2 on the metro.

"You see those wire net fences, there?"

"Yes . . ."

"The mayor of Paris had them put up after displacing the migrants who slept there. Since July 2015, city hall and the Paris prefecture have worked out a policy that is—how should I say?—violent. Yes, violent toward asylum seekers. You will see that, for several kilometers, public space under the metro platforms is sealed off."

I wanted him to see that. This is not a picture of Paris that one often sees, far from the cafés of Oberkampf or the quays Voltaire or Grenelle.

"But then no one can enter?" he asks me.

"No. You see, there are basketball courts and football fields, spaces of life that are now closed."

I continue to speak about the role played by the police in the public spaces of the Goutte d'Or, stop-and-frisk, patrols and canine brigades passing through square Léon and what that produces as affective restriction to public space.

We continue to place de la Chapelle.

I explain to Robert how this was a place of struggle, especially for Sudanese refugees, before their expulsion and the opening of a temporary housing center, briefly self-managed, at the place des Fêtes. We continue our walk. All along the way the wire-mesh fences accompany us, as if they were endless.

"But no one has tried to take them away?" Robert is flabbergasted by such a restrictive infrastructure, as much by its opulence as by the indecency of the device: city of romantic subtlety, Paris also knows how to deal in coarseness.

"Yes, activists and volunteers have tried to remove them. You can even see some graffiti left on the columns." . . . Robert notices posters glued to the walls. One reads there, in Arabic, Pashto, English, and French, calls made for the end of the police presence on asylum seekers' street camps. . . . The poster is dated from over a year ago.

Arriving at avenue de Flandre, we turn left, heading north. I show him that the fences continue here as well. But there, rather than leaving the debris of the camp destroyed by the police and the health services of Paris, the mayor's office preferred to put up an artistic exhibition, promoting the 2024 Olympic Games. We continue our walk along rue d'Ourcq. I notice him being attentive to the spaces we are traversing, to the people and the shops we encounter in the street. Young men in black tracksuits, beards cut like mine, velvet kippahs on their heads, step out of kosher shops and jewelers. . . . Jewish women, dressed in light blue, scarves wrapped around their hair, walk with their children. I smile then lower my gaze in a sign of respect. We continue and turn left on rue Curial, heading south.

I show Robert the public housing in the distance.

"You see the tall buildings there?"

"Yes," he answers.

"They have more or less the same social and political function as the "projects" in the United States. The peculiarity in France is that this type of housing was built for Jewish deportees returning from concentration and extermination camps and other communities displaced by the war, and then for Jewish communities from North Africa who were 'repatriated' along with the *pieds-noirs* and other French settlers following the independence of Algeria. At the time, Algerians, who were called 'natives' or 'French Muslims of Algeria' lived in shanty towns. They were eventually relocated to these blocks. Today these housing projects are home to immigrants from the Eastern Europe, West Africa, the Caribbean, North Africa, Sri Lanka, and Bangladesh. We are walking through what I consider to be one of the densest, richest, and most interesting multicultural spaces in France, both in terms of collective memories and collective experiences."

Robert nods and says to me, "That's right ... Have you ever been to Queens in New York? ... It's true that in the rest of Paris I haven't found a place so close to what I know in the US."

We arrive at rue Riquet. I hesitate: should we continue or turn here? In the moment, I don't understand my hesitation. I grasp its significance later on. At the Villa Curial, a fifty-five-year-old man was shot and killed in his home by a BAC police officer. Shaoyao Liu died instantly in front of his three daughters.

We walk the other way, on rue Riquet toward the quai de la Seine. Old Arab Jewish men play a game of *pétanque* in front of the Sephardic Jewish patisserie Djerba. We continue our walk to the rotunda of Stalingrad, and then, crossing the road, we sit at the Café Jaurès to have coffee and discuss what we have just seen together. Sitting on the terrace, Robert takes out a map of Paris. I trace out our route for him. I show him where I conduct my ethnographic fieldwork in the Goutte d'Or.

"It's a Zone de sécurité prioritaire [ZSP]. A very French thing. They create zones like that, for education, for security. It's presented as a form of positive discrimination, but all right, I don't know where one finds the positive in this. In any case, it's the ZSP that allows, or justifies, the type of police presence that I'm studying."

Robert asks me if the ZSP existed at the time of the massacre of 17 October 1961. I smile and tell him no, but there existed torture centers on rue de la Goutte d'Or, as well as police forces specialized in the surveillance of Arabs in Paris. He stares wide-eyed.

We then speak at length about the Algerian war of independence: Papon, torture, the Harkis, the *pieds-noirs,* the 1870 Cremieux decree and the painful separation between the Jewish and Muslim communities of Algeria in 1962. He asks me to speak more about the ghettoization of the first Algerian immigrants, in the fifties. I take this opportunity to come back to an aspect often forgotten about the Goutte d'Or.

"The Goutte d'Or has always been an immigrant neighborhood. Auvergnats, Savoyards, Italians, Belgians, Picards, and then later Jewish people from France but also from Eastern Europe ... The neighborhood has always been poor, but after the '40s, at the end of the war, parts of the neighborhood gradually fell into ruin. Actually, many disappeared Jewish families never returned from the death camps."

He asks me to point out the Vel d'Hiv on the map.

"So the buildings were falling apart because their inhabitants had been deported, you see? So from here comes Algerian colonial immigration, the so-called sleep merchants that converted the buildings they into hotels for single workers. And then, since we're talking about the Vel d'Hiv: there were the big roundups, the *rafles* in 1943, and then in 1958 the velodrome was again used to intern Algerians suspected of working with the Algerian National Liberation Front."

"Wait," he says in shock, "the French state played out the same scenario after the Second World War?"

Yes, it appears so. Hence the complexity of issues around collective memory in France. . . . We can see, in north Paris, where wounds are barely scarred over before one is cut anew. . . . We have just drifted through the materiality of multiple histories: the history of immigration, the history of colonization and decolonization, the history of genocide and massacres. There are traces of violence on bodies, in minds, and on the walls of buildings. Rather than a competition between distinct memories, this is a cumulative process. . . . We share something in common, a similar sensibility toward hushed familial histories and how we received and transmit them from one generation to the next. . . . This is what I call otherness as a social relation. Zohra, an Algerian elder I met in Château Rouge calls this sensibility the "ghetto." She understands it not only as a spatial restriction but also as a social relation. Abdelmalek Sayad wrote that the existence of immigrants in France was fundamentally political. Maybe that's what he was getting at.


*Conclusion*

Robert and I talked for a long time, addressing many more ideas than I have stated here. I hope to have been faithful not only to our *dérive* but also to the quality of his work. Before we parted, Robert reminded me of a remark I made to him, during our exchanges by email. The word *trace* has an Arabic translation: *ithâr*. This word, which I learned during a conference at the Institute of Islamic Cultures at the Goutte d'Or, is a methodological tool of Muslim historians. Traces of a person who makes history, traces of the calligrapher who inscribes memory as a historical inheritance, traces of the divine, which guides the actions of life and heavens. Jacques Derrida surely had an awareness of this translation, having grown up in colonial Algeria before immigrating to France. . . . The notion of *trace* might find its sources

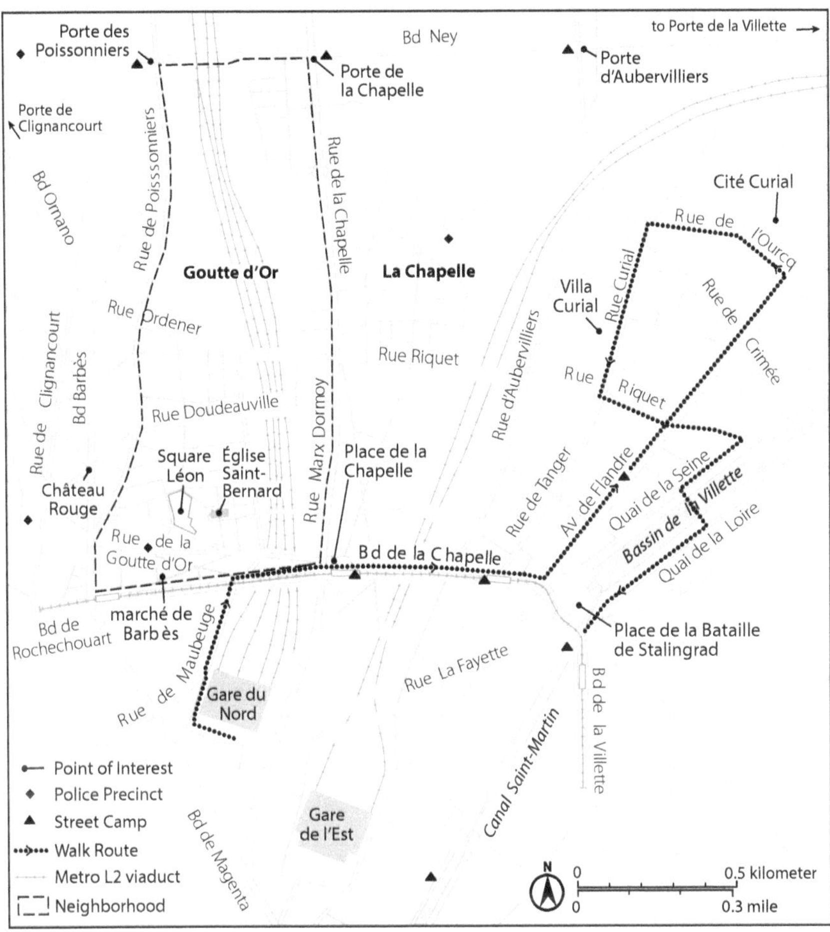


MAP 3. Urban *dérive* in north Paris, July 2017 (Map by Pease Press).

in an inheritance, itself effaced, of Derrida: the concept, itself a trace of lives past and hidden between the lines of the archive.

Robert Desjarlais and I left on a more personal note. . . . I spoke of my family, of my grandparents. I explained how my grandfather had survived the 1945 massacre of Setif, and how, in the late 1950s, he been shot by settler militiamen. He had lived most of his life with shrapnel lodged deep in his back. Robert looked at me and said, "But that's a trace, really. That's exactly what I would like to talk about. You have to write this family history. This is extremely important."

*Saturday, 23 March 2019*

He wanted me to see otherwise, to know of other histories of violence, and through this looking and listening the geographies of pain and displacement familiar to him and others might appear as traces in writing. This engagement became clearer to me when I read the paper that Khalil Habrih wrote for the seminar, in which he spoke of the *dérive urbaine* he and I undertook that Thursday afternoon in July 2017, our drift of a walk through several neighborhoods in north Paris. *"Je tenais à ce qu'il voit cela,"* he wrote of the police eviction of migrants settled in vacant spaces beneath metro platforms and the sealing off of those areas with wire-mesh fences. *I wanted him to see that.* He also wanted me to grasp where violent deaths had taken place, and to know of the hardships people had faced as well as the affective and political sensibilities shared by different marginalized peoples. I sought, in turn, to understand the complicated histories informing his life and those of others, including the welfare of Algerian families who had moved to France during and after the French-Algerian war. These emergent, embodied perceptions took form through walking, and talking, moving bodily through the streets of *Paris nord,* sharing in thoughts along the way, drifting through places and words and histories; and as we walked and spoke of what we encountered I picked up embodied perceptions of the marked terrains that Khalil and others have traversed. Small flint traces of those perceptions are regraphed here, in a series of inscriptions, gashes, and wounds barely scarred over.

There is a cut in the body. Lesions that heal slowly, if at all.

Khalil wanted me to comprehend the specters of violence troubling the lives of many. Our walk that day turned into an education in spectral seeing. Khalil conjured a succession of specters, phantom absences, revenant returns, haunting wounds, violent histories. As of this writing, I have begun to sense these spectral forces in Paris in ways stronger and more acute than I had before. I have since been wandering the city in search of ghostly traces, sensing the edge in their cuts while coming to realize the need for a politics and ethics of spectral memory.

Surfaces and interiors have been sliced into, marked, altered, inscribed upon.

I met Khalil in March 2017, when I gave a talk in a seminar at the École des haute études en science sociales (EHESS), near Montparnasse, far from the northern arrondissements of Paris. Several anthropologists had invited me to present my research on the aftermath of the 13 November 2015 attacks. In a small room set on the third floor of a university building, the morning's light streaming through the windows, some twenty people convened around a combined set of tables. An anthropologist introduced me as the speaker of that session. Reading from a prepared text, she spoke of my research and situated my analytic approach within phenomenological approaches in anthropology.

I framed my talk on the traces of violence evident in the aftermath of the 13 November 2015 attacks. I projected on a screen photographs of the Carillon and the memorials of letters, messages, and flowers that formed there, in the days after the attacks. I also showed images of the commemorative plaque affixed to the hospital wall during the one-year anniversary. Projected as well were photos I had taken of the letters, cards, and books gathered from the memorials and preserved at Les Archives de Paris. I invoked Derrida's contention that "there is always a politics to the archive." In the discussion that followed, those in the room, chiefly professors and students of EHESS, and two members of a team of sociologists who had been studying the memorials that emerged at the sites of the attacks, talked about the political dimensions of memory, writing, and collective memorials. I tried my best to field questions and offer thoughtful responses in French and English. Different languages, histories, and ways of thinking and knowing streamed through those morning hours.

There were cuts to be traced, wounds that called for marking in time and history.

Toward the back of the room, seated among the other students, was a young man, tall and thin, with a slight beard. He looked to be in his early twenties, and reminded me perhaps of myself at that age, starting out in graduate school. His name was Khalil Habrih, I soon learned. Khalil listened intently to my presentation. He kept quiet through much of the discussion, writing now and then in a notebook. Toward the end of the session he raised his hand. He caught my eye and in a calm and measured voice he spoke of the need for considerations of alterity and different historicities and of the "tension about nationalism" surrounding the sites of memory of the 2015 attacks.

"So there is a relation between death and creating a community of people who are alive and belong to the nation," Khalil said. "And the way the attacks happened, I found myself assigned to a position of otherness . . . So there are all these tensions, and I wonder if you're able to see them in your approach."

I hear these words, voiced that March day, as registered on a digital record-ing that the organizers made of the seminar. I hear the specters of voices sounded then, the garbled, phantom strands of my voice, altogether uncanny to me, the speech of others, and Khalil Habrih's voice, which I had no famili-arity with at the time, though now I hear tones smart, *doux,* informed. Khalil's words emerge at 42:16 of the second recording made that day. "I have a question that's maybe off-subject a little bit, but still I want to ask it." Within the recording's acoustics his voice is slightly faint and distant, though his words are clear and to the point. Khalil spoke first in French, and then in English. He was asking if I wanted to portray other perspectives on the after-math of the attacks. Would I want to write about the effects the attacks had on Muslim persons and communities in and around Paris? Would I want to depict other histories of violence in France? Yes, I said, in response, I defi-nitely would like to include these perceptions and histories. But at that time I had not met anyone with whom I could talk in depth about this.

There was no anger or resentment in the tone of Khalil's questions but rather, it struck me, an understanding in sadness of the consequences of colo-nialism, hatred, suspicion, marginalization, police violence and harassment, and Islamophobia in the French Republic. He had observed and lived the damage all around, while certain histories of violence had gone largely unseen, untold.

"There's the question of where to actually capture this," said one of the organizers of the seminar. "Would you have an idea of the location of this?" she asked.

"The thing is, I don't think you can," Khalil said. "I think it's difficult to do so."

"For instance, if we take Barbès [Goutte d'Or]," he continued. "It's a dif-ferentiated territory, as compared to where the attacks happened. I think it's hard to capture it. For instance, on the street where I lived, there used to be a torture center where Algerians were tortured in the 1950s. And then someone went to City Hall to put up a plaque like this one [like the commemorative plaque placed on the wall near Le Carillon], and it was refused.[2] Because the people, you know—the French state had tortured Algerians who wanted their independence in Algeria. So it didn't fit the nar-rative. And you're not going to be able to see it. There's not going to be a spatial-temporal *repère* [landmark] for us to see that there is a different historicity."

"And then, there's things like—on the seventh of January 2016, a man was shot in front of the police precinct of Barbès. It was said to be a terrorist attack, the ministry of the interior came, the army blocked off the whole neighborhood and no one could get out of their homes. It turned out it was just a mentally ill man—*le fou du village,* you know—who was known in the neighborhood. And he was shot as a terrorist and his blood stayed on the ground for a week. And now it's gone. And the memory of it—people don't want to speak about it. I don't know how to capture this."

How can one register remnants of violent events when the state will not permit commemorative plaques at sites of state-sponsored violence, and people do not want to take into lasting memory violent deaths that spilt blood close to where they live? Or when traces of violent acts soon vanish from tangible perception? What kinds of violence might be at work in complicated terrains of different histories and tense, exacting struggles of remembrance and forgetting? And how might someone studying all this be able to follow and write about traces of violence that are scarcely traceable?

"And so the method of phenomenological anthropology," Khalil asked, "at least the way you're doing it, is to access that 'hidden text,' to use James Scott's words—it's all part of it, no?"[3]

"Yes. It should be," I answered. "But it's not easy to do, as you know."

Khalil's critique, conveyed in his subsequent writing, pricked at the conceptual underpinnings of my thought and researches at that time. "During the seminar," he later wrote, "I put forward the question of alterity—as historical production—and its relation to the questions posed by Desjarlais on the attacks of 13 November. As interesting as his questions are, it appeared to me that elements were sorely lacking in the construction of a faithful portrait of traces of violence in Paris."

In question was the validity of a critical phenomenological approach to forces of violence and their effects and lingering traces. If phenomenology is the study of phenomena as they appear, as things that "show" themselves to the world, of that which is "present as such"—as classical definitions of phenomenology tend to parse its reach and import—then how might a phenomenological anthropology attend to forces of violence that do not readily show themselves, that leave little trace in the world, that are not present as such, are not marked and trace out or do not take on tangible, lasting forms? What is involved when it's not just a question of appearance and evident phenomena but also ghostly inklings, fleeting traces, and obscure memories and possibilities?

What if any direct and immediate traces of violence are effaced or denied by others? What if they are gone altogether? How can there be a viable phenomenological anthropology of traces when certain traces cannot be effectively perceived and recorded? The complicated politics of violence and governance in France makes any study of the phenomena of violence—including its histories, traces, erasures, silences, and errant potentialities—an altogether vexed and complicated one.

A viable answer to these concerns is that if a phenomenological anthropology of violence is to work well one has to shift registers. Along with attending to tangible appearances—the directly seen, observed, and recorded, that which is apparent, inscribed, retraced, archived, memorialized, and openly talked about—one also has to consider the less than tangible and the nonevident; one has to attend to erasure and effacement and take heed of the unmarked and the unvoiced, untraced, and untraceable; what goes unrecorded and unmemoralized, politics and poetics of blank absence; the scarcely there, and the not there at all; the "hidden texts," yes, but also that which has never become a text. One has to give careful thought to the absent, the unseen, the intangible, the phantasmal and phantomic as well as haunting reverberations of violence—the spectral, in a word. A critical phenomenology of the spectral is required. To comprehend the specters, one needs to perceive spectrally. And for this to happen, one needs *to be with specters,* to echo a phrase of Derrida's, *être-avec les spectres.*[4]

"The thing is, I don't think you can," Khalil said of the idea of capturing certain traces of violence. Yet what if one attends to the nontangible specters that linger after violent events?

After the seminar ended that day, Khalil and I spoke briefly. I learned he was a graduate student in sociology at EHESS. He was taking the year-long seminar for academic credit. Just then he was trying to complete his master's thesis on the strategies and tactics of the police presence in the Barbès–Château Rouge area of north Paris. I asked Khalil if we might exchange emails, and possibly meet soon, to talk further. He agreed to this, with a smile, and said it might work well if we met one day in north Paris, so that he could show me some of the neighborhoods around there.

Through the next weeks Khalil and I exchanged emails and tried to find a time when we could meet. We were able to do so, finally, in July. Khalil proposed that we meet on the afternoon of the twentieth in front of Gare du Nord.

Gare du Nord is one of the busiest train stations in Europe. It's a transit point for countless travelers as well as an uncertain destination and possible departure point for many migrants from distant parts of the world. These days, most notably peoples from Sudan, Eritrea, Mali, Ethiopia, Afghanistan, Pakistan, Senegal, Côte d'Ivoire, Algeria, Morocco, and Tunisia. Just before 2pm that day I came to the station and walked to its main entrance. I looked up toward the glass and stone facades of the terminus. Numerous peoples walked past, entering or leaving the station. I recalled the words spoken by someone while having lunch at an Indian restaurant close to the terminal: "When I look out at the Gare du Nord and think of all the wealth that went into the making of that immense structure, I think of the colonial exploitation that made it possible." And then there is Emmanuel Macron's caustic comment that a train station "is a place where the successful cross paths with those who are nothing."[5]

I wondered if Khalil and I would recognize each other among the stream of passing strangers. He was smiling when he arrived. We shook hands and said hello. It was good to see him again. I had just returned from Nice and related to him what I had observed during the *journée hommage,* the one-year anniversary of the killings along the promenade.

"Nice is the worst place in France that an attack like that could have happened," Khalil said. The histories of that seaside city were so complicated, fraught, and troubled. Many Algerians living in Nice faced racial prejudices and anti-Islam hatred, going back generations now.

Khalil suggested we pass through the main concourse of the Gare du Nord on the way toward north Paris. We walked through an entrance to the station and stepped past the stairwell leading up to the departure hall for the Eurostar trains to London, where passports and visas are examined and cleared before a passenger can proceed further into the waiting area for the trains. Khalil noted that there is a barrier close to the tracks that deters people from climbing atop any departing train—"the great barrier, white, spiked." This barrier is composed of a series a glass and metal panels, some three meters high, and lined with arrowhead-like spikes along the upper edge. Anyone trying to climb over this wall can be seriously injured, the spikes designed to pierce any encroaching clothing and flesh and to not let go. Posted on the barriers were signs that warned of the *"DANGER D'ELECTROCUTION."* A razor-sharp

FIGURE 31. Controlled entrance near the platforms for trains departing for London, Gare du Nord, July 2017. Photo by R. D.

electrified barrier, slicing through the space of the terminal, signified the dangerous, patrolled border between two nation-states. This border was symptomatic of other militarized walls and barriers in the contemporary world, such as the mile-long wall at Calais, funded by the United Kingdom to prevent migrants from crossing from France into Great Britain; or the four hundred-mile-long Israeli West Bank barrier, made of a concrete wall topped with barbed wire, known in Hebrew as a "separation fence" and in Arabic as a "Wall of Apartheid"; or the various border fences set along the US-Mexico border; or the Ceuta fence at the Morocco-Spain border. Scarred into the land, each of these barriers is designed to deter peoples from moving from one geopolitical domain into another.

The physical symbolic barrier marking the divide between France and Great Britain carries powerful, uneven consequences. For those with the right kinds of passports, the train trip to Great Britain costs time and money, little more than that. For others, the dividing line marks a forbidding limit in movement, life, and well-being. In a quiet voice Khalil told me that one man had recently died trying to pass through that threshold. We passed through the crowds of peoples standing in the concourse of the station, waiting for announcements on trains they would soon be taking.

Khalil's reference to a death did not strike me fully until later on, when, while searching online one night, I found this headline from May 2017: "Man dies after climbing on top of Eurostar train in Paris."

PARIS (Reuters)—A man believed to be a migrant was electrocuted and died at a Paris railway station on Tuesday after climbing on top of a high-speed Eurostar train due to leave for London, disrupting rail services from the busy terminal, officials said.

The man "probably hid" on the Eurostar train at Paris Gare du Nord and was touched by an electric arc, killing him, a police source said.

Police believe the man was probably a migrant trying to reach Britain, the source said.

*Le Parisien* newspaper said the man had been burned beyond recognition and it would be hard to identify him.

The incident happened at about 5 AM (0300 GMT) and led to a power cut that caused congestion at the busy Paris station, a spokesman for SNCF French railways said.

A Eurostar spokeswoman said a few of its departures were briefly delayed early on Tuesday morning but normal service had been quickly restored.[6]

In looking at the train platform and its severe barrier one would never know that someone had died there recently. For Khalil—less for me, then—the landscape of north Paris was marked by tragic, disastrous deaths.

In leaving Gare du Nord, Khalil and I passed by a line of taxis and walked along rue de Maubeuge, toward boulevard de la Chapelle. Along this boulevard—which marks the border between the 10th and 18th arrondissements—runs a *terre-plain* median that supports the viaduct for the elevated train platforms of line 2 of the metro. Starting in late 2014, migrants from East Africa and other countries troubled by war and conflicts and economic hardships, food scarcities and famines, began to take up temporary residence in the *non-lieu* terrain below the viaducts, sleeping in tents and cardboard encampments. Many were seeking asylum and refugee status in France; some must have had hopes of making their way to Great Britain. In early June 2015 a police operation took place in which the camp's residents were expelled from these areas. Concerns about the health and welfare of the residents and poor sanitary conditions in the camp—the threat of epidemics—were cited as reasons for the court order to disband the camps. Eventually, the terrain beneath the train platforms running between the

FIGURE 32. Former site of a camp for migrants and refugees, boulevard de la Chapelle, March 2018. Photo by R. D.

Barbès and Chapelle stations, and on to the Stalingrad station, was fenced off. As Khalil and I walked along rue de la Chapelle, with metro trains barreling along the tracks above us, we could see the metal fences and barriers lining now vacant spaces. Discarded boxes, blankets, and soiled newspapers lay scattered about the muddy ground upon which people had once slept. Khalil stressed the violence in the evacuation—police units had forcibly displaced a number of impoverished, itinerant peoples, *sans-papiers,* and moved them on to detention camps and other temporary facilities, while perhaps deporting some outright. The evictions added to a series of bare life displacements from one zone of indistinction to yet others. While those who arranged and conducted the destruction of the makeshift camp and the relocations of its residents might avow that they were acting in compassionate, humanitarian ways, those displaced were the casualties of such a forceful regime of care.[7]

Weeks later I returned to the former sites of the encampments and took photographs of the places where displaced migrants had once eaten, slept, and rested. Most of the remnant materials had been removed from the spaces, which held scant traces of what had taken place two years earlier. On one large supporting column were written the words, *FROM CALAIS TO GREECE,*

*FUCK THE POLICE!* Toward the base of the column were words painted in red, *FEU AUX CENTRES DE RETENTION*. Burn the detention centers.

Khalil and I walked on. He pointed to where one of the so-called *marchés aux voleurs* (thieves' markets) takes form some days on the sidewalks of a bridge spanning a number of iron train tracks that branch out of the terminals at Gare du Nord, which the police often invade to break up the commerce and arrest merchants selling various goods, some presumably stolen.

Khalil spoke of the ethnographic research he has been conducting on policing techniques in the Zone de sécurité prioritaire of the Barbès–Château Rouge area. There is not, he explained, a continuous, overriding presence of a single police unit in the Goutte d'Or, but, rather, different police forces at different times—as if the ZSP is a training ground for state security forces. These forces are integral to the French war machine, at once flexible and mobile, polymorphous and multifunctional; an assemblage of security forces composed of differentiated bands of soldiers and weaponry, testing their capacities in staged encounters, sharpening skills and military acumen.[8] Combined, the officers exhibit a compound body of strength and potential force and militarized surveillance, like an army occupying a colonial outpost in the heart of the capital.

The police constantly stop and search boys and young men and demand that they show their identification cards. Young men are arrested for minor offenses, with some ending up incarcerated in French prisons. "It's their job," Khalil said of the police efforts to control the territories they have been assigned. "I'm often struck by how banal it all is." Often there is a forced homoerotic dimension to the bodily searches. One male body is touched by a more powerful male body in an invasive, intimidatingly intimate way. "Don't worry, it won't take much longer, though we know you like it," the police might say as they pat down a young man's thighs and crotch.

It's a humiliating experience time and again. Acts of sexual degradation have long been a practice and consequence of colonial regimes. The colonized are made to feel inferior, assaulted, through means of physical or symbolic domination. The violent contact can leave lasting traces—scars, even—in a person's body and psyche. This is a distinct brand of state-secured terrorgraphy: the powers of the state are inscribed into bodies, minds, lives, and deaths. Residents decipher these powers through their wounds. The police hold a legalized monopoly over these acts of force and inscription. The procedures are akin to the security checkpoint stops and searches and surveillance mechanisms wielded against Palestinians in the territories of Israel, and the stop-and-frisk procedures employed by New York City police officers in recent years.[9] Going back further in time—within a time that recurs in people's lives and deaths today—the bodily searches enforced daily by the French police in the Goutte d'Or recall, in a spectral fashion, the bodily searches conducted by French soldiers in Algiers in the 1950s. Photographs from Algiers in 1956 of French *paras* stopping men at gunpoint and forcing them to place their hands against walls so as to search them eerily resemble scenes of French police officers searching young men in Barbès today.

Traces of violence are inscribed into bodies and lives in ways at once indirect, reiterative, recursive, and hauntingly spectral—such that the bodies of those who live in north Paris carry sedimented traces of such violence. This makes the police writing machines of a particular kind, for officers on patrol systematically encode violence and fear onto the subjectiles of bodies. Each instrument of potential force and confinement—body, speech, gun, rifle, batons and truncheons, legal summons, handcuffs, arrest, and detention—serves as an instrument of political inscription. The performance of authorized force inscribes the signature of the sovereign state, writ small onto specific bodies and writ large onto the political body of *Paris nord*.[10] The state stamps its archive onto subjugated subjects, adding indelible marks to the tracework of their lives. The potential for such police interpellations, aggressive stops and searches, and arrest and detention—at any moment, day or night—troubles life in the Goutte d'Or, especially for boys and young men.

Like many living in Paris perceived to be from Africa, or the Middle East, Khalil knows well that he needs to carry his ID card with him at all times. "Oh yes, I learned as a boy—my father taught me—that I needed to have the ID with me at all times." The pressing need for Khalil to carry an ID card with him at all times, to verify his identity while designating him as someone who needs constantly to demonstrate and document his identity, to prove his rightful, legal status as a resident of France, reminds him of the fact that when his grandfather came to France in the 1950s he had to carry a special identity card. His grandfather's formal legal designation at the time was *Français musulman d'Algérie* (French Muslim of Algeria). That was the only formal designation in France based on ethnic and religious identity. The cards were racist in form and implication, as were the intimidating identity checks undertaken in Paris and its impoverished *banlieues*. They marked persons and communities as being racially and religiously other, without the same legal rights as other residents of France.

FIGURE 33. French police forces responding to a collective demonstration along boulevard de Magenta, March 2018. Photo by R. D.

Khalil told me that when he has been searched by the police in the Goutte d'Or, his body patted down in an invasive fashion, he recalled his grandfather being searched years before in France. The grandson's need to submit to the political force of the postcolonial state at the start of the twenty-first century echoes the grandfather's need to submit to the French colonial regime in the twentieth century. With this return of oppressive force, a ritual-like repetition is in effect; through a series of nick impressions bodies reactivate times of hardship.

I realize the risk of taking Khalil Habrih as a "research subject" of sorts, using his words and text as an anthropological resource, shearing language into data and evidence to document the suffering of postcolonial subjects. If care is not taken, any words inscribed could provoke another cut into the skein of wounds Khalil knows and writes about, including the lacerations of social science research on supposedly "exotic" beings living in faraway places. Khalil has conveyed to me that anthropology, at least in France these days, is largely oriented toward others, and ethnological science rests on ideas of cultural difference, tainted by exoticism, the search for otherworldly human beings and ontologies, from Amazonian metaphysics to spirit possession in the Himalayas. That is one of the main reasons Khalil has opted for sociology rather than anthropology as his chosen intellectual vocation. There is also the haunting legacy of French ethnographers conducting research in North Africa in colonial times in order to gain knowledge that could be used to control and subjugate those who were colonized. Knowledge here was power, and colonial orders drew from forms of research, observation, inscription, and control. And so I write tentatively, hesitantly, wary of documenting Khalil's life, wary of further wounding, or branding, wanting the writing instead to be the tangible trace of our thoughts and words together as we traversed north Paris that day—and as we later came to write in dialogic, intersecting ways, without wounding.

As Khalil and I walked along a sidewalk on avenue de Flandre I asked him what he would like me to include in my writing project on the aftermath of the attacks. Khalil thought for a few moments.

"I think there is a need for symmetry," he said. "It would be good if your writing had symmetry."

Symmetry, yes. There should be a proportional balance in portraying the consequences of the attacks in different communities living in France; one should note the violence that sears through many neighborhoods of Paris and its surrounding *banlieues*.

We turned away from avenue de Flandre and walked into a set of smaller streets. We entered a neighborhood unfamiliar to me. A sign for rue d'Ourcq caught my eye. We passed a row of apartment buildings with concrete modernist façades, painted white, and jagged window configurations, and moved on to an intersection of streets lined with a range of shops, *Ikar Market, Chaabi Bank,* with signage in French and Moroccan Arabic, *Au Bontemps Café;* a gift shop with signs in French and Chinese. The streets were busy with pedestrians. I had become disoriented in space; I could not get my bearings in relation to the Gare du Nord or other sites in Paris. I had become lost in space and history, while many of those around us appeared to be right at home.

Khalil and I came to the intersection of rue de Crimée and rue Curial. Across the way stood the architecturally striking figures of two towering buildings, with other similarly "sculptured" buildings in the distance. These buildings formed part of the Cité Curial-Cambrai, the largest social housing complex in Paris. Built in the late 1960s, it is composed of sixteen intra-muros towers, with 1,791 lodgings. At first inhabited chiefly by middle-class families, many of the lodgings are presently occupied by low-income families and individuals. The place is known in the French cultural imaginary as a terrain

FIGURE 34. Cité Curial-Cambrai, March 2018. Photo by R. D.

troubled by rival gangs, the sale of drugs, and petty crime. Khalil stressed the richness of life there and in other neighborhoods along rue Curial.

We crossed the avenue de Flandre, and then approached the flat, slow-moving conduit of water of the Canal de l'Ourcq that led into the Canal Saint-Martin and, from there, into the swirling currents of the Seine. In glimpsing the waters of the canal, I was back in a familiar world. Le Carillon was not far away.

Coming to the rotunda of the place de la Bataille de Stalingrad, and facing the busy rush of vehicles passing through the streets there, I asked Khalil if he would like to get a coffee. He led us to the Juarès Café, where we sat at a table on the terrace. A waiter brought us two espressos. I unfolded a map and asked Khalil if he could trace the route we had taken. He set the map on the table and got his bearings in its crisscrossing weave of streets, avenues, parks, waterways, tourist destinations, and train stations. With a pen he traced out the streets we had walked along. I have since lost track of that singular map. But with Khalil's essay as a guide we have been able to retrace the paths of our walk that day.

In walking and writing further I find myself drifting through the cuts and scarred wounds involved. I have been retracing paths, wandering through texts and films, historical documents and archives, drifting from site to site, wound to wound: Paris 1961; Algiers 1957; Sétif 1945; Paris 1942, 1958; Nanterre and Colombes, 1961; Paris 2005, 2007, 2015. Often it feels like I am not drifting so much as reeling through time and history.

## HISTORIES OF WOUNDING

Khalil and I sat on the café terrace and continued to talk. With the map left open on the table, I asked Khalil if he could note where he was conducting fieldwork in the Goutte d'Or. He took a pen and traced out an area north of Gare du Nord. I also asked him to mark the sites where Algerians were tortured in the late 1950s. Khalil studied the map closely and in black ink underscored the angled intersection of rue de la Goutte d'Or and rue des Gardes. The neighborhood held, for some, lasting cartographies of pain—a terrorgraphy inscribed by forces of the French state, effaced through acts of silence and silencing, erasure, denial, dissimulation, and marked by further acts of reiterative violence.

I asked Khalil a bit about his family, without wanting to pry into his personal life. His grandmother and grandfather moved to France earlier on, he said, in the late 1950s. His grandfather moved from place to place, looking for work in factories. He eventually settled in a town in Savoie, in the French Alps. His father grew up in Savoie. He worked as a French teacher, in several locations, and then lived and worked for a while in Toronto.

Of the years of conflicts and war between Algeria and France, and the Algerian revolution, Khalil said that his grandfather and grandmother do not talk about those days. "The past stays where it is."

For years Khalil's grandfather carried shrapnel in his body from being close to where a bomb exploded, in Algeria. His grandfather had not engaged in fighting any of the sides in the bloody conflict; the wounds suffered were an incidental consequence of violent explosions; collateral damage. "Because the metal was still in his body, he couldn't have CAT scans taken," Khalil said.

Pieces of shrapnel lodged in this man's body were a material trace of violence. The body had become a historiographic volume upon which acts of violence had been inscribed. Notably, these scarified traces were not evident on the surfaces of the body; they could not be perceived through direct optical means. Specific X-ray techniques—a spectral technology, in itself—were required to detect and mark them. Metal cut into the depths of the body and came to be lodged there while the surface wounds healed over; an "exemplum of a wound," these traces fragments were remembered, imagined, and retraced by later generations—much like the wounds of colonialism.[11]

There is a specter of haunting in the recurrence of violence. Algerians are haunted by past actions, including the oppressive, violent actions of the French government, the French military, and police. The histories of violence resound in people's lives. Even when a body does not carry the visible mark of a wound, the life involved is marked, branded, scarred by memories of colonial violence and state terror. The wounds can be imperceptible to most others; they go unseen and unknown.

Khalil spoke of how Algerian families have complicated histories, going back decades, generations. There are different positionings and alliances, which can make relations between brothers tense and difficult. Histories of wounding flow within some families. "I grew up having a sense of this, but I wasn't sure of the reasons for many things," Khalil said.

Something in the tone of Khalil's voice suggested that, now that he was older, past the age of childhood, he had a better understanding of the reasons for strained relations between members of the same families, even if those reasons went unstated.

The wounding is irrevocable. Khalil's words are crucial here. "*On peut voir, dans ce Paris nord où les blessures sont à peine cicatrisées qu'on en entaille de nouvelles . . .*"

There are wounds, *les blessures,* that are barely scarred or healed over; *à peine cicatrisées. Cicatrisé* is the past participle of the verb *cicatriser,* which can be variably translated as "to heal (over), to scar over, to form a scar." The verb is directly related to the French noun *cicatrice,* scar. In the north Paris known to Khalil there are wounds that have started to heal, scar over; I take these wounds to relate to processes of marginalization, domination, and violence in Algeria and other French colonies to specific acts of violence and death in Paris.[12]

Just as these wounds are scarring over, slowly healing, one is cut anew. *Entaille* is the word Khalil used for "cut"; *entailler* is a French verb which can signify "to cut," as when a body is cut; "to gash" or "to nick," depending on the severity or lightness of the cut; or "to notch" something on an object, like a piece of wood. The verb *entailler* is also used by analogy in geological terms, to designate a mark in relief, by a deep cut, as with a quarry that "cuts a gash" in a hill (*carrière qui entaille la colline*). A landscape can bear cuts, gashes, relief marks—*entailles.*

In north Paris there are wounds barely scarred over when one is cut anew. Nicks and gashes are inflicted on the surface of a body, a life, or certain neighborhoods of a city, as if the forceful actions of others pick at the scars or inflict new wounds. *Paris nord* bears a terrain of intercutting nicks, gashes, scars, and open wounds where nothing heals fully.

The recurrence of wounding is evident in north Paris, and elsewhere

- the forceful displacements of itinerant, desperate migrants
- young men killed or seriously injured by the police
- the insulting, injurious speech of politicians and police officers
- offensive journalistic narratives and demeaning cartoon characterizations
- toxic nationalist slogans, such as *"La France aux Français"* (France for the French)
- the policing of residents, space, everyday life and commerce, and of Blackness more generally[13]
- police and security apparatuses that racialize, marginalize, and render suspect
- humiliating routines of stops and bodily searches
- governmental forms of surveillance, monitoring, and profiling
- right-wing threats of internments and deportation
- blatant racism and Islamophobia
- restrictions on public spaces for prayer and spiritual devotion
- restrictions on religious clothing that might be worn in schools and public settings[14]
- acts of othering
- racial profiling
- inscriptions of power and violence on bodies, minds, lands, and histories
- painful inequalities in economic and social resources, and the slow violence of life on the margins
- state apparatuses of marginalization and segregation
- the crowding of poor families into public housing projects
- the de facto segregation of peoples into separate areas of the city
- the historical trauma of colonialism

The wounding is multimodal and multigenerational. Be it within the realms of words, media representations, social policies, police operations, state surveillance, or social and racial categories, painful wounds cut and recut into scars already there. The writing here is a retracing and regrafting of cuts, wounds, scars. The act of writing can be an *entaille,* a gash, relief mark, within a serrated terrain of language, thought, memory. Khalil's words, in turn, have served as gentle, necessary cuts and inter-ruptures into the textures of my thought and writing.

Yet it's not like people passively accept the cuts and incisions and the state's potent inscriptions while nursing wounds or wallowing in despondency or the hardships of the past. Nor do they simply get caught up in paralyzing repetitions of violence and revenge. The shared histories of wounding can offer the basis for a sense of historical affinity and shared community as well as collective efforts in political struggle and engagement.[15] Along with this, women and men act and write anew, fashioning statements and counterstatements through music, song, poetry, fiction, filmmaking, theater, journalism, scholarship, painting, and graffiti and street art, as well as participating in constructive, forward-looking political organizations and relations. There is joy in the everyday, jokes, pleasure, dance, love in family and friendships, strivings for the sacred. From colonial times to the present there has been a generative creativity, poiesis in hardship and in beauty, in which persons and communities signify in new and different ways, refashioning conditions in life in *a will to understand, and a will to fight too.*

### THE CORPSE EXHIBITION

In starting out on the walk with Khalil that July day I thought he might bring me to the Goutte d'Or neighborhood where he had been conducting fieldwork. When it became clear that this was not going to happen I wondered if he was reluctant to go there in my presence. Perhaps those who lived in that neighborhood would take me for a member of the French police force, or a powerful academic who might make a decision or two that had forceful consequences in their lives. It would be better all around, I thought Khalil had decided, to not make an appearance in the place of his fieldwork with an unknown man by his side.

I later decided to go there on my own. Two days after our walk together I set out to locate sites Khalil and I had talked about but did not encounter that day. I wanted to see and sense for myself places that held traces of violence known by Khalil and others. I purchased an all-day metro ticket and rode the line 2 train from Belleville to Barbès-Rochechouart. I left the station through one of the rotating metal gates, passed the crowds mingling about the station on a Saturday morning, heard the calls of young men selling cigarettes, and found my bearings north along boulevard Barbès. Soon I was walking along rue de la Goutte D'Or, counting the numbers noted on small signs fixed to the façades of buildings.

Rue de la Goutte d'Or was once, in the 1940s and 1950s, the location of several low-cost hotels where migrants from North Africa and elsewhere could rent rooms while working in Paris. So-called *marchands de sommeil* (sleep merchants) would crowd single adult males into small shared rooms. In the late 1950s the French police took over a few of these hotels in order to have a base for operations in the Barbès-Chateau area, populated by many Algerians who had migrated from Algeria to France.

The night after I met with Khalil I searched online for details of these events and the specific location of the torture centers. Scattered among postings were references to the fact that 28 rue de la Goutte D'Or was the location of one of the headquarters for police officers and for units of the Auxiliary Police Force. This latter group was composed of men from Algeria, the Harkis, working under the direct supervision of the police. In early 1961, some of these auxiliary police officers apparently tortured a number of Algerians suspected of being members of the Front de Libération Nationale (FLN) in the cellar of that building. Many French police were aware of what was going on, including Maurice Papon, then chief of the Paris Police. The basements in other Parisian quarters of the Auxiliary Police Force served much the same purpose. They were euphemistically called *caves qui chantent* (singing cellars). The French police and the Auxiliary Police strived through infliction of pain to make their captives speak the names and actions of their presumed comrades in arms. The methods used were parallel to those developed and employed by French military and police in Algeria: beatings, the breaking of arms, ribs; electrical shock; impaling on bottles; forced consumption of bleached water. The intent was similar in each situation: to gain information on the enemy, enact revenge, to humiliate, isolate, punish; deter; break and destroy. Apparatuses of torture devised in Algeria "crossed the Mediterranean" and moved from the colony to the metropole.[16]

I came to number 28, where the street intersects with rue des Gardes. The buildings in place there in the 1950s had recently been torn down and new, modernist-looking structures stood in their wake. This building now housed the Brasserie de la Goutte d'Or, a brewery founded in late 2012 that offered the sale of small-batch beer with flavors inspired by the neighborhood's African markets. One spiced red beer was labeled *Château Rouge. Bière Rousse aux accents épicés.*

The taproom was closed just then. I stood between the side of the street and the building. There wasn't much to see. Any observance of past events was phantasmal in nature. The history of the place led me to imagine the cellar once there, a steep stairwell leading down into a dimly lit room. A couple of low-wattage lamps. Empty boxes, bottles of wine. The dank scent of damp mold. Instruments of wounding, electrical devices. A man tied to a chair. Two men standing above him. Blows to a body. Threats voiced in Arabic or in French.[17] All this I glimpsed, in a faint, imagined way, as when one pictures the details of a story told by another. I walked up to the entrance of the building and peered through the glass doors. I could make out the shiny metal of bronze vats and the lightly varnished wood of the bar and taproom. I thought I saw fleeting shadows of human movement toward the back of the room. I wondered if the owners of the brasserie, or any of the workers employed there, knew of what happened years ago in the now vanished cellar of the earlier building.

I stood on the street and looked about. Across the way was a small square with a few scattered trees. Past a flat cobbled surface several elderly men sat on a bench made of a stone base. I began to walk slowly west along rue de la Goutte d'Or. At number 32 was a shop with a deep blue awning called Melia Textiles. Next to it stood the imposing structure of the préfecture de Police de Paris, one of several police precincts in north Paris. A set of interlocking metal fences delimited the entrance to the building along the street. Positioned at an opening permitting passage through the fences were two police officers, standing watch. Dark-blue bulletproof vests protected their torsos. The two men held semiautomatic rifles in their hands. They looked at me as I passed, scoping the movement of an unknown body standing close to the precinct. I tried not to exchange glances with them. The sightlines gunned oblique perceptions.

The police station had the appearance of an urban fortress or a military bunker, six stories tall. The façade of the ground floor was composed of a lattice pattern of small cube-like pieces of dark glass, the mesh pattern designed to withstand forceful blows. Above that ground-level barrier was a smooth flat surface, a massive concrete slab of a wall extending a few feet from another, more interior surface of the building—as though the side of the building facing the street served as a shield protecting the actual substance of the building and its interiors and any materials or persons lodged within it. Each of the windows above was protected by strengthened glass

FIGURE 35. Police station, rue de la Goutte d'Or, March 2018. Photo by R. D.

and metal grating—to deter possible thrown objects, bottles, fireworks. Cutting through this flat shield, running from the metal and glass entrance up another three floors, was a vertical chamber of glass windows; a stairwell was likely beyond that crevice of an opening, which radiated like a gash in the outer shell of the building.

To a spectral mind the dynamics of attack and defense characterized the militarized architecture of this police station, as if the building was continuously bracing for street battles, past, present, or future. Photographs of various police stations in the *banlieues* to the north of Paris reveal variations on militarized themes of defense and deterrence—metal fences set before the buildings; seemingly impenetrable exterior facades, smooth or striated; small slot-like windows and openings, set vertically or horizontally, like the apertures of medieval fortresses; controlled and limited entryways; metal-grated windows; shield-like structures of modernist garrisons.[18] The police precinct on rue de la Goutte d'Or carries a similar defensive aura, as if those who commissioned and designed its fortress structure imagined the phantasm of a full-out attack by enemies on the station and its personnel. If one stands before the station, the militarized architecture makes it easy to imagine such an attack, rocks and bottles thrown from the streets, crowds angered by the killing of their own seeking justice, riot police with gas masks standing firm

FIGURE 36. Police station, rue de la Goutte d'Or, March 2018. Photo by R.D.

behind a phalanx of transparent polycarbonate shields, canisters of tear gas tossed into a surging mass of bodies, phantoms of siege warfare.

Phantasies of the enmity of others can have very real consequences. It was here, at this préfecture, on 7 January 2016, one year to the day of the *Charlie Hebdo* attacks, that a man was killed as he sought to gain entrance to the police headquarters. One newspaper reported the events as such:

> The man arrived in front of the police station on Rue de la Goutte-d'Or at 11:30 a.m. with a meat cleaver, wearing what turned out to be a fake explosives belt. He then brandished the knife and yelled, *"Allahu akbar,"* Arabic for "God is great," before police officers opened fire. Witnesses said the officers had ordered the man several times to stop and step back before shooting him.
>
> The office of the Paris prosecutor, François Molins, on Thursday evening confirmed that the assailant's fingerprints matched those of a man who was convicted of theft in southern France in 2013.
>
> The man told the police at the time that he was named Sallah Ali, that he was born in Casablanca, Morocco, in 1995, and that he was homeless, the prosecutor's office said.
>
> Thursday's attack prompted the temporary closing of schools, shops, and streets. The man's body lay on the sidewalk outside the police station for more than an hour and twenty minutes, covered with a white cloth. A robot was

deployed, and after that, two dogs and then an investigator wearing heavy gear inspected the man's jacket, before determining that it was a fake suicide vest. . . .

Justice Minister Christiane Taubira, speaking on the i-Télé news channel on Thursday evening, said that investigators still needed to clarify whether the attacker was radicalized or if he was mentally unstable.

"A fake explosives belt, the cries, the allegiance in his pocket, these are signs that could link him to a network, but at the same time these could be the signs of someone unbalanced," Ms. Taubira said. "The investigation will clarify all of this."[19]

Photographs from that day show the man's body lying between the metal fences and the entrance to the building. The man's arms lay open on the ground. Two police officers stand above the body. They look stunned, shaken, by what has happened and the disturbing matter of a lifeless body at the entrance of their stronghold headquarters. Another photograph shows a robotic device inspecting the inert body with the use of a camera affixed to what could be called the neck of the robot.

Such images mediate flashpoints in the Republic's state of emergency, which implies, among other legal and police procedures, the sovereign's right to kill or to let live.[20] In operation here was the biopolitics of state security and sovereignty. The sovereign state proclaims a monopoly over apparently justified force within its borders—as though the state holds onto a reserve of legitimate violence, which it actualizes, and sanctions, when deemed necessary. In times of apparent defense against perceived threats, or instances of aggressive force, the sovereign shows its beastly side and launches into kill mode. The state wields an excess of violence, which it justifies on legal, sovereign grounds; in this untimely situation the police officers actualized as a kill team, annihilating a perceived threat. Yet the legitimacy, ethics, limits, and comprehensiveness of those grounds, within the phantasm of the sovereign state and its phantasmal reach, can be questioned and contested.[21]

During the seminar Khalil spoke of how, after the corpse was removed, the man's blood remained on the ground for days after the death. It's not only the miserable death of the man that is disturbing. The uncaring, wounding treatment of the remainders of the man's death relates to the necropolitics of abject dead bodies. The state did not mourn the loss of this life. There would be no commemoration of the death. That singularly complicated, spectacularized death made people uncomfortable all around.

Afterward it became known to the authorities that the deceased's name was Tarek Belgacem and that he was from Tunisia, not Morocco. They said he had taken on various identities while living in Germany and France. I found brief articles online noting that man's death, on the day of the killing and in the next few days. There was little mention at all in newspapers or journals after that; no long-form journalistic accounts of who this man was or what his death implied.

A few short articles appeared when Tarek Belgacem's father arrived in France, from Tunisia, to recover the body of his son. Soon after he arrived in Paris, on 19 January 2016, he spoke with reporters about his interest in talking with the French authorities about his son's death.

"I feel like my son," the father can be heard saying in French, in a video recording posted online. "He felt three bullets in his heart. I want to see the truth about my son's death. And I want to bring back my son again. I want to talk with the French justice system. I want the truth, more than the truth. Something is not quite right. There are too many witnesses that say my son had no chance. He was not a terrorist. I will never debate that [accusation]."[22]

Another article, published on 20 January 2016, noted that Toufik Belgacem wanted to file a formal complaint, accusing the police of voluntary manslaughter.[23] "I'm going to lodge a complaint, because I think there's something wrong," he said. The father spoke of certain inconsistencies between the statements of the police and those of witnesses, including some who said that Tarek had not raised his hand when approaching the police, and that he did not say anything to them. "Why did he fire three or four bullets into his heart?" Toufik Belgacem asked of the police officer who shot his son. "He could have shot him in the leg, or shot him in the hand. Even when he fell, he was still aiming at him. What is that? Is it the French law that says that? The guy who did that is a liar."

The inconsistencies between different accounts of what happened in the moments of the police shooting, and questions raised about the police statements on the death, led to a situation in which Tarek Belgacem's father and other family members sought to seek truth and justice in the event of the death. "*Vérité et justice*," or "*justice et vérité*"—this is often the rallying cry in France for those mourning and protesting the deaths of individuals killed by police under contested or ambiguous circumstances. *Verité et justice pour Adama Traoré. Justice pour Théo.* Entering the words "*verité et justice pour ___*" into the Google search bar brings forth a litany of troubling deaths at the hands of police officers in France. Often, large numbers of people work together to seek the truth about the circumstances of a death, with hopes of obtaining justice for any wrongful deaths. The French legal system usually defends the actions of any police officers involved in a death.[24] The pathways of such deaths might appear to imply misfortunate accidents or tragic circumstances and all too troubled encounters, yet the recursive seriality of the deaths is disturbing. This recurrent, reiterative disaster of violent deaths speaks to an infrastructure of police violence in north Paris and in the poorer *banlieues* on the city outskirts (as in many cities in the United States). The violence runs through everyday police practices and crystallizes, in acute, paroxysmal moments, in the loss of life.

Khalil told me that those who lived in the Goutte d'Or neighborhood where the death took place spoke about it in hushed terms only. It was "too shocking to talk about," he said in trying to explain the concerns here. The residents of the Goutte d'Or worried about bringing trouble onto themselves. It was better to keep quiet, all around. It was as though there was a lingering miasma around the death, a dangerous force at once disconcertingly actual and spectral, and people wanted to stay clear of that.

Khalil said that this killing resembled a "lynching," in which an inert, contorted body is left to hang in the wind, signaling proof of the right to kill, a warning to others. The blood left on the sidewalk and street stood like a remnant trace of the state's power and sovereign authority to kill anyone that its security forces deem a mortal threat to their own lives or the lives of others. The scene had the tone of a *mise à mort,* a state execution, in which the life of a living being was terminated. "He was shot dead like a dog."

It's a question of perspective and memory, and the ways in which histories of violent scarring shape perceptions in the postcolony of the metropole: the killing of the man could be likened to a public execution, while the inert body coldly left on the pavement for several hours and the blood that stained the street for days after was reminiscent of *les expositions de cadavres* (the exhibition of corpses) that the French military performed in sudden, shocking moments during Algeria's war of independence against French rule.[25] As historian Raphaëlle Branche writes in her book on the French army's use of torture in Algeria, "public executions and exhibitions of Algerian corpses clearly reveal a desire to destroy the enemy while establishing power over the population."[26] Such actions, she contends, are intended "to impress, to subjugate, to take possession mentally of the population. Like members of a family forced to witness the torture or death of a loved one to obtain information or rallying, the Algerian population is the chosen public for these executions, veritable displays of military powers."[27]

In his *Journal, 1955–1962*, Kabyle writer Mouloud Feraoun describes one such display of military power in an entry dated 18 June 1957, when he was teaching at a school in Fort National, Algeria. "Around 10:00, we heard a detonation," he begins. A grenade detonated in a hotel; a French captain had been the target of the attack. "There were about six wounded, but the captain had not been touched. The army and the police began to scour the city, rounding up the native population and assembling them in the square outside city hall." What followed was a scene of forced instruction, surveillance, and the grotesque transport of a cadaver, carried unmanageably on a donkey, from which the writer looked away.

> Toward noon, I saw high-ranking officers (a commander and a colonel) arrive at the square. A former fellagha [guerilla fighter opposed to French colonial rule] began to harangue the crowd gathered there. He positioned himself in a jeep near the mess hall and started talking into a loudspeaker. I thought I heard that the aggressor had been shot and that, among the wounded, there were some seriously injured kids. The former fellagha was urging the shopkeepers to be careful; advising them not to offer the terrorists any refuge; and condemning the criminal acts of those who had not hesitated to cause the death of innocent people. Finally, they had the corpse pass by on a small donkey led by a Kabyle, pushed by another, and ridden by a third—who clasped the body as if it were an unmanageable load. On seeing the cadaver's feet, I turned away. At that time or later, I do not remember any more, a soldier was filming the crowd from all angles. Toward 12:30 everybody had been released to go get something to eat. What exactly had happened?[28]

One might ask the same question of the death of Tarek Belgacem before the police prefecture on 7 January 2016, and the treatment of his corpse afterward. What, precisely, had happened?

With this man's death no single event took place. There was no singular death, with a clear and straightforward truth to it, with tangibly apparent reasons and purposes, intentions and motivations. Different occurrences took place, from divergent perspectives, relating to differing histories of life death and violence. There is a vagueness to the death, all around. That vagueness contributes to the miasma that surrounds the death, recollections of it, and the hushed, deterred talk and silence in the days that followed.

It could be said that the police shot and killed a man who approached them in an aggressive way; that the shooting was justifiably in self-defense:

the man would not heed orders to step away, and the trained officers sought in nervous fear and stress to protect themselves and the inhabitants and structure of the precinct and any neighboring buildings. The man looked to have a bomb strapped around his waist; he looked driven, "radicalized" or unbalanced; they could not be sure, the officers had to disable the imminent threat. The Paris police kept the corpse on the pavement for several hours for reasons of safety and forensics—they wanted, first with the aid of the robotic device, to make sure no explosive devices remained on the body, and they needed to gather evidence of the threat and the shooting carefully, procedurally, each trace labeled and recorded. The sudden death triggered an apparatus of security concerns, cool efficiency, techno-forensics, and legal procedures. The disturbing exposure of the crumpled body to passing onlookers, television cameras, and residents of the Goutte d'Or was not the concern of those evaluating the death. The body was by then inert material, less than a person, soon delivered to and autopsied in the morgue. The blood left on the pavement for days after could be taken as resulting from no more than the slow and sporadic pace of street cleanings in the Goutte d'Or.

All this could be said and noted, reasonably so. Yet this is only one possible truth and phantasm to the death. Each truth is phantasmal, and there is truth in each phantasm. Each death is multiply phantasmal, for any death incites torrents of perceptions, affects, imaginings, and ghostly reverberations.

The public manner of the death and the lingering exposure of the corpse invoked the brute power of the state over matters of life and death. The armed forces of the state have the right to kill, when called for, and they coldly opted for killing. Buoyed by the powerful phantasms of state sovereignty and its exceptional potential for violence, the police officers responded with deadly force to the phantom of a siege on the anniversary of catastrophic violence. This was death by phantasm, in effect. The lingering, postdeath exposure of the cadaver was degrading not just to the expired life but to those who could relate to the life and violent death. The blood left on the street was a *tache,* damning stain, profaned body part, degradation of human life and dignity. Blood exhibit.

A sentence of Raphaëlle Branche's applies not just to Algeria in the late 1950s but to north Paris in the early twenty-first century. "The exposure of corpses," she writes, "is part of the same transgressive movement as torture, since it undermines the dignity of the Other—this time beyond death—and affects, through the imposed spectacle of this degradation, the entire population, humiliated or frightened."[29]

The death and its implications are hard to grasp in words or images or through any kind of systematic research. Traces are elusive, and people do not want to talk about it. What remains is a searing unclear mark in people's lives and the terrain of the Goutte d'Or.

How many other lives and deaths have taken, or will assume, a similar form? What killings incite other deaths within a viral spread of violence? What follows a death?

In walking about Paris one is left to consider the art and savvy that goes into exhibiting corpses. It's a worldwide phenomenon and booming industry, with outposts in the military, specialty shops in security brigades. Government regimes and insurgent groups have long been in on the dark arts of warfare and police brutality. Hung bodies, swaying in the wind. Tire necklaces. Severed heads stuck on posts at the far reaches of the empire. Che Guevara's corpse displayed and photographed while set on a concrete slab in the laundry room of a church in Vallegrande, Bolivia, his hands then amputated, placed in formaldehyde, and sent to Buenos Aires for fingerprint analysis. Michael Brown's slain body lies for hours on a blacktop road in the summer heat in Ferguson, Missouri. An army sergeant in a Fifth Stryker brigade "kill team" collects the fingers and bones of his Afghan victims. A Navy SEAL warrior poses in a photograph with a dead Islamic state captive. Video beheadings are performed before black and white banners. Maimed and moribund bodies are spectacularly on show in media installations, while scholars study the corpuses like skilled morticians, with scalpels in their hands.

"Before taking out his knife, he said, 'After studying the client's file you must submit on how you propose to kill your first client and how you will display his body in the city.'"

So begins "The Corpse Exhibition," a troublingly incandescent story of Iraq by writer Hassan Blasim, in which one man relates to another the delicate art of exhibiting corpses. The second man is apparently an applicant or volunteer to a ministry devoted to exhibiting corpses; in explaining how things work there, the first man speaks of specialists, talented and untalented, of archives that hold "brief, poetic reports" of extraordinary works of art, of training "documentaries about the lives of predatory animals" ("Pay particular attention to the images of the victims' bones"), and of the most important office in the institution, "the truth and creativity department."[30]

"Every body you finish off," the man advises his listener, "is a work of art waiting for you to add the final touch, so that you can shine like a precious jewel amid the wreckage of this country. To display a corpse for others to see is the ultimate in the creativity we are seeking and that we are trying to study and benefit from. Personally I can't stand the agents who are unimaginative. . . . I like concision, simplicity, and the striking image."[31]

I have since returned to the Goutte d'Or, a striking image nested in mind. I came close to the police precinct and walked slowly past the building. Two uniformed officers stood by the entrance, a woman and a man. Each carried a gun. What did they think of the killing? Do memories of the dead man and his state-licensed shooters cross their minds as they stand watch? I looked toward the ground, near the metal fences, to see if I could spot where Tarek Belgacem had been killed. It was difficult to know this or see anything distinctive. The cobble stones of the street all looked the same. They looked newly washed, scrubbed clean. There was no apparent trace of the body once there.


## SPECTRAL SEEING

Paris, spectral city. Where it's relatively easy to live alongside ghostly specters and remnants, walk past them on the way to pick up a baguette in the morning, and die, even, among a phantasmagoria of ghosts within a palimpsest metropole that holds layers upon layers of markings and erasures in life and death.

*Et cet être-avec les spectres* . . . In reflecting on the force of hauntings and ghostly reverberations in European history, and on the idea of a hauntology more generally, Derrida wrote of how "this being with specters would be also, not only but also a politics of memory, of heritage and generations."[32] I take this to mean there is political value in cultivating a sense of the spectral, haunting qualities of life and recognizing, in careful, attentive ways, histories of violence and terror. In learning to live with ghosts one can engage with the complexities of the past, present, and future, maintain a sense of multiply haunted, haunting histories, and be aware of the complex intertwinements of the actual and the phantasmal of life-death. This being with specters, in thought and in writing, and in life more generally, can thus also be an ethics, for it offers a way to live in the world, to relate to others, recognize the histories of the dead and the wounded, remember the past and make sense of the present. This spectral awareness, this being with ghosts, can be a daunting, nearly overwhelming one. Avery Gordon writes that one task is "to look for lessons about haunting when there are thousands of ghosts; when entire societies become haunted by terrible deeds that are systematically occurring and are simultaneously denied by every public organ of governance and communication."[33]

Being with specters, so be it. Like others, and like Khalil, I have come to dwell among a number of specters; or, the specters have taken up various haunts in my thought and any words written. Others have lived with spectral traces of violence their entire lives. For some, it could be said that they were born into haunting; they have to contend with trace memories of colonial domination and ghostly reverberations of violence in their lives and communities. As Avery Gordon puts it, "What's distinctive about haunting is that it is an animated state in which a repressed or unresolved social violence is making itself known, sometimes very directly, sometimes more obliquely."[34] And yet, as Khalil himself noted, it's difficult to grasp all this, and so convey the complicated, elusive play of traces and erasures and write in clear and effective ways about how people live and relate to specters of violence. It's all so tricky, elusive—spectral, in a word.

The other day I wrote these sentences: "The wounds are visible in north Paris. 'One can see, in this north Paris . . .' You just need to look. You just need to know how to look. The wounds are tangible; they have material form."

But this isn't quite right. The wounds often do not have visible, tangible, material forms. You can't see or grasp them directly. And so what kind of perception and spectral nonappearance is this in the streets of Paris? What is perceived of state-sanctioned violence that happened last month, or years ago, when there are only a few, if any, remnant traces remaining? Little is apparent, there. The subterranean *cave* where people were tortured in 1961 is now the cellar of a beer brasserie. The blood of that man's death in front of the police station has been washed away. The displaced migrants are long gone. There is nothing to see or sense directly; there is so much to grasp and to notice, but the perception involved is not the seeing of midday light. What is required is a certain kind of *spectral seeing.* Those who know what is there can see the specters. They perceive spectrally, through certain spectral technologies. Some live with the specters, day and night. (Here words like *seeing, perceiving, grasping, sensing, tangible,* and even *specter* and *spectral* strike me as inadequate, limited, all too concrete terms for the complex, elusive processes involved; they are chimera of chimera.)

The word *specter,* from Latin *spectrum,* implies an appearance, vision, apparition, of a certain kind of spectral visibility. *Specĕre,* to look, see. The specter does not involve the clear, distinct, apparently real visibility of daytime appearances. There is something flickering and wavering about specters, something not fully real but still discernible in a certain light. The specter, Derrida notes, "exceeds all the oppositions between visible and invisible, sensible and insensible. A specter is both visible and invisible, both phenomenal and nonphenomenal."[35]

The histories of violence at hand tie into a spectral visibility. This is of a phantasmal, night visibility, of memories, phantasies, obscure potentialities, and haunting dreams and reverberations. The violence is of wounding not necessarily present, any longer, in flesh and blood or in sensate materialities of the world. Usually, it's not directly tangible. The specters here are not the clear, distinct, apparently real visibility or tangibility of daytime appearances. A specter is at once phenomenal and nonphenomenal; it lies somewhere between appearance and nonappearance, the living and the dead. But it's still there, or not, in a spectral, apparitional way. I think it's in this spectral register, within the spectrum of the spectral, that we can find the most truth in Khalil's perception when he writes, "There are traces of violence on the bodies, in the minds, and on the walls of buildings in north Paris."

Khalil wanted me to sense the specters. This was an education in spectral seeing, in which I was learning how to perceive spectral traces of violence. We noted absences and nonappearances as much as we encountered tangible presences. In walking with me in north Paris, talking along the way, and then later in writing about our walk together, Khalil conjured an array of specters. What has emerged in time is a transfer of spectral looking and recognition; the procedures of a spectral seeing have been grafted onto my perceptions, resulting in a shared being and living with ghosts, a politics and ethics of trace and remembrance. I have since been trying to graft those spectral forms and perception into the pages of this text (many have gone unmentioned). It's been a cumulative process, a slow and shaky accretion of spectral phantasms that make the past and present waver.

As I walk about the Goutte D'Or these days, the bulk and sheen of certain buildings, street corners and vacant spaces shimmer like so many mirages, in which I perceive faintly past lives and cruelties. Standing by others, I watch as new cuts appear and then slowly heal over, only to be cut anew.

Who bears such wounds, and who does not? Who lives and perceives the ghosts and specters? To whom do they go unrealized? How do wounds change through time? Who embodies them? Who imagines them? Who is haunted by them? Who is not? Who denies the haunting? Who is spectrally sightless before past woundings? What goes unseen and unsensed?

With this indirect retracing of wounds, and living amidst specters, I'm not sure I'm seeing anything at all. I doubt what I sense and know. That doubt and uncertainty is within the realm of the spectral. Things are not clearly perceived or clearly affirmed.

"Yet must one have a clearly visible—or legible—reality in order for testimony to take place?"[36]


LESS THAN SPECTRAL


Specters do not emerge spontaneously. There is a politics to the forms that specters take or do not take, and the means to which they are sensed, perceived, or not. Certain kinds of relations with ghosts and specters are supported, permitted, sustained, while other relations can be disallowed, diminished, prevented.

I continued to drift through Paris that later day, retracing histories of violence against Algerians. From Barbès I took the line 4 metro to place Saint-Michel. Walking past crowds of tourists I crossed pont Saint-Michel, a bridge spanning the Seine. Arriving at the margins of the Ile de la Cité I found what I was looking for: a memorial plaque set on a wall close to the northern side of the bridge. The metallic surface of this plaque bore a precisely delineated inscription:

> *A LA MEMOIRE*
> *DES NOMBREUX ALGERIENS*
> *TUES LORS DE LA SANGLANT*
> *REPRESSION*
> *DE LA MANIFESTATION PACIFIQUE*
> *DU 17 OCTOBRE 1961*

Which means: "In the memory of the many Algerians killed during the bloody repression of the peaceful demonstration of 17 October 1961."

The plaque was established in 2001, after a contested political effort fueled in part by several memory activist groups, to commemorate the deaths of those killed in Paris on the night of 17 October 1961. On that day thousands of Algerians who lived in various shantytowns on the outskirts of Paris approached the center of the city, by foot, bus, or metro, to demonstrate peacefully against France's colonial rule and illegal curfews imposed upon North Africans by the Paris police force. This collective manifestation was

FIGURE 37. Commemorative plaque, pont Saint-Michel, July 2017. Photo by R. D.

supported and organized by the leaders of the FLN, which strongly encouraged all able-bodied adult Algerians to participate in a unified, peaceful show of defiance and resistance; members of the FLN tried to make sure that no demonstrators carried weapons of any sort. Police officers and Auxiliary Police officers learned about the plans for the demonstration sometime that day; armed with guns and long clubs (*bidules*), they were waiting at bridges, metro stations, and other strategic points when demonstrators arrived and tried to move more fully into the city center. Many of these police officers were enraged by the deaths of colleagues, who had been assassinated by members of the FLN. Their commanding officers, including Maurice Papon, then prefect of the police, reportedly conveyed that there would be no repercussions if they acted in aggressive ways against any Algerians encountered that night. During the violent repression of the protests, through the rainy hours that night, approximately two hundred men and women were killed, apparently by French police forces, chiefly through beatings, shootings, or drownings in the Seine. Many of those killed went unidentified; corpses were buried in unmarked graves in cemeteries outside of Paris. Other bodies were reportedly buried in woods near the city. That same night the police rounded up thousands of Algerian men and transported them to temporary detention centers Paris, where they remained in harrowing, violent conditions for several days or more. Hundreds of those detained were then sent by plane from Orly airport to Algeria, effectively banished from life in France.[37]

In the days following 17 October 1961, the French police and national and city governments worked in concerted ways to prevent and censor any journalist accounts of the state violence and terror, and they denied claims by eyewitnesses to the amount and intensity of violent acts by police officers against unarmed participants in the demonstration. Partly as a result of these forms of state censorship and silence, many of those living in France and elsewhere did not learn of the violent attacks against Algerians in October 1961 until years later, if at all. In conversations with residents of Paris in recent years I have found that most of these acquaintances have heard of the events involved, and they understand that some thirty or fifty persons died the night of 17 October 1961; many did not know that two hundred or more were killed. I learned of the violence only a few years ago. Many participants in the demonstrations have tended not to talk much about those painful times and memories, including with their children or grandchildren. *Li fat met* goes a Kabyle expression: "The past is dead." "One doesn't speak of painful things."[38]

In general, there has been a kind of collective amnesia or aphasia around the events of Paris 1961; for many, it has been difficult to bring to mind, or talk about, what took place in those days, as well as France's colonial conquest and domination of Algeria and the Algerian war of independence.[39] Only from the late 1990s on have there been concerted efforts to delineate a clear historical record of what took place in October 1961, and to establish forms of collective memory around the state violence involved and the resulting deaths, injuries, and trauma. The events of the late 1950s and early 1960s in Paris, and 17 October 1961, specifically—that date lingers as a *cicatrice* in time and memory—now stand as lasting wounds in the memories and political terrains of France, particularly among Algerians living in or around Paris, in Algeria, and elsewhere.

This is one of the wounds that Khalil had in mind when speaking of life in north Paris. Just when it looks like this deep laceration is starting to heal over, one is cut anew. New abrasions repeatedly inscribe and incise past harms in bodies, minds, and in spaces of memory and oblivion.

The streets and quays around boulevard Saint-Michel, and the bridge by that name, were one of the flashpoints of violent clashes between protestors

FIGURE 38. Antiriot police, rue des Trois Bornes. March 2020. Photo by K. H.

and police in 1961. Police officers chased protestors who arrived in the streets there and beat them mercilessly with their clubs. Some demonstrators were shot. Others were thrown into the Seine, alive or dead, their lives lost to its waters. *"Ici on noie les Algériens,"* was a critical graffiti claim painted the night of 5 November 1961 by antiwar activists on the side wall of the quai Conti, photographed by a photojournalist, and then erased by workers of the préfecture de Police: "Here we drown Algerians."[40] For a number of years now, on each October 17th, there have been memorial gatherings at the pont Saint-Michel, to acknowledge and remember the losses of life there. And so when it was decided in 2000, after heated debates in the Paris City Council (Conseil de Paris), that a commemorative plaque should be placed in the center of Paris, in memory of the bloody repression, it made sense that the pont Saint-Michel, spanning the waters of the Seine, would be a good location for it. Fittingly, perhaps, either by design or circumstance, the plaque faces toward the imposing buildings that house the préfecture de Police.

The plaque was unveiled on 17 October 2001, with no government members attending in official capacity. The plaque signified the first "physical inscription of October 1961 within public memory in France."[41] Notably, in the charged, "deliberately vague" words inscribed on the plaque, there is no mention of the main actors responsible for the bloody repression of the peaceful demonstration on 17 October: the Paris police. A statement like that would have been too controversial and inflammatory for the heart of the Republic. In this particular sign of collective memory the agents of the violence go unmentioned. That omission nicks at the lives and consciousnesses of those who recall the violence in direct or indirect ways.[42]

The plaque is set not on the bridge itself but rather on a wall bordering a walkway and, past that, a roadway, a few meters from the start of the bridge. The wall is around a meter high, which means that the plaque, set just below the top of the wall, is not at eye-level; the words are not easily spotted or read. Before I knew of its existence, I must have walked past the plaque numerous times without noticing what was inscribed. I imagine that most others do the same. The plaque is at once of symbolic and political significance and an overlooked marker. It's there, in place and time, and in a way it's not there. The memorial's often unnoticed appearance reflects the play of recognition and oblivion, wounding and the denial of wounding, claims and counter-claims, collective amnesia and anamnesis associated with memories of 17 October and the harsh events that date signifies.

Within the geographical and legal limits of Paris, the commemorative plaque is one of the few material markers that directly and tangibly refer to the state violence against Algerians during the years of French control of Algeria. Most traces of the violence of those times are oblique and diffuse, found within scant marks in the city, or in texts and images, or in the bodies and minds of those living since then. There is a diffuseness to the memories, which are altogether complicated and painful to those involved.

*All of the traces are missing now.* I wrote these words, neither here nor there, later that day while seated in a café down the road. There are so few tangible marks anywhere in the city of the violence against Algerians from that time or other times. There is nothing by the Seine, or the canals. Just a few commemorative plaques in and outside the city. It's not that there were many marks to begin with and then they were effaced. The traces were never there. Just a few marks of blood, or a handful of photographs, film clips, so little was in place, the injured and killed had no time or opportunity to leave marks behind. Few words or images were left for others to encounter and perceive. What has remained are dull, vague placements in a general terrain of death and wounding; a thin opacity of memory, absence, nonappearance.

These nonqualities within a scene of noninscription appeared to mark "a past which has never been present."[43] The remnant features of this absent past, related to a complex field of geographical markers, remnant traces and effacements, reflected, in vague, obscure ways, events that have become relatively invisible and intangible through erosive forces of time, and, likewise, within the same grain of entropic time, events rendered "unvisible" by way of political forces of erasure and occlusion.[44]

At most there was the dull, dim specter of the absence of traces. It was all less than spectral. Perhaps for others the place would invoke a tangible haunting, especially for anyone still alive who could recall the dark violence of that night. For me, there was no sense of ghosts about or restless revenants from a troubled past. I imagined the cries and discomfort of men and women in those anguished days, and I fantastically envisioned bodies tossed into the Seine. Viscerally I sensed nothing of the sort. I perceived nothing but a "ghostless present."[45] This, in itself, is kind of eerie, uncanny, and haunting.

As I walked along a bridge that spanned the Seine I was struck by the incongruity of two disparate perceptions. One was the troubling awareness that this was a site of violence and harm sixty years earlier. The other was that this was a popular site of urban life and leisure pleasures. It's a weird sensation to take in, at once, these two impressions, which sear the flesh of a porous body.

PALIMPSEST OF VIOLENCE

To write is perhaps to bring to the surface something like absent meaning.

MAURICE BLANCHOT,
*Writing of the Disaster*

*Sunday, 17 July 2019*

This is how I perceive Paris these days, specters or not. I see the city in different ways now, especially since meeting Khalil and walking with him through neighborhoods in *Paris nord* and regrafting wounds incised there. Working alongside Khalil has meant a transformative experience on my part, a change of life and becoming in terms at once personal and political. Through our reciprocal engagements I have come to think otherwise about the past and the present, and the future as well.[46] This reperception and resignification of Paris comes with an emergent understanding of myriad forces of violence, wounding, and connection. In her essay "Poetry Is Not a Luxury," Audre Lorde writes, "The quality of light by which we scrutinize our lives has direct bearing upon the product which we live, and upon the changes which we hope to bring about through these lives."[47] The quality of light that elucidates my thought and writing is different than before; the light refracts dissimilarly, and I scrutinize another Paris.

I came upon traces of the 2015 attacks in Paris and became immersed in the tangled matter and fraught atmospherics of what took place within the strands of a critical phenomenology of violence and its effects. This was an effort, a struggle, in sense-making. It was as though I was sorting through shards of broken glass, trying to grasp their reflective surfaces and sharp edges, how they had cut. In writing, I was as if *within the phenomena itself.* The intimacy of that phenomena held nervous intrigues, lasting aporias, dangerous, phantasmal possibilities, and haunting revenants, the likes of which spawned compulsive tracts of writing. I think as well that my thoughts and observations were tied to certain "mainstream" perspectives on Paris and the threat and actuality of violent events. Perhaps it's the case that there were certain occlusions to my thought, categories of thought and ways of knowing and not knowing—at once personal and cultural, political and ideological— that limited my ability to grasp certain histories and contemporary forms of violence and hardship within complex entanglements of past and present. In reading through the earlier texts of mine in this book, I now find that a necessary coefficient is missing from the writing—the coefficient of state violence. In time, I stepped away from the shattered glass and inbent phenomenology and opened up toward other political histories of the city. I now have in mind, in unsettled ways, untold histories of violence in Africa, Europe, the Middle East, and elsewhere. With this, the attacks of November 2015 appear in a different light. Other specters haunt the city. While there is great value in drawing upon a critical phenomenology of violence and its traces, one needs to go beyond such an approach and track the political violence that shades into sensoria. Any effort in a phenomenological anthropology of violence has to proceed in intricate relation with historiographies of violence, so as to take into account complex histories of colonialism, state domination and policing, and the aftereffects of assault, wounding, damage, and harm.

Paris is an apparition of beauty ghosted by past horrors. The glinting lilt of the Seine admits to injured bodies once immersed in its murky waters. Canal Saint-Martin appears calm and peaceful most days, yet corpses were dredged from its locks in the summer of '61. The city's boulevards and

FIGURE 39. Demonstration in support of Adama Traoré's family, avenue de la Porte de Clichy, June 2020. Photo by K. H.

side streets hold faint nebulous traces of torture rooms, detention centers, beatings and deaths, and the absence of such traces. Alongside any luminous boulevard there is the shadow of colonial exploitation and murderous arrogance. When in Paris, while dining at a café or riding the metro, I look at those around me and wonder what their histories are—if they carry the wounding trace of French colonialism, or if their families are of *pied noir* descent and had to leave their "homeland" in Algeria, or if their parents and grandparents were soldiers stationed in *le département français d'Algérie* during the *événements* there. What do they know of, and what do they wish to forget? The city's inhabitants are, themselves, traces of violence.

"The city of a thousand novels," wrote Balzac.[48] And ten thousand histories of violence. André Breton's *Nadja* speaks to this tracework of violence in moments when the narrator writes of the uncommon sensibilities of the novel's namesake, Nadja: "She is disturbed by the thought of what has already occurred in this square and will occur here in the future. Where only two or three couples are at this moment fading into darkness, she seems to see a crowd. 'And the dead, the dead!'"[49] Cuts and scars for centuries now; from the tyrannies of kings to the revolution's reign of terror to the barricades and bloody battles of the Commune of 1871; the German occupation and the

French resistance and fraught collaborations of World War II and the deportation and killing of Jews and many others; the lesions of colonialism and state and police violence against Algerians in Paris and its *bidonvilles* in the late 1950s and early 1960s; the violent police oppression of the peaceful demonstrations on the night of 17 October 1961; Charonne, 1962; May, 1968; the deaths of young men in the *banlieues* in 2005 and 2007 and the resulting "riots"; the *attentats* in 2015; anti-Semitic actions and attacks; all this has taken place within a labyrinth of lines crossing and recrossing one another amidst processes of wounding, scarring, dissolution, disappearance; memory and memorialization; forgetting, dissimulation, erasure and effacement; denial and contestation; grief and mourning, specters and hauntings. Cutting through this brecciated terrain of life-death are forces of fear, suspicion, vigilance, anxiety, sorrow, anger, rage, hatred, grief, care, concern, enmity, and amity. The political and commemorative work of the French state tends to highlight some marks while occluding others. Others in turn try to inscribe alternate histories into the textures of the city, and so create counterarchives of the city's histories, lives, deaths, and voices.

The violent attacks in Paris in November 2015 have emerged as one trace history within this larger palimpsest of scars and abrasions. The violence is tied to other histories in indirect, crosscutting ways. The attacks were not a direct and singular result of French colonialism or imperialist formations; myriad forces and motivations were, and are, at work. But the violence of that night and its aftermath should be understood within this vaster *névralgique* of intercutting life and death. As Khalil Habrih rightly makes clear, any considerations of the violence that night should be thought of in relation to myriad forms of state and societal violence taking place in the metropolis and elsewhere. All this needs to be retraced otherwise.

Through time a body, his, hers, yours, mine, is cut anew—and one writes and acts anew.

Other marks erode in space and time. The other day I found myself near the canal. I came to Le Carillon. The place was quiet, within a return to a semblance of the everyday. A few people were inside, standing by the bar, others seated on the terrace. I walked past the entrance and looked at the wall toward the left. There was no apparent trace of the words *NE PAS ARCHIVER,* once inscribed in dense black ink.

*Do not archive.*

As if those words had never been there, at all.

*R. D.*

INTERRUPTION: PARIS IS AN
APPARITION, SHARING VISIONS

*Wednesday, 8 May 2019*

On a gray and stiff October 2017 afternoon, Robert Desjarlais and I sat in the backroom of a bistro on rue Ordener. As we exchanged notes, reading materials, and photography, we began to wonder what the concepts of traces and specters could help uncover in contexts such as deadly police encounters. As we spoke, I quickly wrote down names on a page Robert had neatly ripped from his notebook. I remained elusive, though, and only gave the paper as such, with little more information: a testament to my will to share and participate in the way Robert constructed his object of study; a point of departure for him to grapple with these spectral traces within his own terms. As I look back on this, I understand my urge to write as a way to conjure up particular ghosts, ones who would tell their own particular stories on the palimpsest of violence that Robert had begun to put into writing.

Last in this list is Tarek Belgacem. I added the name of his father and the indication of an article to read to learn more about the context of his death. On 7 January 2016, Tarek Belgacem, a twenty-five-year-old undocumented Tunisian man, was shot and killed by police officers of the Goutte d'Or precinct. The neighborhood was quickly put on lockdown, and the young man was portrayed as a terrorist in the national media. Soldiers of Opération Sentinelle were on the roofs of rue de la Goutte d'Or and rue Caplat, snipers pointed to the streets. Police officers sealed off the neighborhood, directing people back into their buildings, denizens unable to walk into the neighborhood, shop owners pulling down their metal curtains. Then minister of the interior Bernard Cazeneuve was on the scene, patrolling with soldiers and police officers. By nightfall the whole apparatus had left; there remained the usual police patrols, sirens, and blue lights passing to and fro.

Within hours an eerie stillness settled on the streets of Barbès and Château Rouge. People whispered. *Have you heard?* Another Arab man shot by the police. Then minister of justice Christiane Taubira declared that the man shot did not have the profile of a terrorist of the organization known as the "Islamic State," case closed. His father, Taoufik Belgacem, an olive and almond farmer of central Tunisia, pleaded with the French media: "My son was not a terrorist." In fact, as the story of his life and his migratory path was reconstituted by journalists, Tarek Belgacem appeared as a simple *harrag:* a

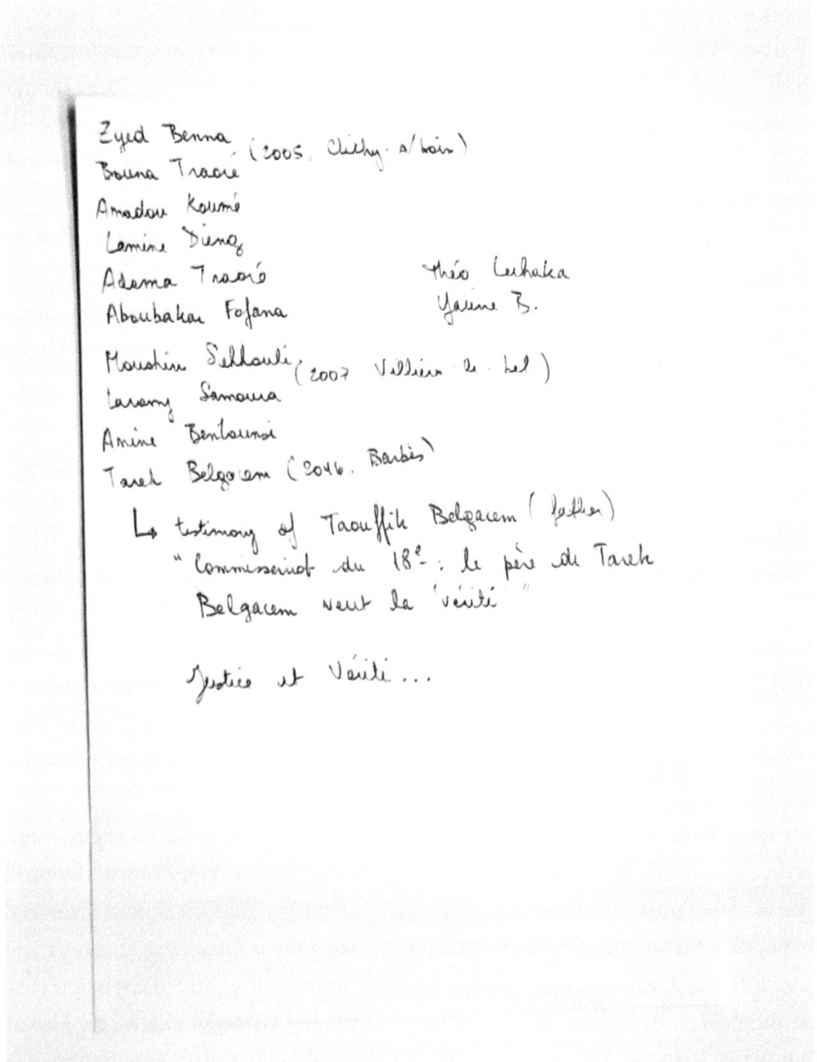

Zyed Benna (2005, Clichy-s/bois)
Bouna Traoré
Amadou Koumé
Lamine Dieng
Adama Traoré          Théo Luhaka
Aboubakar Fofana      Yacine B.

Mouhsin Sellouli (2007 Villiers-le-bel)
Larami Samoura
Amine Bentounsi
Tarek Belgacem (2016. Barbès)
  └ testimony of Taouffik Belgacem (father)
    "Commissariat du 18e : le père de Tarek
      Belgacem veut la 'vérité'"

    Justice et Vérité...

FIGURE 40. List of persons killed or seriously injured by the French police, October 2017. Photo by R. D.

young man who had dreamed of a better, more prosperous, future in Europe, embarking on a makeshift boat to France. He was a young man who had been stopped, frisked, and arrested, and whose existence in the clandestinity of the Schengen space had led him to the detention centers and police precincts of Germany, Italy, Luxembourg, and France.[50] "A delinquent," his father said to *Libération* journalists. "Sure, I can accept that, but not a terrorist."[51]

A year and a half later, in July 2017, as I interviewed a shop owner in Barbès, the death of Tarek Belgacem resurfaced. As we began speaking about police brutality and killings in the neighborhood, Rachid, the shop owner, alluded to the death that had taken place a year prior. I asked what the police had told him that day. Rachid hesitated. He mentioned the body, the blood, which had been left there for days. He hesitated again.

"They just told me to close the shop and leave. I saw the body, like that on the ground. And the police were telling people to leave. But I don't want to get into these things, I don't want any problems. I don't know if he was a terrorist or if this was a police blunder. I don't know, and I don't want to know, I don't want any problems. You know . . . [pause] No, I don't want any problems. I don't have an opinion and I don't want to know."

Rachid did not want to speak on the matter. And in fact, few in the neighborhood dared to speak about it in the framework of my ethnography. Tarek Belgacem's dead body, the Opération Sentinelle soldiers, the difficult dissociation of rumor and truth, haunted our interactions that day. These ghosts, however, were not necessarily *there*. They had an intangible quality to them, until they resurfaced in the present. Less than spectral, they nonetheless thickened the air around us. Rachid, through his hesitations and silence, illustrated the thickness this trace left in and between us: intangible and yet present enough that I quickly wrapped up our conversation and thanked him for his time. To which he responded with gratitude.

The metaphors of specters, haunting, and traces help us to experiment with the margins of semantic availability, as sociologist Avery Gordon would put it. They push us—and our perceptive, affective, analytical, and sensorial capacities—to engage with immaterial materiality. Thinking through the metaphor of haunting is helpful in making sense of the multidimensionality of memories and histories of violence. Thinking through the metaphor of haunting helps us to grapple with the multiple layers that constitutes the palimpsest of violence of the Parisian cityscape. If Tarek Belgacem's exposed dead body had disappeared, the tensions his death had traced within the streets of the Goutte d'Or nonetheless subsisted in a shopkeeper's reluctance to further disclose his thoughts on the matter. This was a trace, in the form of an absence and a silence. These eerie absences are also material, in the sense that they are spatialized and embodied.

Throughout the pages of this book one gets a sense that traces can be found in the form of engravings and graffiti, spontaneous memorials, and in the folds of state archives. But traces are also found in the wake of traumatic events, within the bodies and corporeal dispositions of those who internalize and incorporate them. Traces move from bodies to spaces, and conversely. Individual and collective traumatic events, such as daily occurrences of police violence and the occasional riots and other forms of resistance that take place in France, affect urban space. They change the way administrative and social rhythms interact and shape the city.

On 27 October 2005, in the town of Clichy-sous-Bois (Seine-Saint-Denis, 93), three adolescents, Muhittin Altan (fifteen), Zyed Benna (seventeen), and Bouna Traoré (fifteen), were chased by police officers who were investigating a burglary in the neighboring town of Livry-Gargan. The teenagers, coming home after soccer practice, ran and hid in an electrical substation, next to a live electrical wire. Zyed and Bouna died, Muhittin survived. In the days that followed, demonstrations were organized and teenagers confronted police during nightly riots. Scores of militarized police patrolled during the day while silent demonstrators marched, dressed in white in a sign of mourning. Helicopters flew over at night, shining their lights in the streets and on building façades, while mediators from the neighborhoods walked between rioters and police lines in attempts to negotiate.[52] On 30 October 2005, as the community observed the Taraweeh evening prayer, police shot tear gas canisters at the Bilal Mosque of Clichy-sous-Bois. The demonstrations and riots quickly spread across France's social housing projects. Despite being brief—a few weeks in October and November 2005—the riots of 2005 left their mark on the French Republican polity. On 8 November 2005 the state of emergency was declared and applied in twenty cities across France.

Shortly after, new repressive security laws were passed and eventually centralized in the Code of Homeland Security (Code de la sécurité intérieure), furthering the police's means in technologies and prerogative to occupy public space. Years later, there is little left of the events as such. Traces of violence remain lodged in the tenuous space between individual and collective subjectivities and the arkhē, the state; that is, the laws, decrees, and administrations that structure space and memorialize particular phenomena. The death of children in the context of police surveillance, followed by the revolts, the police, and penal repression, and the stigmatizing media representation participated in the production of a generation of politically conscious subjects.

Saturday, 11 February 2017. A demonstration has been organized in front of the High Court in Bobigny (Seine-Saint-Denis, 93) in reaction to police officers' sexual assault of Théo Luhaka, a young man resident of the housing project la Rose-des-Vents in Aulnay-sous-Bois (93). Several thousand people

FIGURE 41. Young men and women protesting police misconduct in February 2017 in front of the Bobigny High Court, December 2020. Sketch by K. H.

have congregated on the lawn of the tribunal, hidden behind social housing projects and overlooked by bridges that extend out of the surrounding esplanades and buildings. Members of various antiracial profiling collectives, antiracist organizations, members of "Truth and Justice" collectives, and relatives of victims of police brutality are invited to speak to the crowd. Some evoke the histories of immigration and colonization, while others speak on the omnipresence of police patrols in social housing projects and the routinized forms of sexual and racial humiliation young Black and Arab men experience at the hands of the police. The crowd responds with cries, applause, and chants, agreeing with the speakers in a mixture of anger and sadness.

A picture taken that day shows a young Black man holding a French flag in front of him, on which the penal definition of rape has been written. Around the young man, whose face seems mournful as he looks down, young women chant with their arms raised and faces open to the sky. Within this crowd, a new generation grapples with the traces left by past and contemporary violent phenomena. As the speeches are coming to a close, a confrontation with police stationed at the entrance of the court starts. Children, none older than twelve, and police officers stand off on the bridge leading to the tribunal. A speaker calls for everyone to remain calm; another declares the end of the demonstration. The crowd disperses. Some hurriedly leave to catch a metro back to Paris, others begin to demonstrate in the nearby streets. Police officers retreat from the streets and perch themselves on the bridges linking buildings to esplanades, shooting rubber bullets and tear-gas pallets down into the street, apparently aiming at protestors. Shop keepers open their doors one last time, urging bystanders to come in or run away, before sealing their storefront shut. Residents open the backdoors of their buildings, letting people run in and find shelter.

Such epiphenomena leave traces, surely, but they are nonetheless difficult to convey. One would have to be there. One would have to have been there during the event itself, perhaps. But one would also have to be there *now*, to look for particular traces of these events and listen in on life knowingly. One would have to stand within that particular space, amidst the Brutalist architecture of social housing projects and the administrative buildings of the Paris suburbs. The smoke of tear gas, the sound of glass shattering, wounded bodies, cars set on fire, the echoes of police weapons. One would have to be there, to deliberately look for particular ghosts so that place and people may tell their particular stories.

After our first encounters, Robert began to see the streets of Paris differently. It was not necessarily that he had integrated my perspectives into his vision. Rather, he began to sharpen his own gaze in order to perceive what initially appeared to him as nonvisible. In looking for traces of the violence of 17 October 1961, Robert found that the walls no longer had stories to tell, or spontaneous memorials to present for the passer-by. The traces of 17 October, like the traces of police roundups and lockdowns of whole neighborhoods, escape perception; they escape our ability to write and speak. They nonetheless continue to haunt those subjectivities and spatialities which carry them, however silently, unknowingly. The memorial of the 1961 massacre on the pont Saint-Michel, like the memorials dispersed throughout Paris indicating the police roundups of Jewish children in 1942 and 1943, do not convey memory of these events as such. Rather, they are tangible markers of our ability to forget and live on.

In attempting to trace out what appears as "less than spectral," we are forced to contend with the lived materialities of these events: they appear as absent until something or someone (re-)iterates their ubiquity. The relationship Robert Desjarlais and I nurtured relies in part on this sort of copresence; it is much easier to convey one's sensibility of a given space when both stand within that space and contemplate it together. And it was in these attempts to convey our distinct sensibilities that Robert and I began to collaborate.

Our collaboration initially consisted of conversations that we had over email exchanges or as we met in person in Paris. At the time, I navigated Parisian academia with some difficulty and I found Robert's will to understand my perspective refreshing. This did not come without additional self-questioning. Who was I to intervene in a text? Did I represent a collective voice? Was Robert in control of the terms of our relationship? Looking back on my hesitations and unease, I think I was concerned with two things.

One was the symbolic position I would be given within Robert's work. I did not want to be an informant or a consultant. I was wary of becoming a peculiar and lonely voice among ghosts; one that claimed to bring Others to the table. I did not want to find myself becoming "his native," captured in writing as an object of anthropological taxidermy.[53] The other concern was that I was still learning and I could see my perceptions, analyses, and sensibilities evolve. This difficulty resonated through my writing and my subjective experience of authorship.

Finding some sort of stability in my position vis-à-vis Robert did not rely on my ability to write, however. It was only when he encouraged me to pursue doctoral studies in North America that our collaboration truly began. Collaborative research thus starts outside the text, outside the concepts and topic at hand; our collaboration finds its first iteration in the ethical gesture of a professor who, rather than pursue the illusion of textual equality, acted in a way that offered the institutional conditions for my writing to be read *with* his, and conversely.

Collaborative ethnography has long been a topic of discussion in anthropology, as well as for feminist scholars of all fields. In anthropology, collaboration works hand in hand with the researcher's reflexivity and offers a vocabulary (if not a comprehensive method) to frame the deliberate construction of an ethical relationship between the researcher and the participants of fieldwork. Anthropologist Glen D. Hinson writes that "true collaboration entails a sharing of authority and a sharing of visions."[54] One could think here of the work of James Spradley on the "native point of view" of unhousedness and incarceration in Seattle's Skid Road.[55] Or of Mitchell Duneier's work on Black masculinities in *Slim's Table*.[56] One could think here of Paul Rabinow's work on the making of the modern in France and Morocco.[57] All of these authors' critiques were fundamentally reliant on the "emic" categories and experiences of their interlocutors. The sharing of authority and visions is true insofar as the author's initial conception of the object has been considerably altered by participants' own perceptions, experiences, and spontaneous analyses. This, I find, is close to the way I have conceived of my relationship with the participants of my fieldwork. But I would not so easily define it as "collaboration"; it would be misleading to claim that I shared authority and visions with the interlocutors in my fieldwork.[58] Rather, I urged them to partake in the analysis with me, to apply a form of "participant objectivation," wherein the sting of analysis was turned back onto the operations of research rather than solely on the social-life-turned-object-of-study.[59]

The intellectual relationship Robert and I have built over the past few years works as a mutual invitation to reconsider our perspectives and methodologies.[60] As I applied the instruments of critical phenomenology in my research, I centered my own corporeality and documented space as it extended or limited my body and mobility. This worked as a radical shift for me, as I was afforded the possibility to conceive of phenomena from my own subject position and could use my body as a topic of study to understand how racialization imposes itself on the people it racializes. This allowed me to distance myself from the biases and stereotypes of French scholarship on young men in social housing projects, on immigration, security, and Islam. I could bypass the cultural routes through which such racist imaginaries circulate. But I erroneously conceived of the critical nature of my interruptions as reliant on some sort of embodied epistemology that stretched from my subject position to some sort of Algerian experience of colonial displacement. Erroneous, I note, for I do not speak from a "privileged standpoint" and I derive no critical truth from being more or less embedded in the topic at hand. All I could do was suggest a different perspective. Different from Robert's intellectual standpoint and subject position. Different from French academic biases. Different, indeed, but not all encompassing. In other words, my contribution is situated, necessarily partial and incomplete. And our collaboration is one that rests on sharing such partial and incomplete visions. We peered at the same city, through distinct perceptions, methodologies, and historicities. We progressively shifted one another's certainties.

American anthropologist Faye Ginsburg suggests that such collaborative and comparative shifts be understood as a "parallax effect." This "occurs when a change in the position of the observer creates the illusion that an object has been displaced or moved. . . . In optics, the small parallax created by the slightly different angles of vision of each eye enables us to judge distance accurately and see in three dimensions."[61] Much of the collaboration articulated through these pages relied on such a parallax effect. As our understanding of the palimpsestic nature of violence in Paris emerged, renewed, more accurate and more uncertain, we shared visions.

Our collaborative work together has led to other developments. The reflexive practice I tried to develop during my fieldwork and collaboration with Robert Desjarlais eventually led me to an impasse: although I had gotten training in sociology for years, I had felt and continued to feel constrained by the disciplinary vernaculars of sociology. Anthropology, as Robert Desjarlais introduced me to it, has been a generative space for us to meet. Part of my engagements with Robert took on a different dimension as I met anthropologists in North America. I decided to actualize my de facto positioning and to transfer from sociology to doctoral studies in anthropology.

K. H.

---

# EIGHT

# *The histories of these wounds*

In other words, our actions never cease to haunt us.

FRANTZ FANON,
*The Wretched of the Earth*

## A CONFIGURATION OF VIOLENCE

*Monday, 28 September 2020*

When we met, Robert's initial inquiry into the traces of violence around sites of memory had progressively moved toward broader questions on the nature of collective memory. It was by following traces of the *attentats* well into the state production of archived material that Robert began identifying mechanisms of production in the national collective memory of the attacks. Through the process of archiving memorials, state and national culture articulate a synthetic representation of scattered experiences of the trauma of the attacks. Conversely, the Republican commemorations of the attacks constitute the sociopolitical translation of that trauma into an object of national belonging.

This rigorous process of classification and *archivage* of memorials poses the question: who and what does not get consecrated in official *plaques*? And conversely, who and what comes to be represented and treated as a threat to the memorialized national order? These questions invoke a play on representations and collective imaginaries. They also point to actual practices of grief, and how suspicion and vigilance suffused the aftermath of the attacks.

After each terrorist attack, the biographies of the attackers are taken as evidence of collective responsibility. National grief interlocks with vigilance and suspicion, as French Muslim men and women, of North or West African descent, are drawn into a broad cultural and territorial portrait of the "terrorist threat." The exclusionary gesture held within the memorialization of the attacks has practical ramifications in the lives of those who are unjustly represented as threats. It prohibits them from participating in collective grief, as they are required to adhere to certain practices to avoid suspicion.[1] They also come to be at the center of the state's enactment of antiterrorism protocols as the state of emergency collapses into existing administrative categories and legal protocols. The repression of terrorism then takes the shape of stop-and-frisk, home raids, surveillance, house arrests, and detention, with these state capacities concentrated in neighborhoods that, like the Goutte d'Or, make up the preexisting landscape of policing, incarceration, and immigration control.

In reiterating the borders of the nation, the production of state-centered collective memory produces otherness as the nonparticipation in national grief. As otherness becomes an object of intervention onto which the state enacts practices of surveillance, policing, and detainment—in other words, practices of wounding—"we" come to form a community of experience. If I found myself to be more thoroughly perceived as a young Algerian man, it was in institutional settings, with welfare, university, and police officials, that I was most effectively assigned to a spatial and racial category. I found myself belonging to a community of experience that tended to different wounds. I experienced grief differently, not because of cultural specificities necessarily, but rather because I experienced political violence differently. I experienced the attacks along with the collective punishment that antiterrorism put into practice. Allegiance to the Republic did not make sense precisely because it needed to enact collective punishment in order to produce the collectivity against which it fought. I found myself, then, not between enemy lines, but within a vast and complex configuration of political violence.

I take the concept of configuration from the work of German sociologist Norbert Elias, who used it to conceptualize society as a system of interdependent relationships between social actors. A configuration can be understood as a snapshot of a given social context; it highlights the interdependence of antagonistic or otherwise hierarchized subject positions and also accounts for individual dispositions and strategies. Elias applied the notion of configuration to his sociological history of "civilization." He argued, among other things, that the process of state formation in Europe had resulted in a pacified society wherein individuals act conscientiously and with self-control.[2] I would like to reorient the concept of configuration by focusing on the palimpsest of violence Robert Desjarlais and I have described through our ethnographies of Paris.

Civilization, in the words of poet and Martiniquais statesman Aimé Césaire, is no more than a sophisticated word for industrial scales of brutality (*ensauvagement*).[3] If we are to take seriously the process of state formation and of colonial expansion as interdependent, it seems illusory to remain attached to a conception of civilization grounded in notions of legitimate violence and self-control. Indeed, the institutions that emerged out of European modernity consecrated and normalized the brutality of industry and colony. I use the concept of configuration, then, to inform an understanding of political violence as constitutive of our context.[4]

Violence did not begin with the attackers' assault rifles in January and November 2015. Nor are the wounds limited to those who were memorialized in the archives. The contexts of our wounding—the weapons, the perpetrators, the victims—are much broader than the state production of collective memory indicates.

Looking at the trajectories of the objects used in the attacks illustrates how political violence circulates between interdependent actors that are generally represented as fundamentally antagonistic. The weapons that the Kouachi brothers and Amedy Koulibaly used in the January 2015 attacks were sold to them by Claude Hermant, a neo-Nazi organizer based in Lille. Upon his arrest, Hermant explained that he had been working as an "infiltrator" and police informant. Since the early 2000s, Hermant had been working with customs, smuggling weapons and explosives under operations overseen by the police and known as "controlled deliveries" (*livraisons contrôlées*). The weapons were generally brought in from Eastern Europe and the Balkans. Once in France, Hermant reactivated the shotguns, handguns, and automatic rifles and readied them for sale. The young men and women who are indeed caught up in organizations that practice political violence and produce collective trauma are in the midst of processes that surpass them and involve questions of war and sovereignty.

It should go without saying, however, that pointing to the larger historical context and political structures that frame the attacks does not absolve the attackers of their responsibility—a responsibility they had to themselves, to their families, to the spaces where they grew up, and to the people and places that saw them die and take others with them.

Two examples come to mind: one is fictional, and lives through the narration of Algerian author Yasmina Khadra; the other relates to Khaled Kelkal, a young man whose involvement in terrorist attacks in the 1990s coincided with the formal beginning of the antiterrorist Vigipirate plan. Two other examples serve as a historical and textual background: Albert Camus's *The Stranger* and his protagonist Meursault, and Kamel Daoud's 2013 novel *The Meursault Investigation*.

Khaled Kelkal was born 1971 in Mostaganem, Algeria. He emigrated with his mother to Vaulx-en-Velin, near Lyon, in 1973, to live with his father, a factory worker. A smart young man, Kelkal was admitted into the chemistry concentration of a Lyon high school, where he felt out of place, singled out as the only "Arab," an exception to social and ethnic segregation. He continued attending classes but quickly lost interest, feeling alienated from his peers. He wandered around his neighborhood, "zoning around," stealing here and there. In 1990, he was arrested for his alleged complicity in a series of burglaries and released on probation. His criminal charges forced him to drop out of high school. The following year, in 1991, he was sentenced to three years in prison—a sentence that was extended to four years after the state appealed the decision later that same year. While in jail, Khaled Kelkal—who had just turned twenty years old—decided to put his time to generative use: he learned Arabic, began reading the Qur'an, and imagined a family life, marriage, and children after his time in prison.

Despite being acculturated and de facto sociologically French, Kelkal was assigned to a subject position of racial otherness. This exacerbated more fundamental "gaps" he felt within himself, such as his inability to speak Arabic or Algerian Darija, his ignorance of religious practices, or the sense of rupture that exile and immigration procure. Kelkal was "an Arab," but only in the eyes of the French. Incarceration enabled Kelkal's resubjectivation and the exploration of his personhood. The practice of self he developed, however, remained rooted in a form of symbolic relegitimization of his personhood as it appeared to and had been degraded by the phantasmagorias of metropolitan racism. The beauty of Muslim spirituality served the subjective process of gratification and sublimation of wounds rather than an effort of reeducation in collective life, familial or otherwise. In effect, in 1993, after being released on parole, Kelkal became involved with the factions at war in Algeria.[5]

The turn to violence and the participation in the Algerian civil war introduced a rupture within Kelkal's biography. This rupture from familial and collective understandings of self and spirituality paradoxically sealed together distinct processes of racialization, its effects on identity-formation, and subsequent political conversion and action. In that sense, Khaled Kelkal's profile as a French-Algerian youth, living in the interstices of social ascension and carceral spaces, is at odds with the subjective and sociopolitical machinations that propelled him to become the face of homegrown terrorism.[6]

In September 1995, Khaled Kelkal was shot dead in the woodlands near Lyon, some ten miles away from the social housing blocks where he grew up.

Journalists from various television channels had tagged along with the gendarmerie in their deadly chase. On one of the recordings, an officer can be heard yelling, "Finish him, finish him!" as Kelkal lays on the ground, bleeding, his handgun still pointed toward the soldiers that surround him.[7]

In his 2018 novel *Khalil,* Yasmina Khadra offers a narrative that allows us to look into the subjective and affective conflicts that may have coursed through Khaled Kelkal during the last months of his life. With *Khalil,* Khadra explores the inner conflicts that punctuate the life of a young Moroccan man raised in Molenbeek, in the northwest of Brussels. The novel opens on 13 November 2015, as Khalil begins his journey to Paris. When the bomb he had strapped around his chest fails to detonate, thus begins the narration of his personal battle against himself and the world that surrounds him. Forced into hiding, witnessing the onslaught of police operations against Muslims, Khalil reconsiders his choices, commitment, and the spiritual grounding of his political action.

Caught by the beauty of Islam, in which his mentors draped their political project, Khalil had found an endless aesthetic therapy to qualm the ugliness of his life in his housing project. Thinking of one of his friends and mentors, Lyès, he remembers: "He had awoken my senses to my unspeakable internal beauties and had turned me into an enlightened being."[8] His dogged life, his *chienne de vie,* was in the past. But in doing so, Khalil—whose name, in Islam, refers to the friendship between God and the prophets—had used the drapes of inner beauty to build a path toward political violence and his own death.

His family—specifically, his sister Zahra—persisted, tracing their own paths away from self-destruction, and urging him to do so as well. Khadra's work, through its exploration of Khalil's subjectivity, engages with the tensions between freedom and predetermination. What place is there for free will when subject positions are historically constituted? When the sociopolitical positions offered to us are not entirely of our own making? The question here relates to our own personal struggles with life, as we navigate a world we mostly inherit. But it also brings us back to fundamental questions of sociology: the tension between one's individual subjectivity and body and the social structures that press and impress themselves on that individuality. In other words, *Khalil* can be read as the story of one young man's willpower and struggle to escape the conceptual, spiritual, and material prisons we both inherit and enclose ourselves within.

While it is true that we all inherit, in one way or another, the contemporary legacies of past violence, it would be an exaggeration—and a politically dangerous exaggeration at that—to claim that we resort to political violence as a consequence of that inheritance. The violence of colonial conquest haunts the present, from the dynamics of immigrant families to the halls of presidential palaces. But the motivations of young Europeans to take up arms, to kill, and to die in a spectacle of phantasmagoria cannot be reduced to the ghosts that haunt them. This, I find, is clear in Yasmina Khadra's writing. Khalil is not a sublime subject nor does he work toward his own redemption. He is given countless opportunities to stop, to turn to his family, to turn to a collective form of spirituality, to translate his anger and will into something other than death, but still, he chooses not to.

A penchant for killing is nurtured by one's inscription in a configuration of violence; the act of killing relies on one's decision to pull the trigger. In *The Stranger*, Camus's protagonist Meursault is not a subaltern subject: he lives as a settler in French Algeria, benefitting from all the comfort that colonial privilege allows for. And yet, he is haunted by his context, embattled with deeply buried demons. Meursault does not grieve his mother's death. He feels jealousy at times, but does not love. He is a man whose refusal to show empathy for his deceased mother, to ask for forgiveness after having murdered an anonymous Arab, erodes the stability of a society rotten with the very same emptiness that Meursault dares present publicly for the world to see. His mother's death and the murder of a nameless native highlight the absurdity of his existence: an absence of meaning lodged deep within the configuration of violence that made up French Algeria.

Set in context, the absurd gestures of Meursault—to consume without love, to kill without passion or regret, to live without meaning—are all elements of the configuration of violence that he inhabits. Meursault kills seamlessly, for he lives in a land where violence constitutes the norm. "The trigger gave," Meursault narrates, "and the smooth underbelly of the butt jogged my palm. And so, with that crisp, whipcrack sound, it all began. I shook off my sweat and the clinging veil of light. I knew I'd shattered the balance of the day, the spacious calm of this beach on which I had been happy. But I fired four shots more into the inert body, on which they left no visible trace."[9]

In Camus's writing and through Meursault's subjectivity, the Arab killed is unnamed and oddly distant, and Algeria is reduced to an amalgamation of bright lights, heat, and vague *légèreté*. The significance of the dead Arab's anonymity is much better expressed in Algerian novelist Kamel Daoud's *The Meursault Investigation*, in which the narrator Haroun tells us the story of his brother Moussa: the anonymous man that Camus's Mersault has killed.

Daoud introduces another act of violence: Haroun shoots down a neighbor, a *pied-noir* he had known most of his life, as independence from France dawns. The murder is hidden, untold, far from the spectacle of the "wind of history." "That makes seven [bullets] in all," Daoud writes.[10] Five shot by Meursault, and two shot by Haroun as a sort of dispassionate revenge.[11] As violence was constitutive of the privilege of settlers like Meursault, so did French colonization in Algeria end with the act of killing.

Frantz Fanon's clinical cases—as found, for instance, in chapter 5 of *The Wretched of the Earth,* "Colonial War and Mental Disorders"—suggest that both the torturers and the tortured, the colonizer and the colonized, are embedded in an existence of physical and psychological destruction.[12] Colonial situations produce "mental disorders" expressed through sometimes deadly violence. The act of killing does not lead one to liberation or virtue, as Haroun had hoped, but rather accurately illustrates how violence may circulate in a configuration of violence. The two boys who Fanon interviewed, who had decided to kill their French *pied-noir* schoolmate, were unable to explain their gesture; was this a reaction of mimesis as *colon* militias massacred Algerians throughout the countryside? Socialized within a context where violence was constantly perpetrated against them, the murder of the colonizer could be construed as an element of liberation, as Jean-Paul Sartre wrote in the preface to the *Wretched of the Earth.* Perhaps. But such violence, if it can constitute a cry, a claim of one's persistent existence despite colonialism, is *nothing more than violence.* Camus's Meursault and Daoud's Haroun sit in opposed but interdependent relations within a configuration of violence.[13] They allow the violence to course through them without interruption to the extent that they engage in political violence, from a racist killing to a lukewarm act of liberation.

The question remains to be asked: what is it that haunts us so? When considering haunting as an affective *and material* reality, what emerges is the question of transgenerational trauma. Transgenerational trauma is an intimate weight to be carried, one that creates ripples of collective neuralgia. Transgenerational trauma is the manifestation of history and structures of biopolitical constraint within one's own intimacy and networks of kinship. These hauntings take on a more-than-spectral quality when they are accompanied by a "homology of positions" between past and future generations. That is, when the contemporary subject position of otherness inherits the symbolic and sociopolitical position that was once filled by the colonized or the enslaved, expressions of racism in symbolic or material constraints come to be experienced as afterlives of harm committed decades, centuries ago. This reasoning allows us to understand the historical continuity between life and race-making in contemporary carceral and urban settings, on the one hand, and the political economy of enslavement and colonial labor, on the other.[14]

A HISTORY OF THESE WOUNDS . . .

What haunts us so is thus the violence that constituted the material world of the colony and the plantation; it is also the epistemic violence that forced complex subjectivities and societies into hiding. Such claims, however, are of little purpose unless one attempts to ground them in an effort of historiography. That is, unless one attempts to trace out a history of these wounds. Here, I continue to locate the disaster within the overlapping phenomena of policing and urbanization. In doing so, the tracing that I highlight is partial. I write with a certain *inquiétude*—that is, with disquiet and caution.[15] One should read this knowing that there is more to be said, and that what I have written here is not a hidden history; I have, however, attempted to frame it in such a way as to inform a particular historicity urban policing in the Goutte d'Or.

The concepts of *police* and *urban* have a long, shared history in France.[16] In fact, early modern conceptions of the police tended to entirely collapse urbanization and the territorialization of royal executive authority. The police was understood, on the one hand, as the polity, at the center of which stood Paris and the body of the king, and, on the other, as the means to guarantee public order within the king's domain. As roads were being built, soldiers were tasked with their surveillance, and the circulation of agricultural goods, wood, and taxes became centralized under the royal navy and finance ministries of Jean-Baptiste Colbert.

Such a logic was at play when the Black Code (*Code noir*) formalized the French slave-plantation regime in 1685. The Black Code superseded the authority of plantation owners with the authority of the French crown. In expanding France's royal domain to the Caribbean, the Black Code also transposed the metropolitan policing of roads and goods into Martinique, Guadeloupe, and Haiti (Saint-Domingue). In doing so, the French state oversaw, organized, and practiced the systematic surveillance of enslaved peoples, on top of the preexisting system of surveillance and punishment already established by plantation owners and colonial transatlantic companies.

The codification of the slave status as a legal reality had return effects shortly after the promulgation of the Black Code. The edicts of 1716 and 1738, respectively signed by Louis XIV and Louis XV, reinstated the slave status in metropolitan France, allowing French colonists to return to France with the people they enslaved. In 1777, the *Déclaration Royale pour la Police des Noirs* organized the creation of depots to detain Black Caribbean people in France, in the ports of Dunkerque, Le Havre, Saint-Malo, Brest, Nantes, La Rochelle, Bordeaux, and Marseille. Enslaved persons, as well as free "people of color" (*gens de couleur*) who resided in France were forced to register themselves to the state and submit to detention awaiting their deportation back to plantation colonies.[17] It was during this time that racial taxonomy emerged as a science, along with phrenology and craniometry. By the beginning of the nineteenth century, the police and the military would end up playing a significant part in the reinstatement of slavery in the Caribbean colonies, after its abolition during the French revolution (1789–99). With the military invasions of Martinique, Guadeloupe, and Saint-Domingue, as Napoleonic wars raged from Spain to Russia, a system of passports was put in place throughout the French metropole that prohibited Black people from entering Paris.[18]

The professional biography of one Pierre Boyer stands out, both as a bridge between distinct colonial contexts and as an illustration of continuous violence, albeit spread out through time and space. Pierre Boyer joined the French military during the revolution, in 1792. By 1800, he had participated in the military campaigns in Italy, Egypt, and Syria. In 1801, he was made brigade general and served under general Leclerc and Rochambeau in the campaign to reinstate slavery in Haiti (Saint-Domingue) after its abolition in 1794. Back in Europe following Haitian independence (1804), Pierre Boyer earned the nickname of "Pierre the Cruel" during the invasion of Spain by the Napoleonic army. He was reintegrated into active service after the July 1830 revolution in Paris and was dispatched immediately to Algeria. Stationed in the region of Oran, he quickly became notorious for his summary executions of captives and civilians and was sent back to France shortly thereafter.[19]

The invasion of Haiti by the Napoleonic army was notoriously brutal. Scorched earth left indelible traces in the landscapes of the island. From Saint-Domingue to Algeria, colonialism and the territorialization of the French state's authority operated through spectacular displays of violence: coordinated massacres, public executions and torture, and corpse exhibitions. Between 1830 and 1847, as the regions around the cities of Algiers, Oran, and Constantine came under French dominion, a third of the population was exterminated.[20] The circulation of violence and of soldiers' modus operandi illustrates larger continuities. State sovereignty continued to be applied through territorial extensions and the surveillance and corporeal harm and control of specific populations. Similarly, the legal framework of such violence progressively shifted, and for a time overlapped, between the status inscribed in the Black Code and the set of decrees and administrative practices that made up the *Code de l'indigénat* and the Native Status.

On 18 June 1845, in the region of Mostaganem, the Ouled Ryiah tribe was chased by the military columns of Colonel Aimable-Jean-Jacques Pélissier, and took to hiding in the caverns of the Dahra mountain range. As a thousand of women, men, and children found shelter in the caves of the Dahra, the soldiers sealed the five entrances of the cavern with blazing fires. Fed day and night until 20 June 1845, the smoke from the fires left no survivors.[21] In a report submitted to the French parliament in 1848, Republican statesman and political theorist Alexis de Tocqueville wrote that the French conquest had introduced in North Africa forms of violence and barbarism that had been until then unknown to the populations it subjugated. Along with the extermination of tribes, whole cities had been burned to the ground, schools, universities, and seminars dispersed, centers of knowledge and commerce uprooted. And yet, Tocqueville wrote, such a conquest meant that total colonization of the land and the peoples had to be continued. In fact, he argued for the necessity to "destroy anything that may resemble a permanent aggregation of population."[22] The forced sedentarization of formerly nomadic tribes, their dispersal throughout the conquered territory, and the sequestration of land actualized French presence and initiated the making of a settler colony.

In parallel to these military forms of violence, historian and psychiatrist Karima Lazali argues that French colonialism also operated through symbolic violence and the administrative act of naming. The French colonial state changed the toponymy of the land and the patronyms of tribes. Networks of kinship and filiation were replaced with ad hoc names, which blurred the political and genealogical relationships whole peoples had formed over centuries, often over millennia.[23] Just as the French government had sought to monitor the presence of Black people in France decades prior, with this registry the state made "indigenous society" legible to the racial imperatives of colonization and forced labor. From the resistance of Emir Abdelkader ben Mohieddin that ended in 1847 and the last tribal uprising of Cheikh al Mokrani in 1871, the French state—in its various monarchical, imperial, and Republican forms—used war and collective punishment to acquire arable lands and push the Algerian peasantry, merchant, and landed classes into urban ghettos, distant mountains, and infertile plots of land.

French law was thus applied with utmost rigor in conquered territory. But military and administrative authorities also invented new practices to enact the "total colonization" of Algeria, as Tocqueville phrased it. Like the extension of France's royal domain during the colonization of the Caribbean and North America, the expansion of administrative capacities in Algeria had similar return effects in metropolitan France. State-building in the colonies fed into state-building "at home," and vice versa. While in North Africa nomads were fixed to specific localities and entered the French census, on the other side of the Mediterranean such administrative expansion was directed at Roma travelers. Going back to the late seventeenth century, the stigmatization of Roma communities articulated itself hand in hand with the rationalization of French bureaucracy.[24]

By 1895, Roma travelers were forced to register themselves with the authorities, as a systematic census was designed for them specifically. The production of individual files was eventually formalized and organized by the 1912 law mandating travelers be surveilled and monitored by an "anthropometric notebook for nomads" (*carnet anthropométrique*) that all travelers, adults and children alike, were obliged to carry with them.[25] Strengthened by centuries of plantation regime, colonial government, and the racial sciences that structured such polities, the administrative capacities of the French state thus expanded as racist surveillance techniques gained in precision. In 1940, the French identity card (*carte d'identité de français*) worked along similar bureaucratic and racial lines. As the French Demography Services phrased it at the time, it allowed French fascist authorities to "direct the evolution of the race" and organize the registration and deportation of French and foreign Jewish communities.[26]

From 1942 to 1944, as the secretary-general of the Gironde prefecture, high-ranking civil servant Maurice Papon oversaw the transfer of over one thousand Jewish people from Bordeaux to the transit camp of Drancy in the north of Paris, where they awaited deportation to Auschwitz. Immediately after the war, Papon was rehabilitated and integrated into the Algerian section of the French Ministry of the Interior, informing the minister on the massacres of Setif, Kherrata, and Guelma. In reaction to the emergence of Algerian nationalist movements and the display of proindependence flags and slogans during the celebration of German capitulation on 8 May 1945, French military and settler militias "raked over" villages, while more remote mountainous areas were bombed by aircrafts. Bodies were thrown down wells, in the gorges of Kherrata, in mass graves, and some were incinerated in the lime kilns of Heliopolis near Guelma.[27] In 1946, Papon was assigned to Corsica and became the prefect of the island, where he stayed until 1949, when he was then assigned to the Constantine prefecture in Algeria. Moving between Morocco and Algeria, Papon oversaw the military, police, and the psychological repression of anticolonial uprisings. He eventually became regional prefect of Constantine where he coordinated institutional reforms, namely the organization of concentration camps dubbed "regroupment centers," and deployed "operational protection detachments" charged with intelligence, and the interrogation and torture of anticolonial militants and sympathizers. These methods of repression—the surveillance and uprooting of local populations and the creation of archipelagos of "regroupment centers"—was also deployed by French authorities in Cameroon.[28]

Trained by years of high-ranking civil service in the colonies, Maurice Papon was made police prefect of Paris in 1958 and tasked with the surveillance and policing of the Algerian community of Paris. Moving swiftly from colonial to metropolitan settings, Papon's intent to lead a brutal psychological war against Algerian anticolonial militancy eventually led to the massacre of 17 October 1961, during which hundreds of demonstrators were killed, maimed, and thrown in the Seine. From 1958 onward, Maurice Papon introduced new police brigades, such as the Auxiliary Police Force composed primarily of "French Muslims of Algeria." He also operated his "counterrevolutionary war" with preexisting squads and police protocols, such as the Assault and Violence Squads (BAV) tasked with the policing of "Algerian criminality." With the formal independence of Algeria in 1962, these brigades and taskforces were dismantled. They eventually reemerged in the 1970s under the French doctrine of "anticriminality." The Anticrime Squad (BAC) was created by Pierre Bolotte in the 1970s to police immigrant communities in the north of Paris. Bolotte began to work as a civil servant during the German occupation, before pursuing a career as a colonial administrator. He served in French Indochina (Vietnam, Cambodia, Laos), Guadeloupe, Algeria, and La Réunion. While serving as prefect in Guadeloupe, Bolotte oversaw the police repression of the May 1967 Black workers' antiracist uprising, during which scores of people were shot and killed.

Bolotte then went on to become prefect of the newly created Seine-Saint-Denis (93) department, to the north and east of Paris. Experimented on in

Paris throughout the 1970s and 1980s, the BAC was eventually employed in the rest of France in the 1990s, along with a set of anti-immigration laws known as the Pasqua laws. The BAC, a civilian-dress shock-and-awe police force, today patrols public space and social housing blocks in order to surveil and catch offenders red-handed, and provoke "criminal behavior" through relentless harassment.[29]

The process of uncovering the historicity of a given urban space, or a given set of institutional practices, unearths a palimpsest on which the experiences of various peoples have been graphed and erased, sometimes forgotten, at other times consecrated into official national history. The palimpsestic nature of violence in Paris is one within which we can see traces of enslavement, of colonial conquest, of urban surveillance of travelers, performers, and sex workers. In this sense, I have focused on a single layer of this palimpsest of traces, and I invite others to continue such work. Specifically, neighborhoods like the Goutte d'Or should be placed within a larger cartography of corporeal control, which stretches to contemporary colonial settings, such as Martinique, Guadeloupe, La Réunion, Mayotte, and Kanaky/New-Caledonia.[30]

## *ATLAL:* LOOKING AT THE RUINS

Memory and the various phenomena associated with it, such as amnesia, anamnesis, and aphasia, are multidimensional and multidirectional. As Innu scholar Pierrot Ross-Tremblay writes, forgetting is not absolute: those who inherit histories of colonial violence may remember, and they may do so in ways that are often contingent and particular to their own individual path toward remembrance.[31] Yet if such anamnesis is tedious work, it allows for a particular mnemohistory to emerge.

Our relationships to the memories of colonialism, enslavement, and genocide are fraught with conflict and traces of violence. But they are central to understanding the historical processes of erasure and the making of racialized subjectivities and subject positions as painful and degraded ones. Remembering, as Ross-Tremblay writes, is a path toward reformulating this relationship to memory, to pain, and to suffering. It becomes an act of poiesis: as we grapple with these wounded histories, we begin to create something new and, perhaps, beautiful and poetic. Traces of violence do not reveal memory; they allow us to reformulate forgetfulness and to muster new ways of remembering.[32]

Djamel Kerkar's documentary film on the aftermath of the Algerian civil war constitutes such an act of poetics and memory. In *Atlal,* Kerkar embraces the traditional posture of the poet who, facing the ruins, begins to remember, to reformulate their relationship to memory, and in doing begins to look to the future. In the face of the ruins, *atlal* in Arabic, of one's life, of one's dismemberment, one pauses and re-members.[33]

What we have attempted to do in these pages, in a sense, is to look at particular ruins: the traces of the disasters that have graphed themselves into Paris. But *atlal* requires one to do more than look at ruins. It is not simply a question of facing disasters. As the disaster faces us, it requires that we attempt to turn the sting of analysis on ourselves. In other words, *atlal,* or embracing the posture of the poet who gazes at the ruins of one's context, also entails considerations of the conditions that produce one's social position and dispositions. Robert Desjarlais and I did not perceive the same phenomena, we did not apprehend the disaster in the same ways. But we thought to look at ruins, to excavate what they could teach us, and to look again. Our perceptions changed and we reconsidered our methods in light of our ongoing dialogue. More importantly, though, is that we were both forced to properly understand the positions and perspectives from which we spoke. Our collaboration is thus not a universal dialogue. It is a collection of shadows (*esquisses*), a situated perspective enhanced by our will to write and think with mutual respect and amity.

In Kerkar's *Atlal,* the main protagonist of the documentary, a young man named Abdou, not yet twenty years old when the documentary was shot, reflects on his life in Ouled Allal, a village in the Mitidja region in the south of Algiers. The village was almost entirely destroyed by military operations, bombardments, and terrorist attacks during the civil war and of which the ruins, alongside the reconstructed homes and streets, are still there to attest to that history. Standing on the ruins, looking down on them, looking up to the sky, Abdou reflects on the push and pull that structures his life as an afterlife of the war. Pushed by the ruins and the echoes of terrorism and state violence, pulled by the roads of exile to Spain, Italy, France. He finds himself standing there, looking, precisely because he cannot leave. It is also this impossibility that characterizes the poetic posture of *atlal.* The disaster is inextricable. As another protagonist of Kerkar's film says—this time late in the night, as he raps over a small fire—*God traces everything.* In this sense, once it has occurred, the disaster is there and we cannot undo it. Its traces, *athar* in Arabic, are likewise indelible. Traces of violence, in that sense, cannot be unwritten.

*K. H.*

## INTERRUPTION: NERVOUS ACTIVITY

*January 2021*

Time moves nervously. Latent sensations erupt in phantasmagorias. But a stillness remains; a reluctant, restless stillness. Writing is a nervous activity. It moves in jolts, or in relentless moments of silence. The effort to graph the disaster is torn between the fixity of the written form and the constant urgency with which disasters manifest themselves; explosive or unseen, monumental and memorialized, or tucked within the folds of daily catastrophe.

On 7 September 2020, we met on the platform of the Gallieni metro station in Bagnolet, on the eastern perimeter of Paris. Some weeks earlier, in June 2020, a political collective working for the official recognition of colonial crimes had symbolically renamed the station after French communists Maurice and Josette Audin, reminding us by the same token that military commander J. S. Gallieni was most famed for his conquest of Madagascar, in the service of the French colonial enterprise.[34] Gallieni is but one of hundreds of surnames that commemoratively retrace, in the streets and stations of Paris, the military and colonial achievements of France. A mathematician then in his mid-twenties, Maurice Audin was arrested in Algiers, under suspicion of ties with Algerian revolutionaries. He was tortured and killed by members of the French military in June 1957. Soon after the activists placed a banner with the names of Maurice and Josette Audin over the official sign for the metro, subversively renaming it, RATP security agents tore it down. The events marked another tract of inscription, counterinscription, trace, and effacement within the jagged graffs of Paris.

It had been months since we had last met in person. Desjarlais had gone back to the United States to teach, and then had returned to France to undertake a research fellowship in Paris. Habrih had started a PhD program in Canada and had come back to France a few months prior. It was toward the end of the summer, and much had happened in Paris since the beginning of the year.

Following the outbreak of Covid-19 throughout Europe in February, the French government declared a lockdown—or *confinement,* a restriction on mobility in public space—on 16 March 2020. During a televised address the president of the Republic solemnly stated that France was at war (*en guerre*) with the virus. Residents were encouraged to "be vigilant" toward its potential spread. People who could work away from their office were invited to "stay at home" along with children and students, while service and industrial workers continued to attend their workplaces. Anyone stopped by police in public space needed to have a verification form (*attestation dérogatoire de déplacement*) justifying their business in the street.

As a measure imposed throughout metropolitan France, the *confinement* and the threat of illness produced an "illusion of equality," as if vulnerability and mortality, along with the government-decreed constraint, now circulated through society regardless of the privileges afforded by social class, wealth, and institutional access.[35]

A matter of public health, the pandemic was quickly framed as a matter of collective security. The sanitary state of emergency expanded police powers. At the government level, it centralized executive authority over restrictions on mobility and assembly; meaning that restrictions, such as curfews or *confinement,* on all or parts of the "national territory" can be declared by decree. The state of emergency was declared by law on 23 March and lasted until 10 July 2020, before being declared by governmental decree again on 17 October 2020. Not unlike past laws of exception in France, the measures of exception used to "to face the Covid-19 epidemic" reiterated and specified preexisting police *dispositifs.*

On 17 March 2020, a curfew order was decreed in Nice, in fifteen "priority" neighborhoods. Another one was decreed in Saint-Ouen, on 25 March 2020, specifically targeting juveniles. The general order of *confinement* manifested in a renewed police proactivity throughout ZSPs and other stigmatized urban spaces in France, such as street encampments and shantytowns. Images, videos, and testimonies of police brutality circulated on social media daily.

On the night of 19 March 2020, in Villeneuve-la-Garenne, a municipality in the northern suburbs of Paris, a young motorcyclist was hit by a police car. The images went live on various social media platforms. The young man was seen lying on the ground, wounded with an open leg fracture. Riots erupted later that evening in the Hauts-de-Seine (92) department. These images reminded many of the death of Ibrahima Bah, a twenty-two-year-old motorcyclist killed in Villiers-le-Bel (Val-d'Oise, 95) in October 2019. In

FIGURE 42. Gathering at place de la République, organized by families of young men killed in police custody, during ID checks or in prison, June 2020. Photo by K. H.

May 2020, eighteen-year-old Sabri Chouhbi died in similar circumstances in Argenteuil (Val-d'Oise, 95). Both their names could be heard and read during demonstrations organized in the Paris region later that summer (see figure 42).

Later, in March 2020, this time in Les Ulis (Essone, 91), two young men were beaten up by police on their way to work, allegedly for not having respected the confinement order. Stories like these continued to be told, by eyewitnesses, survivors of beatings or collisions, or as anonymous images and videos circulated on the internet. In all the spaces, public or institutional, where constraints on mobility predated the confinement order, the effects of such restrictions were exacerbated. Police escalation in violence mirrored the sealing off of overcrowded prisons and retirement homes, where the virus circulated at alarming rates.

The year 2020, marking the fifth anniversary of the January and November 2015 attacks, thus began in a tumultuous "war" against an invisible but omnipresent enemy. Serendipity would have it that the 2020 curfew order for Paris and other "clusters of contamination" was applied on 17 October 2020.

On Friday, 2 October 2020, French president Emmanuel Macron presented his plan to fight "Islamist *séparatisme*"—outlining a series of measures that would later find their way into the 2020 Law of Sedition (*renforçant les principes républicains*). On Saturday morning, the next day, as children attended an Arabic class at the Omar Mosque of rue Jean-Pierre Timbaud near the Canal Saint-Martin, police officers raided the mosque, investigating seditious ties. The mosque was fined with a fire safety infraction.

On 16 October 2020, a social studies teacher was beheaded in Conflans-Sainte-Honorine, a few yards away from the middle school where he taught. Some days earlier, Samuel Paty, the teacher, had shown caricatures of the prophet Muhammad published by *Charlie Hebdo* during a class session on freedom of speech. Eighteen-year-old Abdullakh Anzorov tracked down the teacher and killed him.

With the teacher's murder ensued an affective, discursive, and legal escalation. Not unlike the *Charlie Hebdo* and anti-Semitic attacks of January 2015 and the attacks of November 2015, the murder of Samuel Paty led to a national movement of affective solidarity, during which state cult and popular affect intertwined. The murder was presented as an attack on French values, specifically freedom of speech (*liberté d'expression*) and French secularism (*laïcité*). To refuse "to be *Charlie*," to distance oneself from the editorial line of *Charlie Hebdo,* has come to be construed as a subversive act against the Republic. Such discourses and governmental policies are in line with a speech that President Emmanuel Macron gave in October 2019, in which he argued that all sectors of French society needed to join forces to "overcome the Islamist hydra." "A society of vigilance, that's what we have to build," said the president, "the vigilance and not the suspicion that corrodes, the vigilance, the attentive listening of the other, the reasonable raising of consciousness, knowing how to identify at school, at work, in places of worship, close to home, the laxity, the deviations, these small gestures that signal a departure from the laws and values of the Republic—a separation." Operation vigilance recurs within the political aims and imaginaries of the French state, intensifying to a nearly panoptic degree. Its nervous concerns work in tandem with an ever-new Islamophobia.

Following the various government declarations, policy decisions, and the murder of Samuel Paty, the lines between the already vague categories of "Islam," "political Islam," and "Islamism" were further blurred by politicians and pundits. New words have come to define the nature of the threat posed by Muslims in France: *séparatisme* (sedition) and *ensauvagement* (a problematic term, signifying hyperviolence and generalized incivility). Both terms involve dangerous phantasms. The legal expansion initiated under the state of emergency (2015–17) culminated with the transfer of the 1955 measures of exception into the Code of Homeland Security (Code de la sécurité intérieure) through the 2017 law no. 2017–1510 "strengthening homeland security and the fight against terrorism." In 2020, two new laws have been presented to parliament: the law on so-called Muslim *separatism,* which "strengthens Republican values," and the law on "global security," which extends administrative and judiciary police powers to private security companies and generalizes the use of firearms.

Since then, associations have been dissolved by government decrees. The first one was BarakaCity, an international NGO based in France dismantled after its president, Idriss Sihamedi, became the centerpiece of antisedition investigations. The only organization in France specialized in assisting victims of anti-Muslim racism, the Collective against Islamophobia in France (Collectif contre l'islamophobie en France; CCIF) was officially disbanded on 2 December 2020. "With the will to send a message," as Minister of the Interior Gérald Darmanin stated on 19 October 2020, raids, arrests, and the disbanding of mosques and associations would continue.

The "society of vigilance" continues to scaffold collective grief. The organic process of grieving death or disappearance moves as if enclosed within a rigid, articulated structure that directs its overall demeanor. Throughout metropolitan France in late October 2020, minutes of silence were organized in memory of the assassinated teacher. Teachers and paraeducators (*surveillants-éducateurs*) were tasked to vigilantly monitor their students' observance of the homage. Four hundred complaints for nonrespect of the minutes of silence were addressed to the district school boards (*rectorats*). Students as young as ten were arrested, interrogated, and their homes investigated for potential ties to seditious or terrorist activities. But behind the curtains of official grief and antiterrorist proactivity, the pandemic continued to work and pressure public health institutions. And in schools where no rigorous sanitary protocol had been prepared, high school students organized blockades. At Paul Éluard High School in Saint-Denis, where students feared they might contaminate their parents and other family members, the protest was met with antiriot police. The images of the dispersal of the protest on 4 November 2020 echoed the mass arrest of over 150 students from the Saint-Exupéry High School in Mantes-la-Jolie on 4 December 2018; the students there were protesting reforms to the exam system and to the admissions procedure in public universities.

The fifth year anniversary of the attacks at the Stade de France, the Bataclan, Le Carillon, and other bars and restaurants in Paris came and went, on 13 November 2020. State-sponsored memorial events were scaled down because of health concerns associated with the pandemic. Premier Jean Castex and Paris mayor Anne Hildago attended small memorial ceremonies at the targeted sites. At the intersection of streets by Le Carillon and Le Petit Cambodge, the dignitaries present laid wreaths at the base of the wall that bears the commemorative plaque, and then, as if in echo of earlier remembrance, looked toward the plaque during a somber moment of silence. "Today, five years on, Paris remembers," Hildago later tweeted. "Let us never forget those who left us," President Macron said in a message on social media that same day. "France was struck to the heart. Horror in the middle of Paris. But the French remained standing. Standing in the face of terror. Standing to defend our freedom and values," he added.[36]

Others spoke of traumatic memories and post-traumatic conditions that have troubled their lives. A survivor of the Bataclan massacre told a reporter, "Five years later, the most difficult thing is still the date of November 13 and all that sounds it. . . . It's really hard for me to say 'today, I'm better or today, that's it.' . . . Post-traumatic stress is not forgotten."[37]

The anniversary thus brought discourses of national memory and a proudly defiant defense of Republican values alongside fragile, stressed words on the disasters lived among survivors of the attacks. Some of those troubled by the attacks might in fact be in favor of less remembrance in their lives.

Others expressed concern over the "shifting threat" of terroristic attacks in France. "The threat is increasingly difficult to pin down," said one former senior intelligence official. "We know how to monitor and infiltrate organized networks and radicalized mosques. But we remain quite helpless when confronted by individuals."[38]

The city pulses on, in its *névralgique* ways.

Writing is a nervous activity. As the palimpsest of violence continues to be etched in the Parisian cityscape, new rhythmic impulses send neuralgia coursing through the streets, arcades, hallways, and homes of the city. Experiences of violence and their aftereffects persist and leave trace impressions in familiar and unfamiliar spaces, in individual and collective subjectivities, and in archival vaults.

Authorship and the claim to have authority over a given topic of study produce sensations of disquiet; a disquiet which prompts heuristic doubt. Disquiet and doubt, unhappy, generative companions of learning and conveying what one has learned, have animated our efforts in this work and pushed us toward considerations of the histories of violence and wounding that inform life and death in Paris, past and present. Finding ourselves in a methodological *dérive*, drifting through critical phenomenology, sociology, anthropology, history—writing is a nervous activity.

This book comes to an end. Yet the writing goes unfinished. Written in a moment; we understand the extent of what we do not yet know with more clarity. Nor do we know what might occur in the coming months and years. While the symbolic space afforded to innocence and willful ignorance collapses unto itself.

Written in a movement; between movements—Paris continues its sleepless night.

*K. H. and R. D.*
*Paris, New York*

## ACKNOWLEDGMENTS

To give thanks for a project to which many have contributed is not an easy task.

For Khalil Habrih, this task is made difficult by years of guidance prior, during, and after the first completion of the manuscript. I would like to thank the friends and professors who, years ago in Oberlin, Ohio, pushed me on the path of research: notably professors Henryatta Ballah, Pamela Brooks, Yveline Alexis, and Darko Opoku; students and friends will hopefully find these lines and recognize themselves. María Elizabeth Membreño, for your kindness and guidance during two visits to Santa Marta, and for your friendship ever since. Sonia Brown, Mike *may he rest in Peace,* and the community at Auntie Na's House, for the time shared in Detroit, thank you.

Since 2015 and life in Paris, others have continued to listen in, answer back, and generate collective reflection. Yasmine Harrison, Amandine S. Bocco, Rym H. Khedjari, Henry Paikin, Alice Duquesnoy, Margaux Cazal, Tammie M. David, Millie Christie-Dervaux, and Ray Camara-Bushell. Thanks also to the people who helped me through my first experiences of fieldwork in Paris: my father, Abdelkader Habrih, for the shyness of his knowledge and the boldness of his pedagogy; my mother, Alina Liegl, for her patience and the understanding that wounds often take the shape of silence; Zahira Ammarguellat, Leila Mehaous, Samir Khirat, uncle Maamar Habrih, aunt Messaouda Karima Habrih, uncle Chamseddine Habrih, aunt Naïma Habrih, my grandmother Corina Liegl, and uncle Robert Liegl. To the anonymous voices and noisemakers that make up the symphony of the 18th arrondissement of Paris, thank you.

To loved ones, who have shaped and nurtured a way of being in the world. Aïssa ben Chérif Habrih, Fatma Habrih Zahoual, and Helmut Liegl.

May God grant you the rest you so deserve. To all of you, my eternal gratitude.

The beginning of doctoral studies at the School of Sociological and Anthropological Studies of the University of Ottawa, Canada, proved to be the best environment possible to repair myself and continue to learn. For their kindness, personal rigor, and persistent encouragement: Souheil Benslimane, Leila Benhadjoudja, Meg Stalcup, David Moffette, Magalie Lefebvre-Jean, Kristen Tole, José Lopez, Nathalie Mondain, Walner Osner, Sonia Ben Soltane, Shoshana Magnet, and the members of the weekly discussion group she facilitated.

This almost goes without saying: thanks to Robert Desjarlais, for his friendship, reliability, and his generous mentorship.


Robert Desjarlais would like to thank a number of friends and colleagues for conversations and exchanges that have contributed in keen ways to the efforts involved with this book, most notably María Elena García, Anne Lovell, Samuel Bordreuil, Anthony Stavrianakis, Laurence Tessier, Nick Bartlett, Michael D. Jackson, Mary Kairidi, Alexa Hagerty, Margaux Fitoussi, Tanja Ahlin, Brian Goldstone, Anand Pandian, Lisa Stevenson, Eduardo Kohn, Christiana Giordano, Stefania Pandolfo, Lawrence Cohen, Mattijs van der Port, Caroline Hoepffner, Jean Hoepffner, Andrew McDowell, Jason Throop, Jarrett Zigon, Aidan Seale-Feldman, Serena Bindi, Maria Speyer, Tanja Ahlin, Dejan Lukić, Jason Bahbak Mohaghegh, Joshua Reno, Sabina Perrino, Tyler Zoanni, Adriana Molina Lopez, James Cerretani, Yasmine Harrison, Peter Skafish, Raphaële Rabanas, Yulia Mylnikova, and Albert Piette. Professor Piette also made possible the publication of *Sur les traces de la violence* with Presses universitaires de Paris Nanterre in 2020. For this work, Céline Curiol deftly translated intricate prose in American English into lucid French. Thanks as well to the Desjarlais family for their warm support, especially my mother, Helen Desjarlais, for her vital poiesis, and my father, Robert C. Desjarlais, in vivid memory.

A stay in Denmark in the spring and summer 2020 as a guest researcher in the Department of Anthropology at the University of Copenhagen provided a supportive climate for research and writing efforts. Thank you in particular to Tine Gammeltoft, Hanne Overgaard Mogensen, Quentin Gausset, Silja and Zephir Gausset, Bjarke Oxlund, Susan Reynolds Whyte, Michael Whyte, Henrik Vigh, Lone Grøn, Susanne Bregnbaek, Anna Lina

Dalsgård, and Tim Flohr Sørenen for friendship and intellectual companionship during those challenging times. A fellowship at the Institut d'études avancées de Paris in the fall of 2020 provided a welcoming and intellectually stimulating setting for work on the present and related research projects. Thank you to the remarkable staff—including Saadi Lahlou, Simon Luck, Cécile Durand, Solène de Bonis, and Claire Jeandal—and our undaunted colleagues there, most notably Colin Jones. Khalil Habrih and I appreciate the fact that we were able to meet at the institute on several occasions in the fall of 2020 to discuss the final steps toward completing the present work. A roundtable organized at l'IEA in November 2020, titled "'Ne Pas Archiver': Traces et mémoire des attentats de 2015," enabled us to converse with Sarah Gensburger and Gérôme Truc on questions of trace, memory, memorials, and archives in the aftermath of the 2015 attacks in Paris. We also valued the opportunity in January 2021 to engage with the participants of the "Team Phenomenology" virtual seminar, organized by Jason Throop and students and colleagues at UCLA.

Responses to presentations I have given in academic settings have been greatly appreciated, including at Humboldt University in Berlin, the University of Copenhagen, New York University, John Jay College of Criminal Justice, Connecticut College, Binghamton University, and University of California, Berkeley. My presentation in the seminar on "La fabrication du sujet politique" at the École des hautes études in sciences sociales, in March 2017, proved highly significant for this project; thank you to Alban Bensa, Manon Capo, Jules Métais, Anna Pomaro, and Daniel Inda, for their invitation to speak in the seminar. Conversations with Manon Capo, on life and atmospherics in Paris after the November 2015 attacks, were very helpful.

My colleagues and students at Sarah Lawrence College have been wonderful interlocutors through the years. Aurora Donzelli, Una Chung, Bella Brodzki, and David Hollander in particular have enriched the thought and language of this book, as have the students who have worked with me at the college. Sophia Lynch assisted in superb ways in research and translation efforts associated with this work. Jennifer Bianca Hook's skilled efforts in image-making have been invaluable. Sarah Lawrence College supported several research stays in France, with funds from the Faith Whitney Ziesing Fund in the Social Sciences, the Faculty Research Fund, the Faculty Publication Fund, and a faculty course release in 2017 providing financial support for the research and writing efforts that have gone into this work.

Lastly, I would like to thank Khalil Habrih, for teaching me so much, and for accompanying me as a true friend in this collaborative endeavor—with grace, intelligence, good humor, and critical acumen.

Together, we would like to thank Kate Marshall and Enrique Ochoa-Kaup at University of California Press for their considerable support in the publication process, and for their masterful efforts in bringing this project to fruition. Thanks as well to Todd Meyers, and a second, anonymous reader, for their keen thoughts and recommendations on an earlier version of the book manuscript. Ben Pease, cartographer at Pease Press, created the three fine maps included here. Christopher Pitts helped to prepare the manuscript for publication. We also would like to thank Farès Yessad [Serdas] for his intuitive understanding of our work and his creative and insightful vision in crafting the artwork for the cover of this book.

GLOSSARY

**attentat.**  "Attempt," attack. More specifically, a violent, terroristic attack.

**BAC.**  Brigade anti-criminalité (Anticrime Squad). A civilian-dress police squad, known for its aggressive tactics, which operates in low-income and majority immigrant neighborhoods in France and overseas territories.

**Bataclan.**  A music hall in the 11th arrondissement of Paris. The site of a terroristic attack and mass shooting on 13 November 2015.

***Charlie Hebdo.***  A French satirical weekly newspaper, published in Paris. The offices of *Charlie Hebdo* were attacked by two men on 7 January 2015. Twelve people were killed and eleven injured.

**contrôle d'identité.**  ID check; stop-and-frisk. Police practice framed primarily by article 78–2 of the Code of Penal Procedure; allows officers to stop, verify identification, and pat down persons who *might* be in infraction of immigration, drug, sex work, or other such laws. ID checks constitute police officers' main activity in the public space; millions are performed by officers yearly. In a 2017 report published by the French Rights' Defensor (Défenseur des droits, a state-funded agency), 80 percent of Black and Arab respondents testified to having been stop-and-frisked at least once in the past five years, while 85 percent of all respondents declared they had never been ID checked.

**CRA.**  Centre de rétention administrative (Immigrant Detention Center; lit., "Administrative Holding Center").

**CRS.**  Compagnie républicaine de sécurité (Antiriot Police; lit., "Republican Security Company"). Police company specialized in crowd control. The CRS is tasked with the policing of public space in low-income majority immigrant neighborhoods categorized as Priority Security Zones.

**dérive.**  Literally, "drift." In an urban *dérive,* a person or group of persons might undertake a drifting, unplanned walk through the streets and neighborhoods of a city.

**état d'urgence.**  State of emergency, a form of state of exception, which in distinction to the state of siege allows for civilian authorities to hold on to governing powers rather than transferring said powers to military authorities. The French state of emergency relies on the 1955 law no. 55–385 "instituting a state of emergency and declaring its application in Algeria." Since the 2017 law no. 2017–1510 "reinforcing homeland security and the fight against terrorism," many measures of exception initially conceived for the state of emergency and used during the state of emergency (2015–17) have been introduced into the Code de la sécurité intérieure and are now part of standard legal and administrative practice, along with other measures of exception tied to antidrug trafficking and anti-immigration legislation.

**GPIS.** Groupement parisien inter-bailleurs de surveillance (Social Housing Surveillance Group; lit., "Parisian Interlandlord Surveillance Group"). This private security company is tasked with the surveillance of social housing blocks (staircases, halls, courtyards) and the surrounding public space.

**hauntology.** The study of hauntings, ghosts, and specters. *Hantologie,* in French.

**hoggra.** From Algerian Darija (North African Arabic). A type of humiliation, arbitrary in nature, practiced in order to dominate the humiliated subject. Originally used to describe colonial authority, it is now widely used to refer both to the military dictatorship in Algeria and to racist police practices in France.

**immigrant centrality.** A (rural or urban) space that concentrates commercial, social, cultural, and religious activities for a given immigrant community; participates in the generational renewal and maintenance of communities' political and symbolic life.

**Le Carillon.** A bar in the 10th arrondissement of Paris. The site of a terroristic attack on 13 November 2015.

**névralgique.** Neuralgic; nerve center or strategic point; the adjectival form of neuralgia, *névralgie,* a sharp and paroxysmal pain along the course of a damaged nerve.

**Opération Sentinelle.** Operation Sentinel. A government program in France in which military soldiers guard and protect key cultural sites in France, and patrol and surveil various streets and neighborhoods in cities throughout the country. Part of the broader Vigipirate program, Opération Sentinelle was launched by President Hollande after the *Charlie Hebdo* attacks in January 2015.

**politique de la ville.** French urban policy, institutionalized most formally through the creation of a Ministry of the City in 1990 and defined as promoting "urban cohesion and solidarity, at the local and national levels, with disadvantaged neighborhoods and their residents" (Law no. 2014–173, art. 1-i).

**PSIG.** Peloton de surveillance et d'intervention de la Gendarmerie (Gendarmerie Surveillance and Intervention Platoons). The Gendarmerie is an armed force composed of military officers and tasked with policing missions in metropolitan France and, notably, in overseas departments. During the 2016 BAC-PSIG training plan, these military police platoons participated in the policing of public space in the Goutte d'Or and other ZSPs.

**spatiality.** From the work of sociologist Maurice Halbwachs; the collected traces of a social group's existence in a given (urban or rural) setting; a distorted window into a social group's collective memory. In this work, the notion is complicated by the absent-presence of exile and colonial history.

**Vigipirate.** Vigilance et protection des installations contre les risques d'attentats terroristes à l'explosif. A nationwide governmental program in France, in which a number of security measures are employed to encourage vigilance against potential terrorist attacks at both the collective and individual level.

**ZSP.** Zone de sécurité prioritaire (Priority Security Zone). Administrative category, which allows the ministries of the interior and justice to coordinate penal and police efforts within designated urban spaces.

NOTES


*AVANT-PROPOS:* A GUIDE TO READING
*TRACES OF VIOLENCE*

*Epigraph:* Derrida (1978:226).

1. See Fassin (2015) for a thoughtful reflection and "discordant voice" on the nationalist fervor and concerns about the "enemy within" that arose in France in the wake of the *Charlie Hebdo* attack. See also Fernando and Raissiguier (2016) on "the impossible subject" of *Charlie Hebdo.*

2. These numbers are provided by the Ministry of the Interior (police and homeland security); see the French Consultative Commission on Human Rights (CNCDH 2017).

3. For an overview of collaborative ethnography see Lassiter (2005). See also Rabinow (2011) for a distinctive collaborative approach in anthropological thought.

4. One trace record of Desjarlais's writing before he began to work with Habrih on the book project can be found with the anthropological reflection *Sur les traces de la violence: Un essai anthropologique après les attentats de Paris* (Desjarlais 2020). The first two chapters of the current work draw, in significantly transformed ways, from that text.

5. The seminar *La fabrication du sujet politique: Réflexivité, subjectivités et pouvoir* was organized by Alban Bensa, Manon Capo, Daniele Inda, Julie Métais, and Anna Pomaro. The title of the presentation by Robert Desjarlais on 24 March 2017 was *Traces de violence: Une anthropologie phénoménologique des attentats du 13 Novembre à Paris.*

6. Charles Baudelaire, "Du vin et du haschisch," *Œuvres, 1:249–50.* As quoted in Benjamin's *The Arcades Project* (1999:349).

7. For Benjamin's use of the concept of the ragpicker, see Benjamin (1999; 2006a) and Gilloch (1997).

8. Benjamin (1998:114).

9. See Sayad (1999a; 1999b).

10. Fanon (1986:111).

11. See Derrida (1994) and Gordon (2008), for instance, as well as the special thematic collection of the journal *Ethos,* in December 2019, on "Hauntology in Psychological Anthropology" (Good and Rahimi 2019).

12. Our consideration of the phantasmal, spectral dimensions of life and violence in Paris draws in part from a recent book by Desjarlais, *The Blind Man: A Phantasmography* (2018a).

13. Jameson (1999:38).

14. See Fanon (2005) and Arendt (1970), as well as Mbembe (2001; 2019). For anthropological writings on violence, see, among others, Appadurai (2006); Asad (2007); Desjarlais et al. (1996); Daniel (1996); Das (2007); Das et al. (2000); Feldman (1991; 2015); Kleinman and Kleinman (1994); Good, Hyde, Pinto, and Good (2008); Gusterson (2017); Han (2012); Jackson (2005); Lukić (2013); Nordstrom and Martin (1992); Nordstrom (1997); Nordstrom and Robben (1996); Scheper-Hughes (1993); Taussig (1987; 1992); Garcia (2015); Wool (2015); and Zani (2019).

15. See Huyssen (2003) and Silverman (2013) for comparable readings of cities as urban palimpsests.

16. To quote Achille Mbembe from his book *Politiques de l'inimitié* (2016:16), translated into English with the title *Necropolitics* (2019:8). The terms *relation, co-composition, return to life,* and *politics of enmity* voiced here also come from Mbembe.


COUNTER-PREFACE: BLUES, FLIGHTS, BEGINNINGS . . .

1. Bocco (2018).


CHAPTER ONE: NÉVRALGIQUE

*Epigraph:* Antonin Artaud, *Le Pèse-nerfs* (1925), "The Nerve Meter," in Artaud (1976:86).

1. Telo and Leclaire (2015). *Trans.*

2. On this see Feldman (2015:74).

3. Desjarlais (2018a:ix).

4. On "fictionalized enemies" see Mbembe (2019:70). See also Derrida (1997:84) and Feldman (2015:1856) on the figure of the enemy as a "'structuring' enemy."

5. Fanon (1986:111).

6. Blanchot (1995a:6).

7. Holland (2013:1); Blanchot (1995a:2).

8. Blanchot (1995a:47), translation modified. We follow here the modified translation of Leslie Hill (2012:303).

9. Blanchot (1995a:47), translation modified. We follow here the modified translation of Hill (2012:303).

10. Blanchot (1995a:39).

11. Blanchot (1995b:333).

12. Blanchot (1995a:38); Blanchot (1980:65).

13. Blanchot (1995a:1).

14. Blanchot (1995a:3).

15. Blanchot (1995a:4).

16. Blanchot (1995a:1).

17. Blanchot (1995a:30).

18. Cf. writings on "the new materialism," such as Coole and Frost (2010); Bennett (2010).

19. To draw from Veena Das, who writes of the ways in which a violent event "attaches itself with its tentacles into everyday life and folds itself into the recesses of the ordinary" (2007:1, 7).

20. On potentiality and "potentiality for darkness" see Agamben (2000:181). See also Malabou (2009; 2012) on plasticity and metamorphic potential; and Zigon (2018:13-17) for "an anthropology of potentiality."

21. Blanchot (1992a:129).

22. Blanchot (1995a:30). On this, see also Desjarlais (2018b).

23. Blanchot (1980:3).

24. I later learned that one reason the scaffolding was put up around the Bataclan was to deter people from writing on the facades of the building or leaving flowers, letters, and other artifacts of mourning and memory near the building itself. While I initially gave thought to focusing my anthropological inquiries on the attack at the Bataclan and its aftereffects, I decided to attend primarily to the setting of Le Carillon, in part because the bar, unlike the music hall, was an important aspect of the everyday lives of many people, and also because it was easier for me to spend time there on a daily basis. But see Gensburger (2017). [R. D.]

25. This point was made by Sarah Gensburger and Gérôme Truc in their talk, "Paris in Shock: Traces and Memory of the 2015 Terrorist Attacks," at La Maison Française at NYU, 17 October 2016. [R. D.]

26. See Truc (2016; 2017; 2019) on the social responses to terrorist attacks in France and elsewhere; and Gensburger (2017; 2019) and Gensburger and Truc (2020) for comprehensive accounts of the memorials that took form in Paris in the wake of the attacks there in 2015.

27. "Paris café hit by terrorist attack reopens to public," *France 24*, 12 December 2015. www.france24.com/en/20151204-paris-cafe-bonne-biere-terrorist-attacks-reopens-public.

28. Ottavi (2016). *Trans.*

29. Ottavi (2016). *Trans.*

30. Telo and Leclaire (2015).

31. *Nuit debout*, which has been translated into English as "Rise up at night," or "Standing night," is a French social movement that began on 31 March 2016, arising out of protests against the government-proposed labor reforms. The movement began at the place de la République in Paris, where protestors held nightly gatherings

following the first protest, and then spread to other cities and towns in France as well as neighboring countries in Europe.

32. Fenby (2016:xix).

33. On this see Karpiak (2016).

34. *"Ça a l'air si paisible . . . du mal à s'imaginer l'horreur qui c'est produit ici . . . merci de mettre une autre image sur ce lieu."* Comments on Eric et Ramzy's Facebook page, www.facebook.com/ericetramzy, 17 November 2015. The link to the film clip can be found at: www.facebook.com/ericetramzy/videos/1183292015018633.

35. *"Nous, on va continuer d'essayer de faire marrer, et vous allez essayer de vous marrer. C'est tout ce qu'on sait faire, c'est tout ce qu'on peut faire aujourd'hui. Continuer."* "Nous, on va continuer d'essayer de faire marrer," *LeMatin,* 18 November 2015. www.lematin.ch/people/Nous-on-va-continuer-d-essayer-de-faire-marrer /story/20049762.

36. Boinet (2015). See also: "Attentats de Paris: L'hommage d'Eric et Ramzy au Carillon," *Allociné,* 18 November 2015.

37. Perez (1998:28).

38. Comments on Eric and Ramzy's Facebook page: www.facebook.com /ericetramzy, 17 November 2015.

39. The temporal and imaginative logic here echoes Roland Barthes's discussion of photography in *Camera Lucida* (Barthes 2010). [R. D.]

40. Bernard Stiegler, in Derrida (2014:86): *"Tout film est hanté par cette 'hantologie.'"*

41. When working on elements of the first draft of the present chapter, it occurred to me that my method of writing about the small events of the everyday echoed a book I had read years ago, namely Georges Perec's *An Attempt at Exhausting a Place in Paris* (2010). Other writings that have influenced the writing this chapter include Michael Taussig's *The Nervous System* (1992) and Kathleen Stewart's *Ordinary Affects* (2007); Georges Didi-Huberman's writings on photographs and other material traces of violence (2012; 2017); and Walter Benjamin's writings on the politics of representation, experience, and sensuous artifacts of cities in the nineteenth and twentieth centuries (Benjamin 1969; 1983; 1999; 2006a; 2006b). [R. D.]

42. Throughout my writing, I mention several urban spaces that overlap. North Paris refers to the urban spaces north of Gare du Nord and stretches from the 18th and 19th arrondissements into the Seine-Saint-Denis department (known colloquially as "ninety-three" [*quatre-vingt-treize*] or "nine-three" [*neuf-trois*] after the department's numerical code). The Goutte d'Or is a neighborhood located in the 18th arrondissement of Paris. The southern part of the Goutte d'Or is called Barbès and has historically served as a central cultural and commercial space for North African immigration to France. From rue Myrha to the barbed-wired wall on rue Ordener, the northern section of the neighborhood is called Château Rouge. Château Rouge, along with Château d'Eau (a neighborhood located in the old arcades and passageways south of Gare de l'Est), is a majority Black, Caribbean, and African cosmopolitan space. The north of Paris is dynamic and these categories shift, with offbeat rhythms of urban fixation and displacement. [K. H.]

43. Toubon and Messamah (1990:53–65).

44. See Chevalier (1969) and Zola ([1877] 2009).

45. For a sociohistory of "the Zone," or the immediate periphery of Paris, see Beauchez, Jérôme, and Djemila Zeneidi (2019).

46. Toubon and Messamah (1990:115, 419).

47. Toubon and Messamah (1990:115, 419).

48. For a historiography of *bidonvilles* in metropolitan France, see Gastaut (2004). For a sociology and history of the *bidonville* of Nanterre, see Sayad and Dupuy (1995). The most acute forms of segregation and the contemporary geography of shantytowns in metropolitan France concern Roma communities; see, for instance, Cousin (2015).

49. While the persecution of Jewish Parisians is often narrated as a tragic effect of German occupation, it is worth stressing that state and popular anti-Semitism are not German imports. In fact, the synagogue on rue Sainte-Isaure, off rue Ordener, was bombed in October 1941 by members of a French fascist organization, the Social Revolutionary Movement. Fascist militancy nonetheless faced active Jewish communist and anarchist resistance. For more on the Jewish communities of contemporary North Paris, see Endelstein (2004); and Simon, Hily, and Meintel (2000); see also the autobiography of Sarah Kofman, *Rue Ordener, rue Labat* (1994). [K. H.]

50. I borrow the expression "battle of Paris" from Einaudi (1991). Although Einaudi refers to the massacre of October 1961 to build his parallel between the 1957 "Battle of Algiers" and early 1960s Paris, the work of police historian Emmanuel Blanchard, most notably *La police parisienne et les Algériens* (2011), highlights how the police procedures and practices tailored to Algerians emerged from over twenty years of racist policing. For an example of colonial representations infusing police practices, see Blanchard (2012) on the 1955 riots in the Goutte d'Or. [K. H.]

51. Péju ([1961] 2000), and Blanchard (2011).

52. Gilmore (2007:28).

53. Sammut (1976).

54. See Fischer (2008; 2017) for a historical and ethnographic overview of the immigration detention system in France.

55. See *La Croix* (2016).

56. Jobard (2005).

57. Monjardet (1996). See also Gauthier and Jobard (2018).

58. Gauthier (2010, 2012). For an analysis of police violence, and its racist and sexist articulations, see Gauthier (2018).

59. The quotes are taken from an opinion piece published in *Le Monde* (Debray et al. 1998), and signed by important figures of National Republicanism in France, such as Alain Finkelkraut and Régis Debray: *"Républicains, n'ayons plus peur !"* Fearless Republicans, imbued with racist psychosis, denigrating non-European immigration. I borrow the term *moral panic* to qualify such phantasmagorical paranoia from Wacquant (2008). [K. H.]

60. For a sociological history of the French Left spearheading of national security policy, and the subsequent legislation on public-private security contracting in France, see Bonelli (2010).

61. For an ethnography of the BAC, see Fassin (2013).

62. Concretely, "judiciary procedures relative to the zone" are stamped with the letters *ZSP* for the prosecutors in order to: (1) monitor these cases as they enter the judiciary process; (2) report them back to coordination meetings with the actors of the ZSP; and (3) maintain the celerity and the severity of due process for these cases as they continue their path to the relevant jurisdictions. See the Paris Police Prefecture's publicly accessible notebooks, the *Cahiers de la préfecture* on the Barbès-Château Rouge ZSP (Communication Service of the Paris Police Prefecture 2013:10–13). [K. H.]

63. See the publicly accessible Parisian Contract for Prevention and Security (Marie de Paris 2015).

64. At the time mayor of the 18th arrondissement, Daniel Vaillant, conceived of the ZSP as a means to build a neighborhood that would be "modern, hygienic, in the norms." In line with this objective of cleansing and normalizing the neighborhood in accord with a vision of a clean, luminous, European city, the ZSP also coordinates the administrative policing of local commerce and a specific targeting of African-owned bars, cafés, restaurants, grocery shops, barbers, and salons, international call shops and cybercafes (with surveillance enforced by police, hygiene and labor inspection, social assistance and tax collection, and customs). The concerted efforts of public authorities in the Goutte d'Or also participate in a progressive transformation of the African cosmopolitan social and cultural makeup of the neighborhood in favor of European, middle-class residents—that is, gentrification. Through the promotion of "social mixing" (*mixité sociale*), civil servants and families with higher income than the neighborhood average are given priority in social housing attributions; businesses that contrast with the African commercial centrality also receive priority attributions from the SEMAVIP (Société d'économie mixte d'aménagement de la ville de Paris) for leases and subsidies. I explore the question of gentrification in a master's thesis (Paris IEP, 2017); see Habrih (2017). [K. H.]

65. This method of police patrol is referred to as *îlotage* or "islanding" and is used to displace a group that has taken to socializing or engaging in commerce in a given, relatively small area. On the place de l'Assommoir, rue des Islettes in Barbès, *îlotage* was used to harass street vendors with daily stop-and-frisk tactics and patrol perimeters tightening around the street. [K. H.]

66. Glissant (1989:65).


CHAPTER TWO: GRAFFS

*Epigraph:* Benjamin (1983:6).

1. Benjamin (2005).

2. On this see Etkind (2013:19–23).

3. Quote: *"choisis minutieusement à l'avance au cœur de la capital française."* "L'Etat islamique revendique les attentats de Paris," 14 Novembre, 2015.

4. Ponniah (2015).

5. As Blanchot writes of friendship (1980:29).

6. See, for instance, Jean Laplanche's discussion of Freud's theory of trauma and seduction in Caruth (2014:29–30).

7. Lacan (1978:52–64).

8. Lukić (2013:viii).

9. Feldman (2019:82–83).

10. Anna (2015).

11. Derrida (2014:60). *Trans.*

12. Derrida (1996b:2).

13. On the concept of destinerrance see, for instance, Derrida (1987).

14. Derrida (1996b:91).

15. Derrida (1996b:91).

16. Fernando and Raissiguier (2016:125–26).

17. Ackerly and Gontarski (2014:16).

18. "Indeed, it is hard to think of an aporia as inducing a static paralytic state, since it leaves an always restless, unresolved remainder" (Wortham 2010:15).

19. To draw from the philosopher Sarah Kofman's writings on the concept of aporia in ancient Greece (1988:21; 1983:49).

20. In December 2001, Don DeLillo wrote of a similar empty bafflement and the struggle to comprehend in the wake of the attacks on the World Trade Center in New York in September of that year: "There is no logic in apocalypse. . . . The writer begins in the towers, trying to imagine the moment, desperately. . . . In its desertion of every basis of comparision, the event asserts its singularity. There is something empty in the sky. The writer tries to give memory, tenderness, and meaning to all that howling space" (2001:34, 29).

21. Blanchot (1980:11). *The Writing of the Disaster* inscribes this aporetic question on one of the most confounding events of the twentieth century: "How is it possible to say: Auschwitz has happened?" (1980:143). Christophe Bident remarks, "This shattering question undoes all the possible relations of memory and oblivion" (2019:407).

22. Blanchot (1995a:7).

23. To draw from words of Derrida (1996a:31).

24. Derrida (1993a:12).

25. For a firsthand history of the Parisian graffiti scene, see the autobiography of graffer COMER OBK (2020).

26. See Chamboredon and Lemaire (1970) for an analysis of the selection process in social housing attributions and the social trajectories of *grands ensembles* residents.

27. Tissot (2007).

28. Tissot (2007).

29. Dikeç (2006:60).

30. Wacquant (2007).

31. Villanueva (2015; 2018).

32. Henni (2017).

33. The French forest code of 1827 (*Code forestier*) partook in the sequestration of land, from the beginning of the conquest in 1830 until the formal end of French colonization. In 1838, the forest service (*service forestier*) was created to enforce the prohibition of controlled fires (then practiced by the nomadic tribes of the Tell and Mitidja regions). Pastoral lands were transformed into forest nurseries, which supplied the French military with wood. Colonization thus articulated itself through the discourse and practice of what came to be defined as policies of "reforestation." The French administration first imposed its presence on territory through the sequestration of land for military use and the dispossession of the pastoral inhabitants (through the spoliation of tribal ownership and common access to land). The tribes of the region, of which a vast majority were nomadic, were then forcefully made sedentary. In 1874, the French legal code applied in Algeria stipulated collective responsibility and collective confiscation of land for "natives" found guilty of violating the colonial and national legislation on forest. By 1885, such spoliation of tribal lands was granted the status of "public utility." The process of uprooting analyzed by Bourdieu and Sayad (1964) can then be understood as a continuation or a dialectic of colonial fixation. See Davis (2007). [K.H.]

34. Sayad (2006:29).

35. Lefebvre ([1974] 1992b; 1992a; 2004).

36. Khatib (1958). See also Debord (1955; 1956).

37. The image that I evoke here takes us back to the "invisible barbed-wire fence of restrictive covenants" in Chicago, studied by Drake and Cayton (1945). See also Duneier (2016). [K.H.]

38. Halbwachs ([1950] 1997).

39. While I engage with Derrida's conception of *trace,* I also ground my understanding in sociologists' use of the term; see Parent and Sabourin (2016). Part of the tension that persists in stigmatized spaces is that the symbolic traces that appear to the social researcher are inscribed in processes of uprooting and fixation. Traces of the past, present, and afterlives of sociocultural collectives—such as the Algerian and Moroccan cultural hub on rue de la Goutte d'Or, or the Haitian and Congolese commercial centrality on rue Doudeauville—are entangled with the symbolic and material traces of their displacement by state authorities. This produces a complication for anyone trying to assemble a representative and relatively exhaustive portrayal of the neighborhood; it forces one to grapple with the "absent presence" of exile (Darwish 2011) within urban forms. I would therefore like to suggest that we conceptualize immigrant and stigmatized urban spaces in terms of "spatialities of exile" wherein the symbolic traces of collective memory encompass both elements of cultural and commercial life *and* state-sanctioned processes of displacement, uprooting and fixation. [K.H.]

*Epigraphs:* Penhoën, as cited with an epigraph in Assia Djebar's novel *Fantasia: An Algerian Calvacade* (1989:1; 1985:1). Blanchot (1986:145; 1980:220): "*Nous ne sommes pas assez éveillés: veiller au-delà de la veille; la vigilance est la nuit qui veille.*"

1. Foucault (2009:20).

2. Jusionyte and Goldstein (2016:6). See also Vigh (2011), who writes of "hyper-vigilance" and "negative potentiality" in situations of violence.

3. On anomaly detection see Feldman, Akthar, and Karlitekin (2017).

4. Gordon (2008:xix); Asad (2017).

5. Geisser (2003:11).

6. Geisser (2010:39).

7. Fernando (2014:45).

8. As of 20 November 2015; to quote from a statement posted on the website of France's Ministère des Armées [Ministry of the Armed Forces]: "*Sont engagés sur le territoire national pour défendre et protéger les Français.*" www.defense.gouv.fr.

9. Foucault (2003:43–62). See also Feldman (2015:70–73).

10. Foucault (2003:47).

11. Masco (2014:1).

12. Fassin (2016).

13. Fassin (2016).

14. Fassin (2016).

15. Lukić (2013:2).

16. Deleuze and Parnet (2011): "*Un animal est un être fondamentalement aux aguets.*"

17. Lukić (2013:1, 15).

18. On this, see Brown (2010).

19. See Rancière (2004:12) on the concept of "the distribution of the sensible."

20. Feldman, Akthar, and Karlitekin (2017).

21. Statements such as these go uncontextualized and anonymized here, unsited in precise identities or situations; they are part of a ragpicker's selection of the city's discourses. [R. D.]

22. See Maguire and Fussey (2016), for instance.

23. The concept of "visceral modes of appraisal" is drawn from Connolly (1999:27); see also Hirschkind (2006:9).

24. The thought that there could be an assemblage of vigilance is inspired, in part, by the seminar led by Nicolas Dodier and Anthony Stavrianiakis on the subject of assemblages [*agencement*] held at L'EHESS in the spring of 2017. See Dodier and Stavrianakis (2018). [R. D.]

25. On the idea of "hauntology," see Derrida (1994).

26. On "phantasmography," see Desjarlais (2016; 2018a).

27. Maurice Blanchot (1995a:121): "The writer: daytime insomniac."

28. Kafka (2016:22).

29. The OAS was a settler terrorist organization that advocated for white European rule in an independent Algeria. Constituted of a network of high-ranking

military officers and doctors, the OAS was responsible for a series of assassinations, bombings, and coups d'état attempts in Algeria and in metropolitan France during the Algerian war of independence. [K. H.]

30. For instance, Dubet (1987).

31. See for instance Lapeyronnie (1999). Others, like Wacquant (2008) or Mohammed (2011), whose work pertained to the formation of youth gangs (*bandes de jeunes*), offer strong counterpoints insofar as they refrain from reiterating homogenizing descriptions of the banlieue as spaces of anomy and violence. They remain, however, committed to a particular commitment to explain and solve "social problems." My overall orientation vis-à-vis this field of study has been contrapuntal. For instance, I understand delinquency not as a form of criminalized *deviance* but as a set of economic activities among many others that make up the neighborhood. Sex work, drug dealing, and contraband interact and make up the immigrant commercial centrality as much as more established, legal businesses. Rather than highlight participants' (as well as my own) involvement or proximity to criminalized activities or stigmatize such activities, I "sociologized" my interlocutors in line with Sayad's sociology of exile and the "double absence" of immigrants-emigrants. For an illustration of this approach after the 2005 urban uprising and the state of emergency, with young French teenagers of Algerian descent, see Mansouri (2013); for a general sociology rooted in reflexive analysis see *The Weight of the World* (Bourdieu 1999). [K. H.]

32. For a discussion on the use of *jeunes de banlieue* as a symbol of broken social ties, see Longhi (2012). For examples of scholarship that reinforces the stigmatization of Black and North-African youth at large and transfers sociosymbolic stigma into scholarship, see Aquatias (1997); and, for more recent examples touching on Islam and antiterrorism, see Kepel (2015) and Rougier (2020). [K. H.]

33. Du Bois ([1903] 2007:11).

34. Haggerty and Ericson (2000).

### CHAPTER FOUR: LEARNING WITH THE BODY

*Epigraph:* Sayad (2004:260).

1. For a theoretical explanation of the concepts, see Bourdieu (1977:72–78); for an operational example of habitus and body hexis, see Bourdieu (2014) on the class habitus and corporeality of middle-class Frenchmen (*les petits bourgeois*).

2. Loïc Wacquant (2018:528–29) writes that the concept of *habitus* finds its roots "in Aristotle's notion of *hexis,* elaborated in his doctrine of virtue in the *Nicomachean Ethics* (ca. 350 BCE), meaning an acquired yet entrenched state of moral character that orients our feelings and desires, and thence our conduct.... It resurged in phenomenology, most prominently in the writings of Edmund Husserl, who designated by habitus the mental conduit between past experiences and forthcoming actions. Husserl also used as a conceptual cognate the term *Habitualität,* later translated into English by his student Alfred Schutz as 'habitual knowledge' (and thence

adopted by ethnomethodology), a notion that resonates with that of *habitude,* as refined by Maurice Merleau-Ponty in his treatment of the 'lived body' as the mute yet intelligent wellspring of social meaning and behavior." For the works referenced by Wacquant, see Husserl (1975), Schutz (1973), and Merleau-Ponty (1962). For more on Bourdieu and phenomenology, see Atkinson (2018); for a more critical engagement with Bourdieu's reading of phenomenologists' work, see Throop and Murphy (2002). [K. H.]

3. Mauss (1973; 1936).

4. Mauss (1973; 1936).

5. See Wacquant (2011). For an example of a body-oriented ethnographic sociology, see also Wacquant (2004).

6. Foucault (1975; 1995).

7. Faubion (2011:4).

8. Ahmed (2006:111).

9. Ahmed (2006:111).

10. Fassin (2011:431).

11. Ahmed (2006:139).

12. Bourdieu (1990).

13. Ahmed (2006:139).

14. Shabazz (2015).

15. This perspective is largely informed by the work of psychologists Kenneth Bancroft Clark and Mamie Phipps Clark; specifically, K. B. Clark's analysis of dispossession in 1960s Harlem. Beyond the structural realities of segregation, spatial closure, restricted access to labor, and exploitation, Clark and Clark pointed to the affective impressions that racism left in young Black persons' subjectivities. See Clark (1965). This, in turn, is a helpful methodological orientation: taking into account these subjective impressions as traces of violence, one can then begin to work with administrative documents, archives, legal texts, and so on in order to identify the practices that have left such impressions. That is, to move from traces of violence toward a study of the practical and institutional articulations of this violence. [K. H.]

16. See Barkat (2005).

17. Sayad (1999b:11–13).

18. The nicknames listed here are not pseudonyms and refer to actual police officers who patrolled the streets of the ZSP at the time. I have retained them because, since the time of these interviews, a number of these officers have had complaints filed against them. Namely, the officer dubbed Karim the Kabyle was arrested on charges of corruption, extortion, and racketeering. See Decugis and Jérémie Pham-Le (2019). [K. H.]

19. Blanchard (2014); see also Garfinkel (1956).

20. Bentounsi, Dieng, Traoré, and Garand all started organizing politically to fight for charges to be brought against the police and *gendarmerie* officers that killed their brothers. Their work, like the work of other families and collectives founded in similar circumstances, is often unsuccessful in terms of the judicial cases brought

against the police. Nevertheless, this grassroots form of political organization continues to leave deep, lasting impressions in immigrant communities and antiracist political action. For more on the feminist perspective that structures women's involvement in antiracist and antiviolence political work, see Ouassak (2020). [K. H.]

21. The sex workers' union STRASS has documented ID checks and pat downs in the northeast neighborhood of Belleville. In the testimonies, working women describe instances of racist and sexist violence comparable in all aspects to the ones described by the young men I interviewed. See the STRASS's report from May 2015, "Police Harassment in Belleville: Testimonies," https://strass-syndicat .org/actualite/harcelement-policier-a-belleville-temoignages. [K. H.]

22. I did not organize interviews with women in the neighborhood. One reason is that, in the case of sex workers, for instance, I did not fully understand how my presence would produce dangerous situations for participants. Whether it be vis-a-vis clients, employers, or police forces, I preferred to cut off part of the fieldwork rather than participate in making women (of varying legal status, racial and gender ascriptions, and housing situations) working in the neighborhood more unsafe. In contradistinction, I had a better sense of how to keep away from police surveillance when the matter at hand was young men who dealt marijuana or hashish on the side. Moreover, I tried a few times to engage in conversations with young women in public space, but I was neither persistent enough nor did I know how to breach certain norms of respect and distance without, as one would, actually breaking them. [K. H.]

23. For more on the way these competing normative imperatives are imposed on women living through racial, gendered, and spatial ascriptions, see the work of Beth Richie (2012) on the "matrix of violence" that Black women face in the US "prison nation."

24. In what is currently referred to as the United States and Canada, practices of congregation and relearning spiritual practices by Indigenous nations and communities is a process of reformulating and reclaiming corporeal autonomy as much as it is a step toward political and territorial sovereignty. See, for instance, Ramirez (2007) or Estes (2019). [K. H.]

25. "*Attentat au Bataclan: La mésentente entre policiers et gendarmes au grand jour.*" *Le Parisian,* 25 March 2016, www.leparisien.fr/faits-divers/attentat-au-bataclan -la-mesentente-entre-policiers-et-gendarmes-au-grand-jour-25-03-2016-5660669 .php.

26. Jünger (1960:54).


CHAPTER FIVE: ARCHIVE SORROW


*Epigraphs:* "*Les archives appartiennent au gouvernement, c'est pour lui qu'elles existent.*" Léon de Laborde (1867:151–52), as cited in Grand (2006:26). Léon de Laborde appears to be quoting the words of Pierre Claude François Daunou, who held the

post of archivist of the empire in France from 1807 to 1814. Blanchot (1980:12):
"*Ce n'est pas toi qui parleras; laisse le désastre parler en toi, fût-ce par oubli ou par silence.*"

1. Blanchot (1995a:75). Blanchot (1980:121): "*Rupture toujours en rupture.*"

2. Blanchot (1995a:75). Blanchot (1980:121): "*vicissitudes harassantes du proche (du voisinage).*"

3. Chrisafis (2016).

4. Judt (2008:197).

5. As Khalil Habrih has pointed out to me. [R. D.]

6. Judt (2008:197; 2005:826).

7. Etkind (2013:176).

8. In Philippe Burin's words, "France has tended to conceive of its conflicts in historical terms, and to conceive of its history in terms of conflict" (Burin 1992; as cited in Judt 2008:200).

9. "From the street to the archives: the case of the homages to the victims of the attacks of Friday 13 November 2015 collected in January 2016," Archives de Paris. https://openagenda.com/jep-2016-ile-de-france/events/le-cas-des-hommages-aux-victimes-des-attentats-du-vendredi-13-novembre-2015-collectes-en-janvier-2016-de-la-rue-aux-archives.

10. Le Mitouard (2016).

11. "It is thus, in this *domiciliation,* in this house arrest, that archives take place" (Derrida 1996b:2).

12. Derrida (1996b:17).

13. Fernando and Raissiguier make a similar point in writing about the public and governmental responses to the Charlie Hebdo attacks in January 2015, including the collective marches and ubiquitous slogans invoked in the days following the attacks: "through performatives like *Je suis Charlie* and the *marche républicaine,* certain subjects are given center stage while others are foreclosed" (2016:128). [R. D.]

14. An archive containing materials collected after the Charlie Hebdo attacks was established in the summer of 2015, at the Harvard University Library—far from the archives of the city of Paris. On the "Charlie Archive" at Harvard University, see, for instance, https://library.harvard.edu/collections/charlie-archive. [R. D.]

15. As quoted in Soullier (2015): "*On a regretté. La première fois, on ne savait pas faire.*"

16. In drawing from this sentence of Jacques Derrida (1995:142): "*C'est n'avoir de cesse, interminablement, de chercher l'archive là où elle se dérobe.*"

17. Le Mitouard (2016). *Trans.*

18. As quoted in Le Mitouard (2016). *Trans.*

19. As quoted in Soullier (2015): "*de créer une matière qui racontera l'histoire dans cent ans.*"

20. Derrida (1996b:36; 1995:60).

21. Derrida (1996b:18; 1995:37).

22. Derrida (1995:132).

23. Archives de Paris. www.archives.paris.fr/r/137/hommages-aux-victimes
-des-attentats-de-2015.

24. *"Un progiciel dédié aux services d'archives publiques départementales ou communales."* See www.arkotheque.fr/r/43/nos-solutions.

25. *"Affichez vos images dans un espace ergonomique, intuitif et séduisant!"* See www.arkotheque.fr/r/102/visionneuse.

26. Derrida (1995:14).

27. Derrida (1996b:11; 1995).

28. On the ideas of a "shadow archive" or "anarchive," see Lippit (2005). Brozgal (2020) writes of the literary and visual representations of the police massacre of Algerian protestors on 17 October 1961 as an "anarchive" that works in contrast to the dominant narratives and representations of the French state and police. See also Torlasco (2013); Azoulay (2012) on a "willful exposure to archive fever"; and Singh (2018) on the idea and possibility of a personal archive of the body as an inventory of historical traces in a body.

29. See Hage (2015).

30. To draw from a phrase and perspective of Jacques Derrida's (1995:103; 1996b:64).

31. Samir had neighbors like DJ Myst and DJ Phaxx.

32. Didier Drogba was the captain of the Ivory Coast national football team. He is also known for his career at the Chelsea Football Club. The neighborhood Samir refers to here is the Baconnets in Antony, in the Hauts-de-Seine (92) department, south of Paris. [K. H.]


CHAPTER SIX: A TRACE IS THE MARK OF
SOMETHING NOT THERE

*Epigraph:* Blanchot (1992b:50).

1. Blanchot (1995a:6; 1980:16).

2. On this see Stoler (2016:5–6).

3. For other scholarly writings on traces see Chamoiseau and Hammadi (1994); Napolitano (2015); Galinon-Mélénec (2011); Galinon-Mélénec, Liénard, and Zlitni (2015); Ladwig (2013); Yoneyama (1999); Navaro-Yashin (2012); Ginzburg (1989; 2012); Crossland (2014); Keller (2015); Weizman (2017); and Bachner (2017). The conceptual orientation to traces developed here is influenced by Jacques Derrida's deconstructive engagements with the concept of "trace" through his scholarly career (from Derrida 1967 to 2014, for instance). [R. D.]

4. By "burning" the border, the man is referring to the practice of crossing international borders without proper administrative status—the papers in question might as well have been burnt. Every day that goes by in Algeria, the *harraga* leave from the northern coast of Africa on makeshift fishing boats and head to the shores of Spain, Sicily, France—often risking death at sea. [K. H.]

5. The French term for "undeclared work" is *travail au noir,* which literally translates to *black labor* or *labor in the black*. [K. H.]

CHAPTER SEVEN: "WHERE WOUNDS ARE BARELY
SCARRED OVER ONE IS CUT ANEW"

*Epigraph:* Fanon (2004:181, 2002:239). *"Mais la guerre continue. Et nous aurons à panser des années encore les plaies multiples et quelquefois indélébiles faites à nos peuples par le déferlement colonialiste."*

1. Recherche, Assistance, Intervention, Dissuasion (Search, Assistance, Intervention, Deterrence), commonly abbreviated RAID, is an elite police special forces unit of the French National Police comparable to the SWAT in the United States.

2. The one trace of this petition that we have found online was published 23 November 2011, on the website for the *Groupe communist—front de Gauche*.

3. Khalil Habrih apparently had in mind here James Scott's *Domination and the Arts of Resistance: Hidden Transcripts* (1992). [R. D.]

4. Derrida (1994:xviii): "And this being with specters [*être-avec les spectres*] would be also, not only but also a politics of memory, of heritage and generations."

5. As noted in Mortimer (2008).

6. Pennetier and Croft (2017).

7. To draw from the title and argument of Miriam Ticktin's 2010 book, *Casualties of Care*. See also Raissiguier (2010) on the politics and cultural history of immigration and persons *sans-papiers* in the Republic of France; and Stevenson (2014) on the politics and complex ambiguities of governmental care in postcolonial settings.

8. On "war machines" see Höller and Mbembe (2007). See Fassin (2013), for an incisive ethnography of urban policing in and around Paris. See also Karpiak and Garriott (2018), for anthropological studies of police more generally.

9. See Shalhoub-Kevorkian (2015) on surveillance and state security practices in Israel, and the "politics of fear" that these practices generate in Palestinian experiences of life and death within the context of Israeli settler colonialism.

10. See Das (2007:162–64) on the signature of the state in India; and Feldman (2015) on the ways in which a sovereign state inscribes its signature of power into the body politic, writ large or small, within the frameworks of contemporary warfare and political visuality.

11. Crapanzano (2011:187).

12. See Crapanzano for an incisive psychoanalytic-anthropological account of the "wounds" that Algerian men known as Harkis have carried through the lives, after siding with the French military during the Algerian war of independence, and the "double wound" that the children of the Harkis carry (2011:187).

13. See Rios (2020) for a comparable account of the formal and informal policing of blackness in St. Louis, Missouri.

14. For scholarly writings on debates around religious clothing and practices, Islam, secularism, and Islamophobia in France, see Bowen (2008); Scott (2010); Fernando (2014).

15. See Feldman (2015:315) on the historically generative potential in "collective scarification" in post-Apartheid South Africa.

16. For details on torture conducted by the French police in Paris in the early 1960s, see House and MacMaster (2006:86–87); Péju ([1961] 2000); Panijel (1962). House and MacMaster write: "Between 17 January and 9 March 1961 at least twenty-seven named individuals claimed they had been tortured in the HQ of the *harkis* at 28 rue de la Goutte d'Or, and 9 rue Harvey in the 18th and 13th arrondissements" (84). Evaluating the historical record, they observe that, "The balance of evidence is that the terrible experiences recorded by FLN suspects in the cellars of central Paris did indeed occur, and that several of them attempted suicide by slashing themselves with shards of glass and by hanging" (87). [R. D.]

17. Such imaginings were informed by the transcribed testimonies of apparent victims of torture at the police precinct in 1959–60, as recorded in Paulette Péju's book, *Ratonnades à Paris, précédé de Les harkis à Paris* ([1961] 2000), which I had been reading closely at the time, along with repeated viewings of Jacques Panijel's film, *Octobre à Paris* (1962), which includes scenes where several persons speak of the ways in which they were tortured. [R. D.]

18. On the "weaponized architecture" of police stations in the *banlieues* of Paris, see Lambert (2016).

19. Breeden and Polonyijan (2016).

20. On sovereignty and the right of death, see Foucault (1984:258–72).

21. See Derrida (2005; 2009); Feldman (2015:117–77). See also Nass (2008:187–212) on the phantasm of the sovereign in Derrida's thought and writings.

22. "La famille de Tarek Belgacem, abattu devant le commissariat de la Goutte d'Or, va porter plainte," *Huffington Post,* France, 19 January 2016, www.huffingtonpost.fr/2016/01/19/famille-tarek-belgacem-commissariat-goutte-dor-plainte_n_9017778.html.

23. Chieze and Quelen (2016).

24. Cases rebelles (2017).

25. See, for example, Branche (2016:396–98).

26. Branche (2016:394–95). *Trans.*

27. Branche (2016:395). *Trans.*

28. Feraoun (2000:214–15).

29. Branche (2016:398). *Trans.*

30. Blasim (2014:1–11).

31. Blasim (2014:5).

32. Derrida (1994: xviii; 1993b:15): "*Et cet être-avec les spectres serait aussi, non seulement mais aussi une politique de la mémoire, de l'héritage et des générations.*"

33. Gordon (2008:64). See also Tuck and Ree (2013:654); and Good and Rahimi (2019).

34. Gordon (2008:xvi).

35. Derrida and Stiegler (2002:116).

36. Didi-Huberman (2017:81).

37. For writings on the events of 17 October 1961, see Péju (2000); Einaudi (1991; 2001; 2009); Tristan (1991); and House and Macmaster's comprehensive account, *Paris 1961: Algerians, State Terror, and Memory* (2006). Documentary films on 17 October 1961 include Panijel (1962) and Adi (2011). See also Leïla Sebbar's novel, *La Seine était rouge* (1999; 2008). Michael Haneke's 2005 film *Caché* reflects in powerful ways the haunting effects of French colonialism, and the events of October 1961, on the lives and memories of French and Algerian peoples. Of the film's first showings in France, Crapanzano remarks, "Tellingly, the film, which played for an exceptionally short time in France, was ignored" (2011:200n4).

38. To quote Algerian-French writer Leïla Sebbar on the matter; Mortimer (2008:xvii).

39. Ann Stoler (2016) aptly speaks of a "colonial aphasia" limiting speech and thought around the unruly histories of colonialism in France. [R. D.]

40. The photographer was Jean Texier, who worked for the newspaper *L'Humanité*.

41. House and Macmaster (2006:318). See House and Macmaster (2006:317–19) for details on the debates around the idea of establishing a memorial plaque, and the establishment of the plaque.

42. Other commemorative plaques set in places on the margins of Paris, such as one close to the Gare de Saint-Denis in the commune of Saint-Denis, do name the Paris police as being the agents responsible for the deadly violence of 17 October 1961. The configuration of political interests in these communes apparently made such statements possible. [R. D.]

43. To invoke a phrase of philosopher Maurice Merleau-Ponty (1962:242). See Al-Saji (2008).

44. Maura Finkelstein develops the term "unvisibility" to write of the ways in which certain features of life and mill work in Mumbai come to be "unrecognized" and "unvisible": "like nonrecognition, 'unvisible' suggests agency and refusal: a practice of unseeing something until it no longer can be seen" (2019:45). Ann Stoler (2016) writes of the "occluded histories of empire," and the ways in which "occlusion" can limit, block, pattern, and channel understandings of history of colonialism past and present, and the politics of contemporary life. One incisive example of an occluded history of empire in Stoler's *Duress* is the way in which the Israeli occupation of Palestine is commonly not seen as a situation of colonial occupation, whereas Stoler and others convincingly argue that it is (Stoler 2016:37–67; see also Shalhoub-Kevorkian 2015). Also to be considered are the ways in which certain forms of the past are "silenced" due to political interests and acts of writing and unwriting on the part of the powerful (see Trouillot 1995). [R. D.]

45. To invoke the words of Austrian writer Peter Handke (2009:182).

46. To draw from the words of Michel Foucault, invoked late in his life, in relating his efforts to "think differently" or "otherwise" (*autrement*) in historiographic and philosophical thought: "There are times in life when the question of knowing if one can think differently than one thinks, and perceive differently than one sees,

is absolutely necessary if one is to go on looking and reflecting at all (Foucault 1990:8–9).

47. Lorde (1984:36).

48. Honoré de Balzac, *Ferragus* (1884). As cited in Colin Jones's *Paris: Biography of a City* (2004), which offers a comprehensive history of Paris.

49. Breton (1960:83).

50. *Harrag* is the nominal form of the verb *harga*, from North African *darija*, "to burn." Irregular border crossing, to cross the Mediterranean by boat, without visa. The *harraga* (plural) are those who burn the border. [K. H.]

51. Macé, Galtier, and Le Devin (2016).

52. For more on this, see the 2007 documentary film *365 jours à Clichy -Montfermeil*, shot by Ladj Ly and produced by the film collective Kourtrajmé.

53. For an informed perspective on anthropological taxidermy and visual ethnography, see Rony (1996:99–126).

54. Hinson (1999). As cited by Lassiter (2005:12).

55. Spradley (1999).

56. Duneier (1992).

57. Rabinow (1977, 1991).

58. That is not to say that anthropological collaboration, in the form of shared authority, vision, *and authorship* does not exist. On the contrary, see, for instance, the collaborative work *Phone and Spear: A Yuta Anthropology*, crafted by the collective Miyrrka Media (2019).

59. Bourdieu (2003).

60. In that sense, could our collaboration be construed as a spontaneous form of "concept work"? See Rabinow (2011:113–53) and Korsby and Stavrianakis (2016). For more on collaboration in anthropology, see the volume edited by Boyer and Marcus (2021).

61. Ginsburg (1995:65).


CHAPTER EIGHT: THE HISTORIES OF THESE WOUNDS

*Epigraph:* Fanon (2004:185; 2002:243): *"Autrement dit, nos actes ne cessent jamais de nous poursuivre."*

1. On the aftermath of the Charlie Hebdo attacks, see Rimbert (2015).

2. Elias (2008); see also Elias (1991:154–61).

3. Césaire ([1954] 2004). See also Dorlin (2009).

4. While in hiding in Paris in 1940, Walter Benjamin wrote his *Theses on the Philosophy of History*. In a striking passage on Paul Klee's *Angelus Novus*, Benjamin writes: "This is how one pictures the angel of history. His face is turned toward the past. Where we perceive a chain of events, he sees one single catastrophe which keeps piling wreckage upon wreckage and hurls it in front of his feet. The angel would like to stay, awaken the dead, and make whole what has been smashed. But a storm is blowing from Paradise; it has got caught in his wings with such violence that the

angel can no longer close them. This storm irresistibly propels him into the future to which his back is turned, while the pile of debris before him grows skyward. This storm is what we call progress" (1969:257–58).

Later in 1940, Walter Benjamin sent a copy of his *Theses* to Hannah Arendt. In September of that year he committed suicide while unsuccessfully seeking safe passage to Spain. German troops entered Paris; the anti-Semitic French government took its seat in Vichy; and Franco had officially put an end to the Spanish Republic. The metaphors Benjamin builds on—ruin, debris, and storm—inform the perspective developed in this chapter. [K.H.]

5. During the 1980s, Algeria was the scene of political movements in a context of dire economic conditions. In October 1988, demonstrations and riots rocked the northern part of country; hundreds of civilians were killed, thousands arrested. Under the auspices of democratic transition and the end of the National Liberation Front one-party system, parliamentary elections were organized in 1991 and saw the Islamic Salvation Front win a majority of the seats in 1992. The Algerian military organized a coup d'état to stop the process and suspend the Constitution. A state of emergency was enforced; with searches, curfews, and disappearances. Armed factions opposed to the Algerian state committed attacks and assassinations throughout the country. By 1997 some factions had entered in negotiations with the state, as civilians died by the hundreds in massacres in the regions of Wahran (Oran) and Dzayer (Algiers). By 1999 and the election of Abdelaziz Bouteflika, close to 200,000 people died or disappeared in what appeared as a senseless, bloody conflict. The end of the civil war, and the amnesty of all parties of the armed conflict—state and guerrilla alike—makes the *fog* of war one that persists to this day. As Karima Lazali (2018) argues, one could see this as a reiteration of the forms of generalized violence deployed throughout French colonization and beginning with the genocidal war of conquest in 1830. For more on the Algerian civil war, see Souaïdia ([2001] 2012) and Aggoun and Rivoire (2005). [K.H.]

6. See Bouamama (2009:19–30) and Rahem (1996). For more on racism and subjectivation, studied through the lens of young Arab and Black men's relationship to Islam and political violence, see the work of Truong (2017).

7. See Johannes and Fromentin (1995).

8. Khadra (2018:14).

9. Camus (1989:159).

10. Daoud (2015:75).

11. Daoud (2014:85–96; 2015).

12. Fanon (2004:181–234).

13. This interdependence is constitutive of colonial privilege and dispossession. For a full discussion of colonial privilege see Memmi ([1957] 2002).

14. See Wacquant (2000).

15. See Fassin (2008).

16. See Foucault (1997; 2003; 2009).

17. Milliot, Blanchard, Denis, and Houte (2020:177–81).

18. Milliot, Blanchard, Denis, and Houte (2020:307).

19. Brière (2008:313–16). For more on the Haitian revolution, see James ([1938] 1989) and Koufinkana (1992).

20. Le Cour Grandmaison (2005:189).

21. Hamida (2008).

22. The quote is excerpted from Tocqueville's "Travail sur l'Algérie," written in 1841. See Tocqueville (1991:705–6). In the same anthology, see also the "Rapport sur le projet de loi relatif aux crédits extraordinaires demandés pour l'Algérie," written in 1848.

23. Lazali (2018).

24. See the *Royal declaration against vagrants, and the people called Bohemians, and those who offer them retreat,* drafted by Jean-Baptiste Colbert for Louis XIV in 1682; accessible online.

25. Browne (2012), Filhol (2011), and Piazza (2004).

26. See Piazza (2006).

27. See Bénot (2005:9–35). On the ovens of Heliopolis, see Mekhaled (1995).

28. Deltombe, Domergue, and Tatsista (2011).

29. For more on the history of French policing and colonial pacification, see Rigouste (2009, 2012).

30. If one is to study the contemporary ramifications of colonialism in the French *métropole,* one can neither ignore nor unsee the contemporary colonial configuration of French "overseas" territories (*les Outre-mer*). Going further with this shift, understanding the contemporary form of French colonialism in active colonies also forces one to step away from concerns of security and policing as such and, in consequence, to focus on broader concerns of life and death, such as questions of race-making and reproductive health. For instance, throughout the 1960s on the island of La Réunion, hundreds of women underwent forced abortions and sterilizations, under the auspices of modernization of the island and the anti-Black racial control of its "demography." The wounding and the death of women within medical institutions ought to be understood with the same gravity as police patrols and incarceration, for they are, in fact, inscribed within the same economy of power and neuralgia. See Vergès (2016). [K. H.]

31. Ross-Tremblay (2015).

32. Ross-Tremblay (2015) suggests that we think of memory as processual; a mnemohistory thus encapsulates not only the facts of history but also a history of memory, or the changing substance of collective memory. Marianne Hirsch proposes the concept of "postmemory" to qualify the "relationship that the generation after those who witnessed cultural or collective trauma bears to the experiences of those who came before" (2008:106), a relationship to the past "not actually mediated by recall but by imaginative investment, projection, and creation" (107). This bares many similarities with the work of Saidiya Hartman (1997; 2008) on critical fabulation and the afterlives of anti-Black enslavement in the Americas; in the same vein of critical historiography, see also the work signed by Christina Sharpe (2016) and Afro-pessimism more generally. [K. H.]

33. Kerkar (2016). For an anthropological method of "ruination," see Navaro-Yashin (2009).

34. Mohammed (2020).

35. See Fassin (2020). Recent data published by the French Statistics Agency (INSEE) have shown how immigrant communities—and specifically immigrants from West Africa—have been affected by preexisting socioracial hierarchies and discrimination, affecting housing, access to labor and the license to work from home, and access to dignified diagnosis and treatment in public health institutions; resulting in inequality as mortality. See Brun and Simon (2020); a note published by the French Demography Agency (INED) relates their findings in English: www .ined.fr/en/everything_about_population/demographic-facts-sheets/focus-on /excess-mortality-due-to-covid-19-seine-saint-denis-invisibility-of-minorities-in -the-figures. [K. H.]

36. *The Local* (2020).

37. *The Local* (2020).

38. Lough and Salaün (2020).

## REFERENCES


### ADMINISTRATIVE AND STATE DOCUMENTS

CNCDH. 2017. *Avis sur le suivi de l'état d'urgence et les mesures anti-terroristes de la loi du 21 juillet 2016* [Opinion on the state of emergency and the antiterrorist measures of the 21 July 2016 law]. Commission nationale consultative des droits de l'homme [French consultative commission on human rights]. 26 January 2017. www.cncdh.fr/fr/actualite/avis-sur-le-suivi-de-letat-durgence-et-les-mesures-anti -terroristes-de-la-loi-du-21.

Communication Service of the Paris Police Prefecture. 2013. *Les cahiers de la préfecture de police. La zone de sécurité prioritaire Barbès-Château Rouge.* Paris: Events Unit of the Police Préfecture.

Mairie de Paris. 2015. *Contrat parisien de prévention et de sécurité 2015–2020.* Parisian Contract for Prevention and Security, signed by the Municipality of Paris, the Police Prefecture, the Paris High Court, the Paris Airports agency, the Paris Academy and Ministry of National Education, Higher Studies, and Research, and the Prefects of Paris and the Ile-de-France region. Retrieved online: www .paris.fr/pages/l-animation-des-politiques-de-prevention-de-la-delinquance -4788#le-contrat-parisien-de-prevention-et-de-securite.


### FILMS

Adi, Yasmina. 2011. *Ici on noie les Algériens.* Paris.
Haneke, Michael. 2005. *Caché.* Culver City, CA: Sony Classics.
Kerkar, Djamel. 2016. *Atlal.* Paris: Capricci.
Ly, Ladj. 2007. *365 jours à Clichy-Montfermeil.* France: Kourtrajmé Productions.
Panijel, Jacques. 1962. *Octobre à Paris.* Paris.

Anna, Cara. 2015. "ISIS expresses fury over French airstrikes in Syria; France says they will continue." *CTV News,* 14 November 2015.

Boinet, Carole. 2015. "Le Carillon, histoire du QG d'un Paris mixte et festif." *Les InRocks.* 22 November 2015.

Breeden, Aurelien, and Anna Polonyijan. 2016. "Man With Fake Explosives Killed in Paris on Charlie Hebdo Anniversary." *New York Times,* 7 January 2016.

Chieze, Guillaume, and Julien Quelen. 2016. "Le père de Tarek Belgacem, l'assaillant du commissariat de Barbès, accuse la police d'homicide volontaire." *RTL.* 20 January 2016.

Chrisafis, Angelique. 2016. "Memorial plaques unveiled in Paris on first anniversary of attacks." *Guardian,* 13 November 2016.

Debray, Régis, et al. 1998. "Républicains, n'ayons plus peur!" *Le Monde,* 4 September 1998.

Decugis, Jean-Michel, and Jérémie Pham-Le. 2019. "Corruption à la BAC du 18e: Révélations sur un policier trop bien note." *Le Parisien,* 7 July 2019.

Hamida, Chaouky. 2008. "Les enfumades du général Bugeaud, un crime contre l'humanité?" *Le Monde,* 14 June 2008.

Johannes, Franck, and Bernard Fromentin. 1995. "La bande-son de la fin de Khaled Kelkal." *Libération,* 3 October 1995.

*La Croix.* 2016. "23 août 1996, l'évacuation musclée des sans-papiers de l'église Saint-Bernard à Paris." 23 August 2016.

Le Mitouard, Eric. 2016. "Paris a sauvegardé tous les messages en homage aux victimes du 13 novembre." *Le Parisien,* 3 November 2016.

*Local.* 2020. "'France was struck to the heart': Survivors remember Paris attacks." 14 November 2020.

Lough, Richard, and Tangi Salaün. 2020. "Five years after Paris attacks, France still scarred and back on alert." *Reuters,* 13 November 2020.

Macé, Célian, Mathieu Galtier, and Willy Le Devin. 2016. "Goutte d'Or: 'Mon fils n'était pas un terroriste." *Libération,* 12 January 2016.

Mohammed, Hajera. 2020. "À Bagnolet, des militants rebaptisent la station de métro Gallieni." *France Bleu Paris,* 18 June 2020.

Mortimer, Gavin. 2017. "How Cool is Macron?" *Spectactor,* 29 July 2017.

Ottavi, Marie. 2016. "Le Carillon fermé, ça plombait le moral et l'ambiance." *Liberation,* 13 January 2016.

Pennetier, Marine, and Adrian Croft. 2017. "Man dies after climbing on top of Eurostar train in Paris." *Reuters,* 2 May 2017.

Ponniah, Kevin. 2015. "Le Carillon: Paris bar regulars left reeling after attack." *BBC News,* 14 November 2015.

Rimbert, Pierre. 2015. "Soyez libres, c'est un ordre." *Le Monde diplomatique,* February 2015.

Seelow, Soren, Simon Piel, and Emeline Cazi. 2015. "Attentats de Paris : L'assaut du Bataclan, raconté heure par heure." *Le Monde,* 30 December 2015.

Soullier, Lucie. 2015. "Attentats du 13 novembre: Le memorial du Bataclan aux Archives de Paris." *Le Monde,* 14 December 2015.

Telo, Laurent, and Philippe Leclaire. 2015. "Dîner au Petit Cambodge et refaire le monde au Carillon." *Le Monde,* 20 November 2015.

## SCHOLARLY WORKS AND LITERATURE


Ackerly, C. J., and S. E. Gontarski. 2014. *The Grove Companion to Samuel Beckett: A Reader's Guide to His Works, Life, and Thought.* New York: Grove Press.

Agamben, Giorgio. 2000. *Potentialities: Collected Essays in Philosophy.* Stanford: Stanford University Press.

Aggoun, Lounis, and Jean-Baptiste Rivoire. 2005. *Françalgérie, crimes et mensonges d'Etats: Une histoire secrète, de la guerre d'indépendance à la "troisième guerre" d'Algérie.* Paris: La Découverte.

Ahmed, Sara. 2006. *Queer Phenomenology.* Durham, NC: Duke University Press.

———. 2010. *The Promise of Happiness.* Durham, NC: Duke University Press.

Al-Saji, Alia. 2008. "'A Past Which Has Never Been Present': Bergsonian Dimensions of Merleau-Ponty's Theory of the Prepersonal." *Research in Phenomenology* 38:41–71.

Appadurai, Arjun. 2006. *Fear of Small Numbers: An Essay on the Geography of Anger.* Durham, NC: Duke University Press.

Aquatias, Sylvain. 1997. "Jeunes de banlieue, entre communauté et societé: Une approche socioanthropologique du lien social." *Socio-anthropologie* 34 (2): 46–60.

Arendt, Hannah. 1970. *On Violence.* New York. Harcourt Brace.

Artaud, Antonin. 1976. *Selected Writings.* New York: Farrar, Straus and Giroux.

Asad, Talal. 2007. *On Suicide Bombing.* New York: Columbia University Press.

———. 2017. "Remarks on Allen Feldman's *Archives of the Insensible.*" *Social Text Online.* https://socialtextjournal.org/periscope_article/remarks-on-allen-feldmans-archives-of-the-insensible.

Atkinson, Will. 2018. "Bourdieu and Schutz: Bringing Together Two Sons of Husserl." In *The Oxford Handbook of Pierre Bourdieu,* edited by Thomas Medvetz and Jeffrey J. Sallaz, 398–420. Oxford: Oxford University Press.

Azoulay, Ariella. 2012. "Archive." *Political Concepts: A Critical Lexicon* (1). www.politicalconcepts.org/archive-ariella-azoulay.

Bachner, Andrea. 2017. *The Mark of Theory: Inscriptive Figures, Poststructuralist Prehistories.* New York: Fordham University Press.

Barkat, Mohammed. 2005. *Le corps d'exception: Les artifices du pouvoir colonial et la destruction de la vie.* Paris: Amsterdam.

Barthes, Roland. 2010. *Camera Lucida: Reflections on Photography.* New York: Hill and Wang.

Beauchez, Jérôme, and Djemila Zeneidi. 2019. "*Sur la Zone:* A Critical Sociology of the Parisian Dangerous Classes (1871–1973)." *Critical Sociology,* 46 (4–5): 693–710.

Benjamin, Walter. 1969. *Illuminations: Essays and Reflections*. New York: Schocken.

———. 1983. *Charles Baudelaire: A Lyric Poet in the Era of High Capitalism*. London: Verso.

———. 1998. "'An Outsider Attracts Attention': On *The Salaried Masses* by S. Kracauer." In *The Salaried Masses: Duty and Distraction in Weimer Germany*, Siegfried Kracauer, 109–14. London: Verso.

———. 1999. *The Arcades Project*. Translated by Howard Eiland and Kevin McLaughlin. Cambridge, MA: Harvard University Press.

———. 2005. "A Little History of Photography." In *Walter Benjamin: Selected Writings*, vol. 2, part 2, *1931–1934*, edited by M. Jennings, H. Eiland, and G. Smith, 507–27. Cambridge, MA: Harvard University Press.

———. 2006a. *The Writer of Modern Life: Essay on Charles Baudelaire*. Cambridge, MA: Harvard University Press.

———. 2006b. *A Berlin Childhood*. Cambridge, MA: Harvard University Press.

Bennett, Jane. 2010. *Vibrant Matter: A Political Ecology of Things*. Durham, NC: Duke University Press.

Bénot, Yves. 2005. *Massacres coloniaux: La IVᵉ République et la mise au pas des colonies françaises*. Paris: La Découverte.

Bident, Christophe. 2019. *Maurice Blanchot: A Critical Biography*. New York: Fordham University Press.

Blanchard, Emmanuel. 2011. *La police parisienne et les Algériens (1944–1962)*. Paris: Nouveau Monde.

———. 2012. "La Goutte d'Or, 30 juillet 1955: Une émeute au cœur de la métropole coloniale." *Actes de la recherche en sciences sociales* 195:98–111.

———. 2014. "Contrôle au faciès: Une cérémonie de dégradation." *Plein Droit* 103:11–15.

———. 2018. "La colonialité des polices françaises." In *Police: questions sensibles*, edited by Jérémie Gauthier and Fabien Jobard, 37–50. Paris: PUF.

Blanchot, Maurice. 1980. *L'écriture du désastre*. Paris: Gallimard.

———. 1992a. *The Infinite Conversation*. Minneapolis: University of Minnesota Press.

———. 1992b. *The Step Not Beyond*. Buffalo, NY: SUNY University Press.

———. 1995a. *The Writing of the Disaster*. Lincoln: University of Nebraska Press.

———. 1995b. *The Work of Fire*. Stanford: Stanford University Press.

Blasim, Hassan. 2014. *The Corpse Exhibition*. New York: Penguin.

Bocco, Amandine. 2018. "Les 'politiques de la terre' au lendemain de l'abolition de l'esclavage: L'étude d'une révolte de cultivateurs affranchis sur l'habitation domaniale 'La Gabrielle,' Roura, Guyane française (1845–1856)." Master's thesis, Institut d'études politiques de Paris.

Bonelli, Laurent. 2010. *La France a peur: Une histoire sociale de l' "insécurité."* Paris: La Découverte.

Bouamama, Saïd. 2009. "Khaled Kelkal: Une production française." In *Les classes et quartiers populaires: Paupérisation, ethnicisation et discrimination*, edited by S. Bouamama, 19–30. Paris: Éditions du Cygne.

Bourdieu, Pierre. 1977. *Outline of a Theory of Practice*. Cambridge: Cambridge University Press.

———. 1990. *In Other Words: Essays toward Reflexive Anthropology*. Stanford, CA: Stanford University Press.

———, ed. 1999. *The Weight of the World: Social Suffering in Contemporary Society*. Cambridge: Polity Press.

———. 2003. "Participant Objectivation." *Journal of the Royal Anthropological Institute* 9:281–94.

———. 2014. "The Future of Class and the Causality of the Probable." In *Rethinking Economics: Exploring the Work of Pierre Bourdieu*, edited by Christoforou Asimina and Michael Lainé, 233–70. New York: Routledge.

Bourdieu, Pierre, and Abdelmalek Sayad. 1964. *Le déracinement: La crise de l'agriculture traditionnelle en Algérie*. Paris: Éditions de Minuit.

Bowen, John. 2008. *Why the French Don't Like Headscarves: Islam, the State, and Public Space*. Princeton: Princeton University Press.

Boyer, Dominique, and George E. Marcus, eds. 2021. *Collaborative Anthropology Today: A Collection of Exceptions*. Ithaca, NY: Cornell University Press.

Branche, Raphaëlle. 2016. *La torture et l'armée pendant la guerre d'Algérie, 1954–1962*. Paris: Gallimard.

Breton, André. 1960. *Nadja*. New York: Grove Press.

Brière, Jean-François. 2008. *Haïti et la France, 1804–1848: Le rêve brisé*. Paris: Karthala.

Brown, Wendy. 2010. *Walled States, Waning Sovereignty*. Cambridge, MA: Zone Books.

Browne, Simone. 2012. "Race and Surveillance." In *Routledge Handbook of Surveillance Studies*, edited by Kristie Ball, Kevin Haggerty, and David Lyon, 72–79. New York: Routledge.

Brozgal, Lia. 2020. *Absent the Archive: Cultural Traces of a Massacre in Paris, 17 October 1961*. Liverpool: Liverpool University Press.

Brun, Solène, and Patrick Simon. 2020. "L'invisibilité des minorités dans les chiffres du Coronavirus: Le détour par la Seine-Saint-Denis." *De facto* 19:68–78.

Burin, Philippe. 1992. "Vichy." In *Les lieux de mémoire*, vol. 3, *Les France*, edited by Pierre Nora, 321–45. Paris: Gallimard.

Camus, Albert. (1942) 1957. *L'étranger*. Paris: Gallimard.

———. 1989. *The Stranger*. New York: Vintage.

Caruth, Cathy. 2014. *Listening to Trauma: Conversations with Leaders in the Theory and Treatment of Catastrophic Experience*. Baltimore: Johns Hopkins University Press.

Cases Rebelles (collective). 2017. *100 portraits contre l'État policier*. Paris: Syllepse.

Césaire, Aimé. (1954) 2004. *Discours sur le colonialisme*. Paris: Présence Africaine.

Chamboredon, Jean-Claude, and Madeleine Lemaire. 1970. "Proximité spatiale et distance sociale: Les grands ensembles et leur peuplement." *Revue française de sociologie* 11:3–33.

Chamoiseau, Patrick, and Rodolphe Hammadi. 1994. *Guyane: Traces-mémoire du bagne.* Paris: Caisse nationale des monuments historiques et des sites.

Chevalier, Louis. (1958) 1969. *Classes laborieuses et classes dangereuses à Paris pendant la première moitié du 19e siècle.* Paris: Plon.

Clark, Kenneth B. 1965. *Dark Ghetto: Dilemmas of Social Power.* Middletown, CT: Wesleyan University Press.

Comer, Obk. 2020. *Marqué à vie! 30 ans de graffiti "vandal."* Paris: Da Real.

Connolly, William. 1999. *Why I Am Not a Secularist.* Minneapolis: University of Minnesota Press.

Coole, Diana, and Samantha Frost, eds. 2010. *New Materialisms: Ontology, Agency, and Politics.* Durham, NC: Duke University Press.

Cousin, Grégoire. 2015. "Le platz des Roms." *Revue Projet* 348:31–37.

Crapanzano, Vincent. 2011. *The Harkis: The Wound That Never Heals.* Chicago: University of Chicago Press.

Crossland, Zöe. 2014. *Ancestral Encounters in Highland Madagascar: Material Signs and Traces of the Dead.* Cambridge: Cambridge University Press.

Daniel, E. Valentine. 1996. *Charred Lullabies: Chapters in an Anthropography of Violence.* Princeton: Princeton University Press.

Daoud, Kamel. 2014. *Meursault, contre-enquête.* Arles: Actes Sud.

———. 2015. *The Meursault Investigation.* New York: Other Press.

Darwish, Mahmoud. 2011. *In the Presence of Absence.* Translated by Sinan Antoon. Brooklyn: Archipelago Books.

Das, Veena. 2007. *Life and Words: Violence and the Descent into the Ordinary.* Berkeley: University of California Press.

Das, Veena, Arthur Kleinman, Mamphela Ramphele, and Pamela Reynolds, eds. 2000. *Violence and Subjectivity.* Berkeley: University of California Press.

Davis, Diana K. 2007. *Resurrecting the Granary of Rome: Environmental History and French Colonial Expansion in North Africa.* Athens: Ohio University Press.

Debord, Guy. 1955. "Introduction to a Critique of Urban Geography." *Les Lèvres Nues* (6). Translated by Ken Knabb.

———. 1956. "Theory of the Dérive." *Les Lèvres Nues* (9).

Deleuze, Gilles, and Claire Parnet. 2011. *L'abécédaire de Gilles Deleuze.* Cambridge, MA: Semiotext(e).

DeLillo, Don. 2001. "In the Ruins of the Future." *Harper's Magazine* 303 (1819): 33-40.

Deltombe, Thomas, Manuel Domergue, and Jacob Tatsitsa. 2011. *Kamerun! Une guerre cachée aux origins de la Françafrique, 1948–1971.* Paris: La Découverte.

Derrida, Jacques. 1967. *De la grammatologie.* Paris: Éditions de Minuit.

———. 1978. *Writing and Difference.* Chicago: University of Chicago Press.

———. 1987. *The Postcard: From Socrates to Freud and Beyond.* Chicago: University of Chicago Press.

———. 1993a. *Aporias.* Stanford, CA: Stanford University Press.

———. 1993b. *Spectres de Marx: L'état de la dette, le travail du deuil et la nouvelle Internationale.* Paris: Éditions Galilee.

———. 1994. *Specters of Marx, the State of the Debt, the Work of Mourning, and the New International.* New York: Routledge.

———. 1995. *Mal d'archive: Une impression freudienne.* Paris: Galilée.

———. 1996a. *Apories.* Paris: Galilée.

———. 1996b. *Archive Fever: A Freudian Impression.* Chicago: University of Chicago Press.

———. 1997. *The Politics of Friendship.* New York: Verso.

———. 2005. *Rogues: Two Essays on Reason.* Stanford, CA: Stanford University Press.

———. 2009. *The Beast and the Sovereign, Volume 1.* Chicago: University of Chicago Press.

———. 2014. *Trace et archive, image et art.* Bry-sur Marne: INA Éditions.

Derrida, Jacques, and Bernard Stiegler. 2002. *Echographies of Television.* Cambridge: Polity Press.

Desjarlais, Robert. 2016. "Phantasmography." *American Anthropologist* 118:400–407.

———. 2018a. *The Blind Man: A Phantasmography.* New York: Fordham University Press.

———. 2018b. "Learning How to Die." In *A Companion to the Anthropology of Death,* edited by Antonius C. G. M. Robbens, 251–64. Oxford: Wiley-Blackwell.

———. 2020. *Sur les traces de la violence: Un essai anthropologique après les attentats de Paris.* Paris: Presses Universitaires de Paris Nanterre.

Desjarlais, Robert, Leon Eisenberg, Byron Good, and Arthur Kleinman, eds. 1996. *World Mental Health: Problems and Priorities in Low-Income Countries.* Oxford: Oxford University Press.

Didi-Huberman, Georges. 2012. *Images in Spite of All: Four Photographs from Auschwitz.* Chicago: University of Chicago Press.

———. 2017. *Bark.* Cambridge, MA: MIT Press.

Dikeç, Mustafa. 2006. "Two Decades of French Urban Policy: From Social Development of Neighborhoods to the Republican Penal State." *Antipode* 38:59–81.

Djebar, Assia. 1985. *L'amour, la fantasia.* Paris: Éditions Jean-Claude Lattès.

———. 1989. *Fantasia: An Algerian Calvacade.* London: Quartet.

Dodier, Nicolas, and Anthony Stavrianakis, eds. 2018. *Les objets composés: Agencements, dispositifs, assemblages.* Paris: Éditions de l'École des Hautes Études en Sciences Sociales.

Dorlin, Elsa. 2009. *La matrice de la race: Généalogie sexuelle et coloniale de la Nation française.* Paris: La Découverte.

Drake, St. Clair, and Horace Cayton. (1945) 2015. *Black Metropolis: A Study of Negro Life in a Northern City.* Chicago: University of Chicago Press.

Du Bois, William E. B. (1903) 2007. *The Souls of Black Folk.* New York: Oxford University Press.

Dubet, François. 1987. *La Galère: Jeunes en survie.* Paris: Fayard.

Duneier, Mitchell. 1992. *Slim's Table: Race, Respectability, and Masculinity.* Chicago: University of Chicago Press.

———. 2016. *The Ghetto: The Invention of a Place, the History of an Idea.* New York: Farrar, Strauss, and Giroux.

Einaudi, Jean-Luc. 1991. *La bataille de Paris: 17 Octobre 1961*. Paris: Éditions du Seuil.

———. 2001. *Octobre 1961: Un massacre à Paris*. Paris: Fayard.

———. 2009. *Scènes de la guerre d'Algérie en France: Automne 1961*. Paris: Le Cherche Midi.

Elias, Norbert. (1970) 1991. *Qu'est-ce que la sociologie?* Translated by Yasmin Hoffman. La Tour d'Aigues: Éditions de l'Aube.

———. 2008. "Power and Civilisation." *Journal of Power* 1:135–42.

Endelstein, Lucine. 2004. "Le judaïsme dans un quartier parisien populaire." *Hommes and Migrations* 1250:49–60.

Estes, Nick. 2019. *Our History Is the Future: Standing Rock versus the Dakota Access Pipeline, and the Long Tradition of Indigenous Resistance*. Brooklyn: Verso.

Etkind, Alexander. 2013. *Warped Mourning: Stories of the Undead in the Land of the Unburied*. Stanford, CA: Stanford University Press.

Fanon, Frantz. (1952) 1986. *Black Skin, White Masks*. New York: Grove Press.

———. (1961) 2002. *Les Damnés de la terre*. Paris: Éditions la Découverte.

———. (1961) 2004. *The Wretched of the Earth*. New York: Grove.

———. 2011. *Œuvres*. Paris: La Découverte.

Fassin, Didier. 2008. "L'inquiétude ethnographique." In *Les politiques de l'enquête*, edited by Alban Bensa and Didier Fassin, 7–15. Paris: La Découverte.

———. 2011. "Racialization: How to do Races with Bodies." In *A Companion to the Anthropology of the Body and Embodiment*, edited by Frances Mascia-Lees, 419–34. Hoboken, NJ: Wiley-Blackwell.

———. 2013. *Enforcing Order: An Ethnography of Urban Policing*. Cambridge: Polity Press.

———. 2015. "In the Name of the Republic: Untimely Meditations on the Aftermath of the *Charlie Hebdo* Attack." *Anthropology Today* 31 (2): 3–7.

———. 2016. "Permanent State of Emergency." *London Review of Books* 38 (5).

———. 2020. "La dangeureuse illusion de l'égalité devant l'épidémie." *Collège de France* online publication: www.college-de-france.fr/site/didier-fassin/L-illusion -dangereuse-de-legalite-devant-lepidemie.htm.

Faubion, James. 2011. *An Anthropology of Ethics*. Cambridge: Cambridge University Press.

Feldman, Allen. 1991. *Formations of Violence: The Narrative of the Body and Political Terror in Northern Ireland*. Chicago: University of Chicago Press.

———. 2015. *Archives of the Insensible: Of War, Photopolitics, and Dead Memory*. Chicago: University of Chicago Press.

———. 2019. "War under Erasure: Contretemps, Disappearance, Anthropophagy, Survivance." *Theory and Event* 22:175–203.

Feldman, Allen, with Asif Akthar and Selim Karlitekin. 2017. "On War, Photopolitics, White Public-Space and the Body: A Conversation with Allen Feldman." *Naked Punch,* 17 October 2017. http://nakedpunch.com/articles/273?fbclid= IwAR2LR3KMyLloNXLpzcEuKzaIGdokTXJxJsUBWcnu3F3so8rn7 CchFRHL6NU.

Fenby, Jonathan. 2016. *France: A Modern History from the Revolution to the War with Terror.* New York: St. Martin's Press.

Feraoun, Mouloud. 2000. *Journal 1955–1962.* Lincoln: University of Nebraska Press.

Fernando, Mayanthi. 2014. *The Republic Unsettled: Muslim French the Contradictions of Secularism.* Durham, NC: Duke University Press.

Fernando, Mayanthi, and Catherine Raissiguier. 2016. "The Impossible Subject of *Charlie Hebdo.*" *Contemporary French Civilization* 41:125–44.

Filhol, Emmanuel. 2011. "Le carnet anthropométrique des nomades." In *Aux origines de la police scientifique,* edited by Pierre Piazza, 252–73. Paris: Karthala.

Finkelstein, Maura. 2019. *The Archive of Loss: Lively Ruination in Mill Land Mumbai.* Durham, NC: Duke University Press.

Fischer, Nicolas. 2008. "Une industrie de l'éloignement: La retention administrative." *Après-demain* 6:18–21.

———. 2017. *Le territoire de l'expulsion: La retention administrative des étrangers et l'État de droit en France.* Lyon: ENS Éditions.

Foucault, Michel. 1975. *Surveiller et punir.* Paris: Gallimard.

———. 1984. "The Right of Death and the Power over Life." In *The Foucault Reader,* edited by Paul Rabinow, 258–72. New York: Pantheon.

———. 1990. *The History of Sexuality.* Vol. 2, *The Use of Pleasure.* New York: Vintage.

———. 1995. *Discipline and Punish: The Birth of the Prison.* New York: Vintage.

———. 1997. *"Il faut défendre la société": Cours au Collège de France, 1976.* Paris: Seuil.

———. 2003. *"Society Must Be Defended": Lectures at the Collège de France, 1975–1976.* New York: Picador.

———. 2009. *Security, Territory, Population: Lectures at the Collège de France, 1977–1978.* New York: Picador.

Galinon-Mélénec, Béatrice. 2011. *L'homme trace: Perspectives anthropologiques des traces contemporaines.* Paris: CNRS.

Galinon-Mélénec, Béatrice, Fabien Liénard, and Sami Zlitni, eds. 2015. *L'homme-trace: Inscriptions corporelles et techniques.* Paris: CNRS.

Garcia, Angela. 2015. "Serenity: Violence, Inequality, and Recovery on the Edge of Mexico City." *Medical Anthropology Quarterly* 29:455–72.

Garfinkel, Harold. 1956. "Conditions of Successful Degradation Ceremonies." *American Journal of Sociology* 61:420–24.

Gastaut, Yvan. 2004. "Les bidonvilles, lieux d'exclusion et de marginalité en France durant les trentes glorieuses." *Cahiers de la Méditerranée* 69:233–50.

Gauthier, Jérémie. 2010. "Esquisse du pouvoir policier discriminant: Une analyse interactionniste des cadres de l'expérience policière." *Déviance et Société* 34:267–78.

———. 2012. "Origines contrôlées: La police à l'épreuve de la question minoritaire à Paris et à Berlin." PhD diss., University of Versailles (UVSQ).

———. 2018. "L'art français de la violence policière." In *Police: Questions sensibles,* edited by Jérémie Gauthier and Fabien Jobard, 51–64. Paris: PUF.

Gauthier, Jérémie, and Fabien Jobard, eds. 2018. *Police: Questions sensibles.* Paris: PUF.

Geisser, Vincent. 2003. *La nouvelle islamophobie.* Paris: La Découverte.

———. 2010. "Islamophobia: A French Specificity in Europe?" *Human Architecture* 8 (2): 39–46.

Gensburger, Sarah. 2017. *Mémoire vive: Chroniques d'un quartier, Bataclan 2015–2016.* Paris: Anamosa.

———. 2019. *Memory on My Doorstep: Chronicles of the Bataclan Neighborhood, Paris 2015–2016.* Leuven, Belgium: Leuven University Press.

Gensburger, Sarah, and Gérôme Truc, eds. 2020. *Les mémoriaux du 13 novembre.* Paris: Éditions de l'École des Hautes Études en Sciences Sociales.

Gilloch, Graeme. 1997. *Myth and Metropolis: Walter Benjamin and the City.* Cambridge: Polity Press.

Gilmore, Ruth W. 2007. *Golden Gulag: Prisons, Surplus, Crisis, and Opposition in Globalizing California.* Berkeley: University of California Press.

Ginsburg, Faye. 1995. "The Parallax Effect: The Impact of Aboriginal Media on Ethnographic Film." *Visual Anthropology Review* 11 (2): 64–76.

Ginzburg, Carlo. 1989. *Clues, Myths, and the Historical Method.* Baltimore, MD: Johns Hopkins University Press.

———. 2012. *Threads and Traces: True, False, Fictive.* Berkeley: University of California Press.

Glissant, Édouard, 1989. *Caribbean Discourse: Selected Essays.* Charlottesville: University of Virginia Press.

Good, Byron, and Sadeq Rahimi. 2019. "Special Thematic Collection: Hauntology in Psychological Anthropology." *Ethos* 47:407–529.

Good, Mary-Jo, Sandra Hyde, Sarah Pinto, and Byron Good, eds. 2008. *Postcolonial Disorders.* Berkeley: University of California Press.

Gordon, Avery. 2008. *Ghostly Matters: Haunting and the Sociological Imagination.* 2nd ed. Minneapolis: University of Minnesota Press.

Grand, Philippe. 2006. "État, nation, archives." *Matériaux pour l'histoire de notre temps* 82:26–36.

Gusterson, Hugh. 2017. *Drone: Remote Control Warfare.* Cambridge, MA: MIT Press.

Habrih, Khalil. 2017. *De la gentrification à la Goutte d'Or de Paris-Nord: Proximité physique et segregation fine.* Paris: Institut d'études politiques.

Hage, Ghassen. 2015. *Alter-Politics: Critical Anthropology and the Radical Imagination.* Melbourne: Melbourne University Press.

Haggerty, Kevin D., and Richard V. Ericson. 2000. "The Surveillant Assemblage." *British Journal of Sociology* 51:605–39.

Halbwachs, Maurice. (1950) 1997. *La mémoire collective.* Paris: Albin Michel.

Han, Clara. 2012. *Life in Debt: Times of Care and Violence in Neoliberal Chile.* Berkeley: University of California Press.

Handke, Peter. 2009. *Slow Homecoming.* New York: New York Review Books Classics.

Hartman, Saidiya V. 1997. *Scenes of Subjection: Terror, Slavery, and Self-Making in Nineteenth-Century America.* New York: Oxford University Press

———. 2008. "Venus in Two Acts." *Small Axe* 26:1–14.

Henni, Samia. 2017. *Architecture of Couterrevolution: The French Army in Northern Algeria.* Chicago: University of Chicago Press.

Hill, Leslie. 2012. *Maurice Blanchot and Fragmentary Writing: A Change of Epoch.* London: Continuum.

Hinson, Glen D. 1999. "'You've Got to Include an Invitation': Engaged Reciprocity and Negotiated Purpose in Collaborative Ethnography." Paper presented at the 98th Annual Meeting of the American Anthropological Association, Chicago.

Hirsch, Marianne. 2008. "The Generation of Postmemory." *Poetics Today* 29 (1): 103–25.

Hirschkind, Charles. 2006. *The Ethical Soundscape: Cassette Sermons and Islamic Counterpublics.* New York: Columbia University Press.

Holland, Michael. 2013. "Introduction." In Maurice Blanchot, *Into Disaster: Chronicles of Intellectual Life,* 1–7. New York: Fordham University Press.

Höller, Christian, and Achille Mbembe. 2007. "Africa in Motion: An Interview with the Post-Colonialism Theoretician Achille Mbembe." *Mute,* 17 March 2007. www.metamute.org/editorial/articles/africa-motion-interview-post-colonialism -theoretician-achille-mbembe.

House, Jim, and Neil Macmaster. 2006. *Paris 1961: Algerians, State Terror, and Memory.* Oxford: Oxford University Press.

Husserl, Edmund. (1947) 1975. *Experience and Judgment.* Evanston, IL: Northwestern University Press.

Huyssen, Andreas. 2003. *Present Pasts: Urban Palimpsests and the Politics of Memory.* Stanford, CA: Stanford University Press.

Jackson, Michael D. 2005. *In Sierra Leone.* Durham, NC: Duke University Press.

James, Cyril L. R. (1938) 1989. *The Black Jacobins: Toussaint L'Ouverture and the San Domingo Revolution.* New York: Vintage.

Jameson, Fredric. 1999. "Marx's Purloined Letter." In *Ghostly Demarcations: A Symposium on Jacques Derrida's Specters of Marx,* edited by Michael Sprinker, 26–67. New York: Verso.

Jobard, Fabien. 2005. "Le nouveau mandat policier: Faire la police dans les zones dite de 'non-droit.'" *Criminologie* 38 (2): 103–21.

Jones, Colin. 2004. *Paris: Biography of a City.* London: Penguin.

Judt, Tony. 2005. *Postwar: A History of Europe Since 1945.* New York: Penguin.

———. 2008. *Reappraisals: Reflections on the Forgotten Twentieth Century.* New York: Penguin.

Jünger, Ernst. 1960. *The Glass Bees.* New York: Farrar, Strauss, and Giroux.

Jusionyte, Ieva, and Daniel M. Goldstein. 2016. "In/visible—In/secure: Optics of Regulation and Control." *Focaal: Journal of Global and Historical Anthropology* 75:3–13.

Kafka, Franz. 2016. "At Night." In *Konundrum: Selected Prose of Franz Kafka.* Translated by Peter Wortsman. New York: Archipelago Books.

Karpiak, Kevin. 2016. "Vectors of Police and Public in France after *Charlie Hebdo* and La Bataclan." *Anthropology Now* 8:69–70.

Karpiak, Kevin, and William Garriot, eds. 2018. *The Anthropology of Police.* London: Routledge.

Keller, Richard. 2015. *Fatal Isolation: The Devastating Paris Heat Wave of 2003.* Chicago: University of Chicago Press.

Kepel, Gilles, with Antoine Jardin. 2015. *Terreur dans l'Hexagone: Genèse du djihad français.* Paris: Gallimard.

Khadra, Yasmina. 2018. *Khalil.* Paris: Julliard.

Khatib, Abdelhafid. 1958. "Essai de description psychogéographique des Halles." *Internationale Situationniste* (2): 13–17.

Kleinman, Arthur, and Joan Kleinman. 1994. "How Bodies Remember: Social Memory and Bodily Experience of Criticism, Resistance, and Delegitimation following China's Cultural Revolution." *New Literary History* 25:707–23.

Kofman, Sarah. 1983. *Comment s'en sortir?* Paris: Galilée.

———. 1988. "Beyond Aporia?" In *Post-Structuralist Classics,* edited by Andrew Benjamin, 7–44. London: Routledge.

———. 1994. *Rue Ordener, rue Labat.* Paris : Galilée.

Koufinkana, Marcel. 1992. "Les esclaves noirs en France et la Révolution (1700–1794)." *Horizons Maghrébins* 18/19:144–61.

Kosby, Trine Mygind, and Anthrony Stavrianakis. 2018. "Moments in Collaboration: Experiments in Concept Work." *Journal of Anthropology* 83 (1): 39–57.

Lacan, Jacques. 1979. *The Four Fundamental Concepts of Psycho-analysis.* New York: Norton.

Ladwig, Patrice. 2013. "Ontology, materiality, and spectral traces: Methodological thoughts on studying Lao Buddhist festivals for ghosts and ancestral spirits." *Anthropological Theory* 12:427–47.

Lambert, Léopold. 2016. "The Weaponized Architecture of Police Stations in the Paris Banlieues." *Funambulist,* posted 20 December 2016. https:// thefunambulist.net/architectural-projects/weaponized-architecture-police -stations-paris-banlieues.

Lapeyronnie, Didier. 1999. "Contre-monde: Imitation, opposition, exclusion." *Les annales de la recherche urbaine* 83/84:53–58.

Lassiter, Luke E. 2005. *The Chicago Guide to Collaborative Ethnography.* Chicago: University of Chicago Press.

Lazali, Karima. 2018. *Le trauma colonial: Une enquête sur les effets psychiques et politiques contemporains de l'oppression coloniale en Algérie.* Paris: La Découverte.

Le Cour Grandmaison, Olivier. 2005. *Exterminer, coloniser: Sur la guerre et l'Etat colonial.* Paris: Fayard.

Lefebvre, Henri. 1992a. *Eléments de rythmanalyse: Introduction à la connaissance des rythmes.* Paris: Syllepse.

———. (1974) 1992b. *The Production of Space.* New York: Wiley-Blackwell.

———. 2004. *Rhythmanalysis: Space, Time, and Everyday Life.* London: Continuum Press.

Léon de Laborde, Maquis de. 1867. *Les archives de la France: Leurs vicissitudes pendant la Révolution, leur régénération sous l'Empire*. Paris: J. Claye.

Lippit, Akira Mizuta. 2005. *Atomic Light (Shadow Optics)*. Minneapolis: University of Minnesota Press.

Longhi, Julien. 2012. "Imaginaires, représentations et stéréotypes dans la sémiotisation du mythe de la banlieue et des jeunes de banlieue." In *Discours et sémiotisation de l'espace: Les représentations de la banlieue et de sa jeunesse,* edited by Béatrice Turpin, 123–42. Paris: Harmattan.

Lorde, Audre. 1984. *Sister Outsider: Essays and Speeches*. Trumansburg, NY: Crossing Press.

Lukić, Dejan. 2013. *Hostage Spaces of the Contemporary Islamicate World: Phantom Territoriality*. London: Bloomsbury.

Maguire, Mark, and Pete Fussey. 2016. "Sensing Evil: Counterterrorism, Technoscience, and the Cultural Reproduction of Security." *Focaal: Journal of Global and Historical Anthropology* 75:31–44.

Malabou, Catherine. 2009. *Plasticity at the Dusk of Writing: Dialectic, Destruction, Deconstruction*. New York: Columbia University Press.

———. 2012. *The Ontology of the Accident: An Essay on Destructive Plasticity*. Cambridge: Polity Press.

Mansouri, Malika. 2013. *Révoltes postcoloniales au coeur de l'Hexagone: Voix d'adolescents*. Paris: PUF.

Mark, Bernard. 1982. *Des voix dans la nuit: La résistance juive à Auschwitz-Birkenau*. Paris: Plon.

Masco, Joseph. 2014. *The Theatre of Operations: National Security Affect from the Cold War to the War on Terror*. Durham, NC: Duke University Press.

Mauss, Marcel. (1934) 1936. "Les techniques du corps." *Journal de psychologie* 32 (3–4), 271–93.

———. 1973. "Techniques of the Body." *Economy and Society* 2 (1): 70–88.

Mbembe, Achille. 2001. *On the Postcolony*. Berkeley: University of California Press.

———. 2016. *Politiques de l'inimitié*. Paris: La Découverte.

———. 2019. *Necropolitics*. Duke: Duke University Press.

Mekhaled, Boucif. 1995. *Chronique d'un massacre: 8 mai 1945, Sétif, Guelma, Kerrata*. Paris: Syros.

Memmi, Albert. (1957) 2002. *Portrait du colonisé / Portrait du colonisateur*. Paris: Gallimard.

Merleau-Ponty, Maurice. 1962. *Phenomenology of Perception*. London: Routledge.

Milliot, Vincent, Emmanuel Blanchard, Vincent Denis, and Dominique Houte. 2020. *Histoire des polices en France: Des guerres de religion à nos jours*. Paris: Belin.

Miyarrka Media (collective). 2019. *Phone & Spear: A Yuta Anthropology*. Cambridge, MA: MIT Press.

Mohammed, Marwan. 2011. *La formation des bandes: Entre la famille, l'école et la rue*. Paris: PUF.

Monjardet, Dominique. 1996. *Ce que fait la police: Sociologie de la force publique*. Paris: La Découverte.

Mortimer, Mildred. 2008. "Introduction: Unearthing Hidden History." In Leïla Sebbar, *The Seine Was Red: Paris, October 1961*, translated by Mildred Montimer, xiii–xxiv. Bloomington: Indiana University Press.

Naas, Michael. 2008. *Derrida from Now On*. New York: Fordham University Press.

Napolitano, Valentina. 2015. "Anthropology and traces." *Anthropological Theory* 15:47–67.

Navaro-Yashin, Yael. 2009. "Affective Spaces, Melancholic Objects: Ruination and the Production of Anthropological Knowledge." *Journal of the Royal Anthropological Institute* 15:1–18.

———. 2012. *The Make-Believe Space: Affective Geography in a Postwar Polity*. Durham, NC: Duke University Press.

Nordstrom, Carolyn. 1997. *A Different Kind of War Story*. Philadelphia: University of Pennsylvania Press.

Nordstrom, Carolyn, and Antonius C. G. M. Robben, eds. 1996. *Fieldwork Under Fire: Contemporary Studies of Violence and Culture*. Berkeley: University of California Press.

Nordstrom, Carolyn, and Joann Martin. 1992. *The Paths to Domination, Resistance, and Terror*. Berkeley: University of California Press.

Ouassak, Fatima. 2020. *La puissance des mères: Pour un nouveau sujet révolutionnaire*. Paris: La Découverte.

Parent, Frédéric, and Paul Sabourin. 2016. "Ethnographie et théorie de la description: La construction des données sociologiques." *Cahiers de recherche sociologique* 61:109–26.

Péju, Paulette. (1961) 2000. *Ratonnades à Paris, précédé de Les harkis à Paris*. Paris: Éditions la Découverte and Syros.

Perec, Georges. 2010. *An Attempt at Exhausting a Place in Paris*. Cambridge, MA: Wakefield Press.

Perez, Gilberto. 1998. *The Material Ghost: Films and their Medium*. Baltimore, MD: Johns Hopkins University Press.

Piazza, Pierre. 2004. *Histoire de la carte nationale d'identité*. Paris: Odile Jacob.

———. 2006. "La 'carte d'identité de français' sous Vichy." In *Du papier à la biométrie: Identifier les individus*, edited by Xavier Crettiez and Pierre Piazza, 51–69. Paris: Presses de Sciences Po.

Rabinow, Paul. 1977. *Reflections on Fieldwork in Morocco*. Berkeley: University of California Press.

———. 1991. *French Modern: Norms and Forms of the Social Environment*. Cambridge, MA: MIT Press.

———. 2011. *The Accompaniment: Assembling the Contemporary*. Chicago: University of Chicago Press.

Rahem, Karim. 1996. "Kelkal, un enfant de la République française?" *Journal des anthropologues* 63:125–40.

Raissiguier, Catherine. 2010. *Reinventing the Republic: Gender, Migration, and Citizenship in France*. Stanford, CA: Stanford University Press.

Ramirez, Renya K. 2007. *Native Hubs: Culture, Community, and Belonging in Silicon Valley and Beyond.* Durham, NC: Duke University Press

Rancière, Jacques. 2004. *The Politics of Aesthetics: The Distribution of the Sensible.* New York: Continuum International Publishing Group.

Richie, Beth. 2012. *Arrested Justice: Black Women, Violence, and America's Prison Nation.* New York: NYU Press.

Rigouste, Mathieu. 2009. *L'ennemi intérieur: La généalogie coloniale et militaire de l'ordre sécuritaire dans la France contemporaine.* Paris: La Découverte.

————. 2012. *La domination policière: Une violence industrielle.* Paris: La Fabrique.

Rios, Jodi. 2000. *Black Lives and Spatial Matters: Policing Blackness and Practicing Freedom in Suburban St. Louis.* Ithaca, NY: Cornell University Press.

Rony, Fatimah Tobing. 1996. *The Third Eye: Race, Cinema, and Ethnographic Spectacle.* Durham, NC: Duke University Press.

Ross-Tremblay, Pierrot. 2015. "L'oubli n'est pas absolu: Réminiscences et prise de parole chez les Premiers peuples de la francophonie des Amériques." *Minorités linguistiques et société* 5:214–31.

Rougier, Bernard, ed. 2020. *Les territoires conquis de l'islamisme.* Paris: Presses universitaires de France.

Roy, Olivier. 2016. *Le djihad et la mort.* Paris: Éditions du Seuil.

Sammut, Carmel. 1976. "L'immigration clandestine en France depuis les circulaires Fontanet, Marcellin et Gorse." In *Les travailleurs étrangers en Europe occidentale: Actes du colloque tenu à la Sorbonne, Paris du 5 au 7 juin 1974,* edited by Philippe J. Bernard, 379–97. Nice, France: Institute of Interethnic and Intercultural Studies and Research.

Sayad, Abdelmalek. 1977. "Les trois âges de l'immigration algérienne en France." *Actes de la recherche en sciences sociales* 15:59–77.

————. 1999a. *La double absence: Des illusions de l'émigré aux souffrances de l'immigré.* Paris: Éditions du Seuil.

————. 1999b. "Immigration et 'pensée d'état.'" *Actes de la recherche en sciences sociales* 129:5–14.

————. 2004. *The Suffering of the Immigrant.* Cambridge: Polity Press.

————. 2006. *L'immigration ou les paradoxes de l'altérité,* vol. 2, *Les enfants illégitimes.* Paris: Raisons d'agir.

Sayad, Abdelmalek, and Elianne Dupuy. 1995. *Un Nanterre algérien, terre de bidonvilles.* Paris: Autrement.

Scheper-Hughes, Nancy. 1993. *Death without Weeping: The Violence of Everyday Life in Brazil.* Berkeley: University of California Press.

Schutz, Alfred. 1973. *Structures of the Lifeworld.* Evanston, IL: Northwestern University Press.

Scott, James. 1992. *Domination and the Arts of Resistance: Hidden Transcripts.* New Haven, CT: Yale University Press.

Scott, Joan. 2010. *The Politics of the Veil.* Princeton: Princeton University Press.

Sebbar, Leïla. 1999. *La Seine était rouge.* Paris: Magnier.

———. 2008. *The Seine Was Red: Paris, October 1961.* Translated by Mildred Mortimer. Bloomington: Indiana University Press.

Shabazz, Rashad. 2015. *Spatializing Blackness: Architectures of Confinement and Black Masculinity in Chicago.* Champaign: University of Illinois Press.

Shalhoub-Kevorkian, Nadera. 2015. *Security Theology, Surveillance, and the Politics of Fear.* Cambridge: Cambridge University Press.

Sharpe, Christina. 2016. *In the Wake: On Blackness and Being.* Durham: Duke University Press.

Silverman, Max. 2013. *Palimpsestic Memory: The Holocaust and Colonialism in French and Francophone Fiction and Film.* New York: Berghahn.

Simon, Patrick, Marie-Antoinette Hily, and Deirdre Meintel. 2000. "L'invention de l'authenticité: Belleville, quartier juif tunisien." *Revue européenne des migrations internationales* 16 (2): 9–41.

Singh, Julietta. 2018. *No Archive Will Restore You.* New York: Punctum Books.

Souaïdia, Habib. (2001) 2012. *La sale guerre: Le témoignage d'un ancien officier des forces spéciales de l'armée algérienne.* Paris: La Découverte.

Spradley, James. (1970) 1999. *You Owe Yourself a Drunk: An Ethnography of Urban Nomads.* Long Grove, IL: Waveland Press.

Stevenson, Lisa. 2014. *Life Beside Itself: Imagining Care in the Canadian Arctic.* Berkeley: University of California Press.

Stewart, Kathleen. 2007. *Ordinary Affects.* Durham, NC: Duke University Press.

Stoler, Ann. 2016. *Duress: Imperial Durabilities in our Times.* Durham, NC: Duke University Press.

Taussig, Michael. 1987. *Shamanism, Colonialism, and the Wild Man: A Study in Terror and Healing.* Chicago: University of Chicago Press.

———. 1992. *The Nervous System.* New York: Routledge.

Throop, Jason, and Keith M. Murphy. 2002. "Bourdieu and Phenomenology: A Critical Assessment." *Anthropological Theory* 2 (2): 185–207.

Ticktin, Miriam. 2010. *Casualties of Care: Immigration and the Politics of Humanitarianism in France.* Berkeley: University of California Press.

Tissot, Sylvie. 2007. *L'État et les quartiers: Genèse d'une catégorie de l'action publique.* Paris: Éditions du Seuil.

Tocqueville, Alexis de. 1991. *Oeuvre complète.* Paris: Gallimard.

Torlasco, Domietta. 2013. *The Heretical Archive: Digital Memory at the End of Film.* Minneapolis: University of Minnesota Press.

Toubon, Jean-Claude, and Khelifa Messamah. 1990. *Centralité immigrée.* Paris: L'Harmattan.

Tristan, Anne. 1991. *Le silence du fleuve.* Paris: Au Nom de la Mémoire.

Trouillot, Michel-Rolph. 1995. *Silencing the Past: Power and the Production of History.* Boston: Beacon Press.

Truc, Gérôme. 2016. *Sidérations: Une sociologie des attentats.* Paris: Presses Universitaires de France.

———. 2017. *Shell Shocked: The Social Response to Terrorist Attacks.* New York: Polity Press.

———. 2019. "What Terror Attacks Do to Societies: Fieldwork and Case Studies." *Ethnologie française* 173:5–19.

Truong, Fabien. 2017. *Loyautés radicales: L'islam et les "mauvais garçons" de la Nation.* Paris: La Découverte.

Tuck, Eve, and C. Ree. 2013. "A Glossary of Haunting." In *Handbook of Autoethnography,* edited by Stacey Holman Jones, Tony E. Adams, and Carolyn Ellis, 639–58. Walnut Creek, CA: Left Coast Press.

Vergès, Françoise. 2016. *Le ventre des femmes: Capitalisme, racialisation, féminisme.* Paris: Albin Michel.

Vigh, Henrik. 2011. "Vigilance: On Conflict, Social Invisibility, and Negative Potentiality." *Social Analysis* 55 (3): 93–114.

Villanueva, Joaquin. 2015. "The Territorialization of the 'Republican Law': Judicial Presence in Seine-Saint-Denis, France." PhD diss., Syracuse University.

———. 2018. "Pathways of Confinement: The Legal Constitution of Carceral Spaces in France's Social Housing Estates." *Social and Cultural Geography* 19:963–83.

Wacquant, Loïc. 2000. "The New 'Peculiar Institution': On the Prison as Surrogate Ghetto." *Theoretical Criminology* 4:377–89.

———. 2004. *Body and Soul: Notesbooks of an Apprentice Boxer.* Oxford: Oxford University Press.

———. 2007. "Territorial Stigmatization in the Age of Advanced Marginality." *Thesis Eleven* 91:66–77.

———. 2008. *Urban Outcasts: A Comparative Sociology of Advanced Marginality.* Cambridge: Polity Press.

———. 2011. "Habitus as Topic and Tool: Reflections on Becoming a Prizefighter." *Qualitative Research in Psychology* 8 (1): 81–92.

———. 2018. "A Concise Genealogy and Anatomy of Habitus." In *The Oxford Handbook of Pierre Bourdieu,* edited by Thomas Medvetz and Jeffrey J. Sallaz, 528–36. Oxford: Oxford University Press.

Weizman, Eyal. 2017. *Forensic Architecture: Violence at the Threshold of Detectability.* Cambridge, MA: Zone Books.

Wool, Zoë. 2015. *After War: The Weight of Life at Walter Reed.* Durham, NC: Duke University Press.

Wortham, Simon. 2010. *The Derrida Dictionary.* London: Bloomsbury Academic.

Yoneyama, Lisa. 1999. *Hiroshima Traces: Time, Space, and the Dialectics of Memory.* Berkeley: University of California Press.

Zani, Leah. 2019. *Bomb Children: Life in the Former Battlefields of Laos.* Durham, NC: Duke University Press.

Zigon, Jarrett. 2018. *A War on People: Drug User Politics and a New Ethics of Community.* Berkeley: University of California Press.

Zola, Emile. (1877) 2009. *L'assommoir.* Translated by Margaret Mauldon. Oxford: Oxford University Press.

INDEX

photography, 18*fig.*, 119, 121, 124, 127, 157, 164, 166; and traces, 141; and violence, 5, 22, 42–43, 178, 183
poiesis, 9, 91, 92, 173; of masculinity, 108; and praxis, 93, 109; of traces, 140, 141
police, 23, 83, 87–88, 155*map*, 165–67, 175–80, 231–33; and colonial/racial violence, 174, 187–91, 195, 213, 216, 239n50, 250n17, 254n30; and modern state formation, 70, 153, 212–13, 216–17; and police imperatives of urbanization, 59, 66; and police informant Claude Hermant, 207; and police officers' habitus, 90; and profiling, 82, 94–95, 96–98, 132–33, 165, 209; and racial typologies, 32–33; and rhythms of policing, 62–64, 94, 240n65; and the sanitary state of emergency, 220–21, 223; state of emergency, 72–73, 84; and state vigilance, 71, 78, 112, 172, 183; and targeting of women and feminine persons, 245n20, 246n21, 246n22; violence of the, 65, 98, 101–3, 104–8, 152–53, 158, 196–201. *See also* "being stopped"; ID checks; stop-and-search/frisk
politique de la ville, 59, 232

Rabinow, Paul, 202
Raissiguier, Catherine, 53–54, 247n13
Republic of France: and anti-Islamic racism, 71, 158; and colonialism, 84; and immigrant communities, 66; and memorialization, 120; militarization of, 72; and responses to terroristic attacks, xiv, xxxii, 16–17, 72–73, 206; state of emergency in, 84–85; and surveillance, 84, 86, 96; urban planning in, 59; and vigilance, 60–70, 79–80, 220, 222
rhythms/rhythmanalysis, xx, 24, 58, 60, 62–67, 92, 94, 108, 114, 129, 199, 224; of military vigilance, 69, 112
Ross-Tremblay, Pierrot, 217
ruins, xix, 217–18

Saint-Bernard Church, 7, 31, 155*map*
Saint-Denis, xiv, xxxii, 3, 150
Sartre, Jean-Paul, 211

Sayad, Abdelkmalek, xx, 61–62, 89, 90, 96, 154, 244n31
Scred Connexion, 130–31, 135, 137
security; biopolitics of, 178; and cybersecurity, 76; and death, 186; in France, 69–70, 71–72, 74, 199, 223; and "global war on terror," 70; in modern nation-states, 69; and pandemic, 220; in Paris, 82, 153, 165, 172, 219; as potentiality, 69. *See also* ZSP
"*séparatisme*," 221–23
Shabazz, Rashad, 93–94, 108
social death, 90
spatiality, 66, 233; of exile, 66, 242n39; and urban geography, 93
spectral anthropology, xix, xxiii, 4, 11, 22, 115, 176, 184
spectrality/specters, xvi, 5, 17, 43, 189, 196, 198; and "being with specters," 184, 187; critical phenomenology of, 160; and film, 20–21; the future as, 126; and haunting, xxi, xxviii, 171, 211; and imagining, 45; and Le Carillon, 144; and "less than spectral," 187–91, 198, 201; and Paris, 184, 192, 193; politics of, 187; and seeing, 156, 184–87; of the state, 76; of terror, 68; and traces, 142–44; and vigilance, 81; and violence, 46, 48, 156, 166, 180, 186; and writing, 122. *See also* spectral anthropology
Spradley, James, 202
Stade de France, xiii, xxv*map*, 3, 223
state of emergency, xiv, xxxi, xxxii, 38, 37*fig.*, 48, 71, 72, 83, 84–86, 96, 116, 124, 178, 199, 206, 222–23, 231–32; and Algerian civil war, 253n5; a history of, 84; and public health, 220
stop-and-search/frisk, 38, 72, 96, 99, 165
subjectivation, 91, 93, 150; and experiences of police violence, 106–7. *See also* ethics
subject position(s), 130–31, 135, 137, 203, 206, 208–9; of authors, xviii; of immigrants, 62; of otherness, 211; and spatiality, 91; and vigilance, 80
surveillance, 165–66; as assemblage, 33; and colonialism, 212; in France, 70, 71, 75, 84–85, 172, 206, 214–15; genealogy of, 70; and Opération Sentinelle, 71–73; in

Founded in 1893,
UNIVERSITY OF CALIFORNIA PRESS
publishes bold, progressive books and journals
on topics in the arts, humanities, social sciences,
and natural sciences—with a focus on social
justice issues—that inspire thought and action
among readers worldwide.

The UC PRESS FOUNDATION
raises funds to uphold the press's vital role
as an independent, nonprofit publisher, and
receives philanthropic support from a wide
range of individuals and institutions—and from
committed readers like you. To learn more, visit
ucpress.edu/supportus.